HAUNTED
LAKE HURON

by Frederick Stonehouse

Lake Superior
Port Cities Inc.

First Edition: June 2007

LAKE SUPERIOR PORT CITIES INC.
P.O. Box 16417
Duluth, Minnesota 55816-0417 USA
Lake Superior 1-888-BIG LAKE (888-244-5253) • www.lakesuperior.com
Port Cities Inc. Publishers of *Lake Superior Magazine* and *Lake Superior Travel Guide*

5 4 3 2 1

Library of Congress Cataloging-in-Publication Data

Stonehouse, Frederick, 1948-
   Haunted Lake Huron : lake myths, wrecks & spirits / by Frederick Stonehouse. – 1st ed.
      p. cm.
   Includes bibliographical references and index.
   ISBN 978-0-942235-79-1
   1. Ghosts – Huron, Lake (Mich. and Ont.) Region. 2. Shipwrecks – Huron, Lake (Mich. and Ont.) Region. 3. Ghosts – North America. 4. Shipwrecks – North America. I. Title
   BF 1472.N7S76 2007
   133.109774 – dc22   2007015405

Printed in the United States of America

            Editors: Paul L. Hayden, Konnie LeMay, Robert Berg
      Book Design: Mathew Pawlak
     Cover Design: Joy Morgan Dey, Mathew Pawlak
Inside Illustrations: Joy Morgan Dey
            Printer: Sheridan Books, Ann Arbor, Michigan

This book is dedicated to
those who seek the magnificent
folklore of Lake Huron.

Lake Huron Region

Michigan	9. Bois Blanc Island	17. Lake Muskoka
1. Port Huron	10. Mackinac Island	18. Parry Sound
2. Point Aux Barques	11. St. Ignace	19. Georgian Bay
3. Bay City	12. Drummond Island	20. Christian Island
4. Saginaw Bay		21. Collingwood
5. Tawas City	**Ontario**	22. Owen Sound
6. Alpena	13. St. Joseph Island	23. White Cloud Island
7. Thunder Bay Island	14. North Channel	24. Bayfield
8. Mackinaw City	15. Little Current	25. Sarnia
	16. Manitoulin Island	

Contents

Introduction

In many ways Lake Huron is the forgotten Great Lake. While it is huge, ranking third in size behind lakes Michigan and Superior, she never, as the late comedian Rodney Dangerfield lamented, "gets no respect."

Perhaps it is because she has no large cities on her shores. Port Huron and Sarnia are really on the St. Clair River. Bay City sits at the foot of shallow Saginaw Bay far off the real lake and Owen Sound on the Canadian side is on the east shore of Bruce Peninsula fronting Georgian Bay. The old cement town of Alpena is the only community of any size on Lake Huron proper. Now they are all nice places, but they aren't, as former Vice President John Nance Garner said, "worth a bucket of warm spit" when compared to Chicago, Milwaukee, Cleveland or Toronto in terms of vibrancy or national recognition. Even Mackinac Island doesn't even cause a ripple. It's so close to Lake Michigan that most visitors don't even realize the island is part of Lake Huron! And, of course, the folks visiting Mackinac are on the path of fudge, not the beauty and mystery of Lake Huron.

Lake Huron is often credited as the first Great Lake discovered by Europeans. Samuel de Champlain, the "Father of New France," is said to have reached it in July 1615 when he emerged from the mouth of the French River into Georgian Bay. It certainly took a while before he realized he was only in a bay and that a fresh-water sea lay just beyond to the west. Not cognizant that there were four other "seas," he dubbed his discovery "La Mer Douce" or "Sweetwater Sea." Father Le Caron, a wandering Recollect missionary, may have reached the lake a few days before Champlain but he was more interested in finding innocent Indians to harangue into "conversion" than discovery of new inland oceans. Entienne Brule, the illiterate voyageur, could have seen the big lake years earlier but also had no interest in discovery. When all was said and done, Champlain got the credit. By contrast, Brule was killed in a drunken brawl in 1632 and "eaten" by the Huron, whether as a mark of respect or a source of added protein can be conjectured. Personally, I think they just threw him on the "barbie," as my Australian friends would say. The name of the lake is in honor of the Hurons but certainly not in recognition of their culinary skills (Brule sauté anyone?). The voyageur had become so debauched in Champlain's eyes that he considered his demise as "good riddance."

The lake became a vital link in the French highway between old Lower Canada and the new upper reaches of the vast land. Oddly, perhaps, the French pushed northwest up the St. Marys River to Lake Superior and points beyond as well as west through the Straits of Mackinac into Lake Michigan well before ever roaming into the southern waters of Lake Huron. There simply wasn't any reason to go south. The beaver was westward and that miserable fur-bearing creature was their gold. What did Lake Huron offer beyond a highway for their canoes?

The comparative desolation of the lake today clearly dates from the days of the old French. The east shore of the lake is mostly uninhabited, just a long stretch of Canada dotted with small isolated communities. Even Georgian Bay hangs off Huron like an unwanted appendage. The Michigan coast is equally without anything remarkable. A few lighthouses and small burgs but nothing worth a second look as is evidenced by the lack of economic development or even a vibrant tourist trade when compared to the west shore of Michigan. The eastern shore of Michigan may bill itself as the "sunrise coast" in contrast to the western shore's "sunset coast," but most folks willingly enjoy a cocktail watching the sun slowly drop into Lake Michigan with the spectacular "red sky" cloud reflections. Damn few drag themselves out of a warm and comfortable bed to watch a sunrise. And from a marketing perspective, therein is the problem.

The shoreline of Lake Huron is stunning in its variation. In the south, the beaches are sand, pleasant to the eye and made for lounging on a warm summer day. Sailing north they change to rock. Finally, at the upper end is the southern edge of the great Laurentian Shield.[1]

Even recreational sailors tend to avoid Lake Huron proper, concentrating their cruising in Georgian Bay or the picturesque North Channel. Although the big freighters plow her waters throughout the season, their passages are without comment, just commercial boats earning a quiet living. The exception, of course, is the annual Port Huron to Mackinac Island sailboat race. Upwards of 300 wind wagons make the trek, but I suspect the real agenda is the great party at the island rather than the lake in between.

In terms of maritime-related ghost tales, Lake Huron is equal to any of her watery sisters. There are many things that "go splash in the night" on Huron and she is fertile ground for readers interested in such stories. While I have been collecting Great Lakes ghost stories, superstitions, sea monster tales and folklore for many years, it was not until I began to assemble this book that I realized the rich collection of material relating to Lake Huron. Readers will be impressed with it all.

Lake Huron's relative obscure popularity is a shame. She is a remarkable lake, filled with enough history, beauty, awe and mystery to stand tall among her sisters but, again paraphrasing old Rodney, "She don't get no respect."

I hope you enjoy reading *Haunted Lake Huron*.

Frederick Stonehouse

CHAPTER 1

Cursed Ships

Superstition always played a strong role in an old-time sailor's life. Some superstitions were unique to the profession, like the comparative value of rats and cats aboard a ship. Others were general to the population at large, for example bad luck associated with the number 13. Regardless, it is fair to say that sailors are some of the most superstitious people on earth.

Captain William Bonnah of Toledo, Ohio, sailed the lakes a long time and owned and mastered many vessels. It wasn't until he looked back on his career that he realized that the schooner he was in the process of buying was his 13th and that the date he had scheduled to close the deal was March 13th! He couldn't change the fact that it would be his 13th ship, but he could change the date for closing the deal, shifting it to the next day, just to be on the safe side. Why tempt fate?

Bonnah must have thought he cheated the 13th superstition, since for four months all was peaceful. Nothing marred the effective operation of his new schooner the *John Schuette*. On July 2, 1909, fate finally called in its marker. The schooner was upbound in the Detroit River from Cleveland, Ohio, with a cargo of coal. She was just passing Ecorse, Michigan, at 7 p.m. when a powerful squall knocked her off course. Bonnah and his crew struggled to bring the ship back on track, but it wasn't a quick process for a heavily loaded sailing vessel. They took too long and the *Schuette* drifted across the course of the big excursion steamer *Columbia*. She was coming back from Bois Blanc Island and her decks were crowded with an estimated 2,500 Presbyterian Sunday school picnickers. The

Columbia easily swung clear of the schooner and continued on up river. The steamer *Alfred Mitchell*, however, was close behind the *Columbia* and partially blinded by her thick black smoke. Unable to turn in time, the *Mitchell* drove hard into the old schooner, sinking the *Schuette* so quickly that the crew barely had time to launch her yawl and pull to safety. So ended Captain Bonnah's 13th ship![1]

While the propeller *Troy* had more luck than most ships, in her case it was all bad. It fact, it was very bad!

Her beginning was common enough, built in 1849 in Cleveland by Laffeiner and Stevens. The 163-foot wooden steamer was described by one reporter as a "beautiful vessel ... almost flawless in her design." Certainly this was all true, but he mentioned nothing of her luck.

Her list of disasters is indeed impressive. A bare two weeks after launching, she started to write her journal of perhaps unparalleled groundings, fires, scrapes, collisions, sinkings and just general mayhem. On April 10, 1849, she smashed into the schooner *Ariel* off Chicago, sinking her in shallow water. The *Troy* also suffered damage requiring the attention of shipyard workers.

In February 1850, while fitting out in Erie, Pennsylvania, she burned to the water's edge, necessitating $11,500 in repairs.

Reportedly when she was in Buffalo in March 1850, her boiler exploded killing six crewmen.

On September 30, 1850, she collided with the schooner *Almeda* off Erie, sinking her in shallow water.

In 1853, she lost her rudder on Lake Erie and had to be towed by another steamer into Buffalo for repair.

The following September her boiler exploded killing a fireman and injuring several others. The disabled vessel was towed to Chicago for repair. Expenses were heavy.

Early in the 1856 season she ran aground at Belle Isle, running up a $300 repair bill to set her right.

In August, she ran up on a reef off Bois Blanc Island in northern Lake Huron. Uncertain of either salvage or seaworthiness, the passengers were offloaded and taken to Traverse City. Several days later the *Troy* was towed to Mackinac Island for temporary repair.

Early in the 1858 season the hoodoo ship plowed hard on a shoal at Round Island, just a few miles to the north of her Bois Blanc grounding. Salvage tugs hauled her free and after repairs she was back to work.

It was a remarkable list of disasters, far more than could be expected of a normal working vessel. It seemed what could go wrong did go wrong. One result was that the *Troy* developed a reputation for being a "black cat" boat and getting men to crew her became very difficult. No sailor wants to work on a ship without luck. Sailing was dangerous enough without doing it on a bad luck boat.

The final straw came in October 1859. After loading passengers and a cargo of wheat in Racine, Wisconsin, she headed north on Lake Michigan bound for Port Colborne, Ontario. She stopped at Grand Traverse and Mackinac Island before turning southeasterly on Lake Huron. By the time she reached Presque Isle midway down the lake she was bucking into strong headwinds, but she gamely continued on course. Early on the 18th, as she was crossing Saginaw Bay, the winds veered to the northwest and, as the mate later stated, "blew a perfect hurricane."

Under the constant pounding of the building seas, the *Troy* started to break up. Waves stove in gangway doors, battered down her upper works and smashed her hatches. When the boiler flooded out and she was left without power, everyone knew that the end was near.

At 7:30 a.m., the captain ordered his passengers and crew to abandon ship. Now everything really went to hell! He directed the eight passengers, chambermaid and first engineer into the lifeboat where he would join them. The rest of the crew was ordered to take the quarter boat. It was a good plan, but the men panicked and instead of helping to launch the big lifeboat, ran for the smaller quarter boat and hurriedly shoved it into the lake where it promptly swamped. The captain and engineer managed to get the lifeboat into the water but the crew, now that they had lost the quarter boat, rushed for it as their only salvation. Madly they jumped aboard nearly swamping it. The seas drove the overloaded boat away from the *Troy* without her oars. It was truly at the mercy of the lake and Huron was not in a forgiving mood.

In the chaos of abandoning ship, the mate, second engineer and wheelman found themselves left on the *Troy*. With no other option, they launched an old yawl as the *Troy* dove for the bottom. The decrepit boat was in sad condition, leaking and with only one oar. Bailing constantly, they managed to keep afloat until finally being blown ashore on the Canadian side of the Lake, about four miles south of Goderich. Their survival was a near miracle. They were also the only survivors.

The death toll for the *Troy* was high, taking 23 of her passengers and crew down with her. Reportedly, none of the bodies was ever recovered. All remain forever on the bottom of Lake Huron. The wreck was located in 100 feet of water in 1998. She is badly smashed, evidently hitting the bottom very hard as she plunged. Considering her sad reputation, her loss was long overdue.[2]

Most people think of the old propeller *Meteor* in context of her deadly collision with her sister ship *Pewabic*. When the two wooden ships smacked together on Thunder Bay in August 1865, the *Pewabic* came off with the short end of the stick, diving for the bottom with the loss of roughly 100 people. The two ships were in a passing situation and came too close while trying to "speak" to each other. Both were relatively new, built only two years prior.

But the *Meteor* caused another disaster eight years later that is usually forgotten, eclipsed by her *Pewabic* incident. On June 8, 1873, the *Meteor* arrived in Detroit from Buffalo bound for Duluth. As is typical, she moored at the Buckley and Company dock to discharge and load passengers and freight. In the early afternoon, smoke was seen curling skyward from her cargo hold. The *Meteor* was burning. Panicked passengers ran for the dock while the crew attempted to battle the fire. The blaze had too much of a jump, however, and soon upper deck cabins were burning. It spread to the docks and nearby warehouses. When the Detroit Fire Department arrived complete with horse-drawn pump engines belching black smoke, it was a conflagration clearly out of control. The tinder dry wood docks and stacked freight all provided rich fuel for the ravenous flames. Eventually eight big Detroit Fire Department steam pumpers and two hook and ladder companies were on the scene, devoting their full efforts to stopping the spread of the blaze.

The *Meteor* wasn't done causing trouble. When her hawsers burned through, the swift current pushed the nautical inferno out into the river and she happily bumped along from dock to dock setting each on fire in turn. A fire fighting crew dutifully followed along snuffing out the resulting fires.

Eventually the *Meteor* came up against the Michigan Central Freight House dock where it threatened to torch the huge facility. Although it certainly was known early on by the officers on the ship, about now the firefighters realized (or were finally told) that the *Meteor* carried several barrels of gunpowder. With everything on

the ship merrily burning like a college pre-game bonfire, it was only a matter of time before it exploded.

Responding to the threat, Captain Joseph Nicholson and the tug *Favorite* with two crewmen rushed to the *Meteor* and rigged a towing hawser to her bow. Nicholson firewalled his throttles and headed across the river to Canada. Given a choice it is always better to have a ship detonate in Canada than the U.S.

The *Favorite* and *Meteor* almost made it. Just shy of a nice shallow bar on the Canadian side of the river, the gunpowder exploded with an earsplitting roar. The entire upper works of the steamer blew off, bits and pieces whizzing away into space. Surprisingly, the *Favorite* was not damaged although the crew likely had their wits scared out of them. More surprisingly, the *Meteor* was still afloat! The force of the blast was directed upward, thus causing little damage to the hull. Incredibly, there was enough left of her for the salvers to rebuilt her and send her out again.

One man died in the conflagration. Waiter Andrew Briggs apparently over indulged in cheap redeye and passed out in the linen room. In the confusion of the fire no one missed him until it was too late.

The *Meteor* suffered through a long list of other catastrophes. A few days after sinking the *Pewabic* she suffered a fire at the dock in the Sault. In 1871, she sank after hitting a rock in Put-In-Bay on

Lake Erie. After major repairs she returned to service. After wrecking again in 1882, she was again rebuilt, but now as the schooner-barge *Nelson Bloom*. She was finally abandoned in 1925, certainly an unlucky ship to the end.[3]

The old steamer *Globe* was another notorious hoodoo. Her entire career was seemingly dogged by ill fortune.

She was built in 1846 in Maumee, Ohio, as a propeller. Three years later she sank in Buffalo requiring a rebuilding cost of a $100,000, a massive sum for the time. In August 1863, she burned and sank on Saginaw Bay near Big Charity Island. Four years later she was salvaged and converted to a barge. Sold to Canadian interests in 1856, she wrecked on Lake Superior in 1860. Recovered by a United States salver, she ended up back in on the U.S. list.

Her end came in October 1873 when she was under tow of the steamer *T.U. Bradbury* on Lake Erie. Gale force winds and seas snapped her towing hawser and blew her ashore at Pigeon Bay, near Point Pelee. The hoodoo was finally finished.[4]

Captain Stephen B. Grummond is a great example of a self-made man. Starting with virtually nothing, shipping out as a sailor at age 15 and attending school in the winter, he was able to own his own ship at age 18. He parlayed one ship into another and soon owned a fleet, eventually operating an extensive shipping, tug and salvage business. He plowed his profits into Detroit real estate and grew even wealthier. Eventually he also served as mayor, a remarkable achievement for someone who started life as a penniless sailor.

Regardless of his business and political success, he did have a strange run of bad luck with his tugs. When he went on vacation during the summer of 1882 his tug *Swain* was sunk in a collision. When he went to Mackinac Island on another holiday the following year, his tug *J.P. Clark* sank in another collision. When he returned from a trip on the propeller *Atlantic* a few weeks later, his tug *Mocking Bird* was on the bottom after colliding with the steamer *Gladiator*. It would seem, thereafter, that he decided to stay in town and thereby avoid additional tug accidents.[5]

The Canadian tug *Fred A. Lee* really flaunted superstition – launched on a 13th, lost on a Friday the 13th and sinking 13 miles off Pointe aux Barques, Lake Huron. Other than also having a crew of 13, what could be more eerie?

The 70-foot tug slid down the ways on June 13, 1896. (Ways are supports on which a ship is built and on which it slides in launching.) While at least it wasn't a Friday the 13th, but a Saturday, doubtless many old-timers considered it a mistake to conduct such an important ceremony on the 13th. Why take chances? Despite their fears, her working career was relatively long and uneventful, certainly at odds with such an unlucky beginning. But in the end, the 13th curse struck anyway.

The *Lee* left Sarnia, Ontario, during the morning of November 12, 1936, bound for winter quarters at Sault Ste. Marie, Canada. She spent the season working in the St. Clair and Detroit rivers for the Wallaceburg Sand and Gravel Company of Wallaceburg, Ontario. The job was done and the five-man crew was eager to get home and be with their families.

During the night of the 12th, the tug managed to stray off course and run aground near Harbor Beach, Michigan, about 60 miles north of Sarnia. The Harbor Beach Coast Guard pulled her free without great effort and the *Lee* continued north for the Sault.

The crew of the freighter *John G. Munson* next picks up the story. About 4 p.m. on November 13, The *Munson* was coming southward around Pointe aux Barques and her mate was watching the tug coming north, about two miles distant. There were no other ships visible, so the tug naturally drew his full attention. He looked away for a minute, and then glanced back. The tug was gone! Grabbing his binoculars he searched for it but found only empty lake. The captain swung the ship toward where the tug had been and a quarter of an hour later they passed through a small wreckage field. There wasn't much left. Some wood from the pilothouse, a mattress, wood chair and a few pillows were all they found. There were neither survivors nor bodies.

The best theory of the cause of the disaster was a boiler explosion. It could have been caused by a leak started when she went aground, the water rising unnoticed until it hit the hot boilers. The explosion also could have been caused by mud pumped in while aground and plugging some boiler tubes, then letting go while under way, sending a shot of cold water into the hot boiler resulting in an explosion.

But when all was said and done, the tug was launched on a 13th and sunk 13 miles off Pointe aux Barques on a Friday the 13th. Was it all coincidence or something else?[6]

Some ships are hoodoos during their active sailing careers. The schooner-barge *Fontana* was different. She waited until being sunk before using her sharp fangs to snare other ships.

During the night of August 3, 1900, she was under tow of the steamer *Kaliyuga* and just entering the St. Clair Rapids, just where today's Bluewater Bridge is located. The *Kaliyuga*, of course, carried her own demons. Both vessels were downbound from Marquette for Cleveland with full loads of rich iron ore. As luck would have it, the steamer *Appomattox* with the schooner-barge *Santiago* was upbound and approaching the rapids. It was unclear why, but the *Santiago* smashed into the *Fontana*, sending the downbound ship to the bottom. One *Fontana* sailor was lost, apparently asleep in the forecastle when the bow of the *Santiago* cut into it, likely crushing him instantly.

Since the stern of the *Fontana* was still above water and the channel was very narrow, a couple of buoys were quickly laid to warn shipping of the danger. Lights were also installed. None of the warnings did any good. The river was a very busy artery for shipping and the accident had an accordion effect, much like an accident on a busy Interstate highway has today. There were also no police to guide traffic safely past.

Several ships narrowly missed the hull, veering clear just in time to avoid hitting it. The schooner-barge *Kingfisher* wasn't so lucky. Under tow of the steamer *Samuel Marshall*, she struck the *Fontana* hull hard, damaging herself considerably. As soon as the tug *George Brockway* managed to drag her free, she went into dry-dock for repair.

With the danger of the *Fontana* so obvious, the federal government gave a contract to the Harris Baker Company of Detroit for salvage. The experts gave it a try, but the current was too swift and they finally gave up. The only alternative was to demolish her with dynamite. Before she could be blown into splinters, there was another accident. The steamer *Maurice B. Grover* was towing the schooner-barge *John Martin*, both downbound with Minnesota ore, when everything went to hell in the congested water around the *Fontana*. The upbound steamer *Yuma* drew abreast on the port side of the *Grover* when she suddenly swerved smacking into the *Martin*, sending her to the river bottom. The accident also killed four of the *Martin*'s crew, drowned in the confusion of her sinking. To try to keep other ships from joining the new underwater fleet, an illuminated tug was kept on site to act as a floating warning signal.

The tug was only marginally effective. Before the divers and dynamite could go to work, the schooner *A.J. McBrier* banged into the *Fontana*, the shock of the impact knocking one of her sailors into the river drowning him. A tug eventually pulled the *McBrier* free and into Port Huron for repair.

The stream of accidents choked the normal river traffic to a trickle. At one point more than 90 ships were held up for days, all because of the mayhem around the *Fontana* wreck.

Finally the demolition divers got the job done. Their powerful charges of dynamite reduced the wreck to a level deep enough to allow ships to safely pass overhead. But the blasts didn't absolutely eliminate the *Fontana*. Scuba divers today can still find structure from her deep in the mud.

The 234-foot *Fontana* was built in St. Clair in 1888 as a four-masted schooner. In a desperate effort to compete with the big and efficient steamers, some shipbuilders built very large schooners like the *Fontana*. However the big schooners proved too large for viable operation and all were reduced to tow barges.[7]

The Lakes are well known for quick and vicious ship-killing squalls. Seeming to boil up out of another dimension, they can strike with incredible ferocity.

On the evening of June 20, 1872, the schooner *Jamaica* was sailing on Lake Huron just off Rock Falls on Michigan's Thumb, when a sudden squall capsized her. Demonstrating the capricious nature of the squall, a couple of nearby ships were damaged, but other vessels nearby were unaffected. The battered *Jamaica* soon dove for the bottom.

The *Jamaica* was loaded with grain and bound from Milwaukee to Oswego. Before the squall hit, the weather was beautiful with light and variable winds. There was no warning of what was coming. The crew had just finished supper and lounged quietly on deck when she went over. The cook was trapped below and was the only death.

The nearby schooner *Starlight* quickly rescued the *Jamaica* crew.

Since the water was only 50 feet deep and the schooner righted herself as she sank, her masts ended up sticking out of the water, clear markers of her location. However, the grain in the holds swelled from the water and burst open part of the deck and hull.

The Coast Wrecking Company came out a few days later to recover the schooner. To prepare her for lifting, a hard-hat diver dropped on the wreck to attach a pair of large steel pontoons to the sides of the hull. Once air was pumped into the chambers, the schooner would float to the surface where other pumps would expel the water in her hull. After he chained the pontoons to the hull the diver carefully worked his way into the galley where he found the missing cook. She was standing upright, her arms reaching out and hands clenched tight. Her face was frozen in a contortion of purest horror. He said it was an image of death he would remember forever.

The 138-foot schooner was built in 1867 in Oswego, New York. Her end came in August 1885 on Lake Michigan, when she was blown ashore between Evanston and Glencoe, Illinois. The local Life-Saving Service rescued her crew and passengers. What made it all a bit "eerie" was she went ashore in the identical location the year before.[8]

The failure of a ship to slide smoothly down the launchway is usually considered by old-time sailors to be sure proof of a cursed ship, but not always. Sometimes the gods smiled on adversity. The launching of the propeller *Montana* is a case in point.

The big 236-foot package freighter *Montana* was all set to launch when the crowds arrived at the Port Huron shipyard of Alexander Muir. Launchings were always a festive occasion and people expected a real show. Following the inevitable speeches and breaking of the bottle across her stem, a large buffet was usually laid out, including a keg or two of "Old Undercoat" or similar hooch. As traditional on the Lakes, the *Montana* would be launched sideways so when she hit the river there would be a large and satisfying splash.

On signal, the dockyard workers knocked loose the wedges and the *Montana* started to slide down the greased ways. And then she stopped cold! A period of drought had caused low water in the river and, as a result, mud built up on the bottom of the launchway preventing her from slipping off her platform. The propeller was stuck and going nowhere soon. The disappointed crowd left and a deeply embarrassed shipbuilder went to work to get her afloat.

Three salvage tugs pulled on hawsers without success other than churning up the muddy river bottom. Yard workers shoveled away the mud without making a difference. Heavy salvage pontoons were used to lift the hull free without result. Tugs pulled again, the thick clouds of black smoke pouring from their stacks demonstrating their obsession to move the reluctant *Montana*, but she stayed fast to the ways. Finally the big wrecking tug *Prindiville* arrived on the scene, took a hawser and in combination with the other tugs, managed to drag the reluctant *Montana* into the river. It took three days of work and expense to do what should have taken 30 seconds on launch day.

Regardless of the launching problems, the *Montana* had a long and relatively problem free career. In September 1895, she struck an underwater obstruction in the Portage Canal on the Keweenaw Peninsula and sank, but was soon recovered. Her end came on September 6, 1914, when she burned and sank off Thunder Bay Island, Lake Huron.[9]

Ships aren't inanimate objects. Each has a life and soul of its own. It comes from the very material used to build her and is wakened during the launching ceremony. The crash of the bottle of spirits across the bow energizes her much as pouring acid into a lead automotive battery brings it to "life," or at least that's the belief of many shipmasters.

Some ships are lucky. Everything seems to go right. They never "kiss" a dock, find bottom or break free from a mooring. Repairs are limited to those required of fair wear and tear, not accidental damage. Machinery always works and never fails. Passengers and crew are happy aboard her.

While the old sidewheeler *Tashmoo* was a happy ship, she wasn't a lucky one. Some writers claim that she was the most popular vessel on the busy Detroit River. There is no reason to dispute such claims.

Legendary Great Lakes naval architect Frank Kirby designed her to be the fastest and best-equipped day boat on the lakes, if not the world. Launched on December 30, 1899, at the Wyandotte yard of the Detroit Shipbuilding Company, she gave every indication of meeting his lofty goals. Her sleek 300-foot hull promised speed just as the famous Gar-Wood boats would a decade later. She was a greyhound ready to cut loose as soon as the engineer pushed open her throttles.

Kirby designed her to carry 4,000 people, but her owner, the White Star Line, limited capacity to 2,800 to assure that no passenger felt unduly crowded.

Throughout the long winter, workers finished her upper works. Cabin exteriors were painted white, the same as her steel hull. The dining room featured dark mahogany as did the grand saloon and male-only smoking room lined with chestnut stained malachite. The most visible feature was her huge glass windows allowing passengers to gaze at the passing scenery without leaving the comfort of the interior accommodations. Even private parlors had large glass windows. An estimated 600 windows adorned her, giving her a unique recognition on the Detroit-Toledo-Port Huron run.

During the season, the *Tashmoo* ran hard and fast not only on the water but also during her frequent stops. For example, in 1908 her schedule required her to leave Detroit promptly at 8:30 a.m., reaching Port Huron at 2 p.m. sharp after 20 stops! Some of the halts were relatively long, a full half-hour at St. Clair, for example, but the Gus Trautz Hotel on Harsens Island rated only three minutes. After a short stay in Port Huron she reversed the trip.

Harsens Island, often called "America's Venice" in recognition of its many canals, was a vital stopping point for the steamer, picking up and dropping passengers at a variety of hotels and resorts. She made 10 stops on the island in less than an hour. Tashmoo Park was a key destination for many travelers. Opening in 1897, it was a pleasure spot of stately old trees, picnic tables, a baseball field, various swings and numerous rides. A gambling casino and huge dancing pavilion were also part of the attraction. Canadian Indians from Walpole Island just across the channel often canoed over to sell various native trinkets to the tourists.

The *Tashmoo* carried a host of famous passengers. On a trial run in 1900, Admiral George Dewey, the recent hero of the Battle of Manila Bay in the Spanish-American War, and his bride, Susan, graced her decks. A couple of years later the indomitable President Teddy Roosevelt took a trip on her.

As mentioned, the old sidewheeler may have been very popular but she never was a lucky ship. Perhaps it was her name. Old-timers held that naming a ship after an Indian was not good business, but then again old-timers always complain about something.

The first showing of the curse was the infamous race between the *Tashmoo* and *City of Erie* on June 4, 1901. Racing passenger ships was fairly common and drew large crowds and larger wagers. Although the *Tashmoo* was considered the faster ship and dubbed the "White Flyer," the *City of Erie* beat her by three lengths over the 100-mile course from Cleveland east to Erie, Pennsylvania. "Lucky" ships don't lose races.

When business decreased in the 1920s as more and more folks learned the joys of motoring rather than taking the boat, the company sold its other steamers but kept the *Tashmoo* running as usual. She was still popular with the public and, most important, earning money.

It was as if the *Tashmoo* curse was simply waiting to strike and it did so with a vengeance on December 8, 1927. A powerful 60-

mile-an-hour storm hammered the Detroit River hitting the *Tashmoo* hard. Even though the *Tashmoo* was moored for the season to her dock with 14 heavy steel cables, they snapped like dried macaroni sending the steamer out into the wild river. Blown upriver by icy blasts, she smacked into the ferry *Promise*, causing her crew to jump to the dock to escape seeming death. Since visibility was near nil, the white monster soon disappeared into the gloom. A short time later she slammed into the concrete abutments of the Belle Isle Bridge. Two tugs were able to get some hawsers on her, pulling her from immediate danger, but as they came up to the Detroit Shipbuilding Company dock another blast parted the cables. She was again free and drifting fast for the bridge. Again the tugs managed to make fast to her and this time were successful in laying her into her dock. After repair, she was ready to start a new season.

The curse was quiet for a while, but on August 3, 1934, it reared up again. The *Tashmoo* was near Algonac downbound from Port Huron when a series of powerful wind blasts buffeted her. Instead of trying to dock in the difficult conditions, her captain safely held her offshore until the blasts passed, or he thought they did. When he started to dock her during what turned out to be a lull, a suddenly violent wind forced her into the shallows and hard aground, breaking a paddlewheel in the process. Her passengers were eventually taken ashore by the Coast Guard and a host of small craft. The following day she was refloated and towed to the yard for repair.

Less than two years later the curse bit again. On June 18, 1936, she was running a moonlight charter on the Detroit River when she hit what was called a "submerged rock" about midnight. Fourteen hundred members of a Hamtramck social club were enjoying themselves when she struck the object just off the Sugar Island Channel. Many revelers remember it as a jolt that knocked the lights out, but since Jean Calloway and her orchestra was still merrily playing in the ballroom, who cared? Ironically the last song was "Old Man River." Inquiring passengers who asked about the bump and sudden change in course were just told that it was engine difficulty.

The captain immediately knew he was in deep trouble. Water was coming in faster than his pumps could expel it. Either he quickly put his passengers ashore or the ship sank in the river with Lord knows how many casualties. He immediately headed for the nearest place to make a safe landing, the Brunner-Mond Company coal dock just above Amherstburg on the Canadian side of the river. He just made it. No sooner did the last passenger stagger down the gangway then the *Tashmoo* squatted to the bottom, putting her lower decks awash.

Streetcars from Detroit and the passenger steamer *Columbia* eventually arrived to return the passengers to Detroit. The salvagers, however, proved to be utterly incompetent. Instead of bringing her up slowly and carefully on an even keel, they let the bow rise too quickly, breaking her keel. It was more bad luck. The damage was too extensive to economically repair, spelling the end of the old steamer.

The ghouls had yet to pick her bones clean, however. Eventually her various parts were auctioned off. Captain J.A. McKenty, a tugboat captain from Chatham, Ontario, bought her pilothouse. The innovative tug man converted it into a summer cabin near Chatham. *Tashmoo* cottage became a local tourism attraction.

But the curse still stalked the steamer. On June 10, 1951, the cottage burned to the ground.[10]

Small craft could also be jinxed. The Bois Blanc Island Coast Guard's 36-foot motor lifeboat is a case in point. The boat was considered the hoodoo of the Tenth Coast Guard District when it set out from the island in January 1939 with a crew of five to rescue three fishermen from Detour, Michigan, adrift on the ice in northern Lake Huron. Bois Blanc Island is about 30 miles to the west of Detour. Forced back by the thick and drifting ice, the Coast Guard lifeboat crew attempted to return to the safety of the station, but the ever-thickening ice blocked their way. Unable to make progress, the crew shut the boat down hoping for better weather in the morning. During the night temperatures plummeted to 20 degrees below zero and the men suffered terribly from the piercing cold. With the engine off, there was no heat from any source. Had it been left running they could have huddled in the noisy but at least warm engine room. With fuel low, there was no choice but to shut it down and bear the unforgiving cold.

The Coast Guard boat was caught tight in a moving sheet of ice and the first rays of the gray dawn found them pushed far to the south of the station. Even worse, the recalcitrant engine refused to start, leaving them totally to the mercy of the moving ice. Eventually the boat was forced against the shore ice pack 20 miles south of Cheboygan, Michigan. Stiff with cold, the men abandoned the lifeboat and scrambled over three miles of rough ice to reach shore. There they began their desperate trek to Cheboygan, finally staggering into the city the following day. All of the crew had second-degree frostbite on their hands and feet. Had they been out much longer, death would have been inevitable. As events played out, their valiant effort in a jinxed boat was all for nothing. The fishermen had been rescued earlier by some friends who manhandled a small boat over the ice and brought them ashore.

Before its assignment to Bois Blanc, the lifeboat had been at Muskegon where it was used in the ill-fated attempt to rescue the crew of the steamer *Henry Cort*. Reportedly one of the Coast Guard crew was thrown from the boat in the wave action while responding to the call for help. The crew later claimed that it was as though the boat didn't want any of the men to stay aboard, that it was trying to buck them out. This was very odd behavior for a design that had proven itself over many years as the finest lifeboat in the world. Even worse during the attempted rescue, one of the Coast Guardsmen drowned. The boat had a long history of problems and old-timers often called it the "boat that wouldn't go." Any station having it assigned knew there would be trouble. It was just a hoodoo boat. Regardless, it was government property and could not simply be abandoned even though it lay forlornly on the Huron shore. The Coast Guard eventually used a bulldozer to drag the boat over the ice to the beach at Grace Harbor. Damaged beyond repair, but also perhaps with a touch of belated but inspired management, they officially declared it beyond salvage and stripped it of any useful equipment. A Coast Guard crew returned in the spring, soaked it in gasoline and burned the cursed thing to embers. Doubtlessly Coast Guardsmen throughout the district were relieved the boat wouldn't turn up in their boathouse.[11]

Some ships had trouble staying above water. They dove for the bottom every chance they had, as evidenced by the antics of the wood propeller *John Duncan*. Built in Green Bay, Wisconsin, by A.J. Johnson in 1891, at 225 feet in length, she was a large vessel for the period.

It is reported that she sank four times during her career! One occurrence was just off the piers at Harrisville, Michigan, on Lake Huron in August 1903. She sprang a leak in a northeast gale and ran up a distress flag, which was spotted by the lookout at the Sturgeon Point U.S. Life-Saving Service Station, six miles distant. After a hard pull of more than two hours the lifesavers reached the sinking steamer, which had dropped anchor to hold her head to sea. With the lifesavers standing by, the captain slipped his anchor and let the *Duncan* drift towards the beach, finally grounding in 20 feet of water. The life-savers ran up alongside and brought off the crew without undue trouble, including the female cook. After the gale blew itself out the life-savers helped the salvagers recover the steamer.

She wrecked for the last time in 1919 in the St. Lawrence River. Although recovered, she was finally declared a constructive loss and allowed to rot away in the boneyard in 1920. Considering her troubled career, it was a peaceful end.[12]

CHAPTER 2

Ghost Ships

Over the years I have done a number of public programs on shipwrecks as well as Great Lakes maritime history in general. Invariably afterwards a number of people will come up to me and volunteer various information and old stories. This is especially enjoyable for me and a highlight of the presentation. Anytime I can "capture" good stories is important.

Quite some time ago, I don't remember when or where, after I finished a program, I was approached by a man about 60 years old who related a story that, at the time, while interesting, I frankly blew off. The gentleman intended it to illustrate how easily even modern sailboats can get into trouble on the lakes. When I began to assemble material for this book, I realized that it is a most remarkable tale. At the time I had no particular interest in the Great Lakes supernatural and had not yet been deeply enough involved in Life-Saving Service research and history to fully put two and two together. In any case, this is the story as I remember he related it to me.

"This happened about 1965, although it could have been a year later or earlier. It was April and I was sailing north with my family along the Michigan coast of Lake Huron. We had a good breeze, nothing great but we were going along very well. It was late in the day, just a little before dusk.

"Visibility was really terrible, one of those gray days of fog and mist. We kept waiting for it to blow off, but it never did.

"I wasn't real certain where we were (remember, this was prior to LORAN and GPS). Our depth gauge was showing good water,

several hundred feet or so, and figured we were well out in the lake, probably approaching the mouth of Saginaw Bay. Once we cleared Pointe aux Barques, I thought I'd be pretty clear up to Alpena.

"I was at the helm and my son was up forward. We were getting ready to fly the Jenny, when suddenly this white rowing boat just appeared dead ahead of us. I don't think it was 50 yards away! It was full of men, eight anyway. All were rowing except for one standing in the stern. He had his left arm and shoulder cradled over a long steering oar. He looked right at me and waved slowly with his right arm. I was in the Navy during the war and I remember the chiefs had us do lifeboat drill, but this boat was different. The sides were a lot lower. There was some lettering on the bow, but I could not see it clearly enough to read. It was definitely a wooden boat.

"I thought for sure we would hit them. I yelled to my son to hold on and threw the helm over, heading more northeast. It was pretty frantic for a minute. This unknown boat in front of me, my son hanging on, me trying to steer and trim up on the new course. My wife was below making supper and my quick turn overturned her stew, so I had her yells ringing in my ears, too!

"When I looked again to be certain we would clear the boat, it was gone. Visibility was bad, but I still should have seen it. I always wondered what happened to it.

"A shout from my son brought me back with a start. He said he could see bottom! A glance at the depth gauge showed a bare five foot under the keel. I thought what the hell, had we blundered into Pointe aux Barques Reef?

"In any case, within a minute the depth increased and we soon were in good water. Whatever it was, we just cut the edge of it.

"After an hour or so, the fog finally blew off and I could make out Pointe aux Barques Light. Handing the helm to my son, I went below and pulled out my chart and using the bearing from the light tried to figure out what happened.

"As best I can guess, we almost hit Pointe aux Barques Reef. If we didn't run across that strange rowing boat and turn when we did, I'm certain we would have run right up on it and wrecked. I don't know where that little white boat came from, but it saved us from a very dangerous situation."

The story was meant to illustrate how easy it is to get into real trouble on the lakes, even in a modern yacht. As I mentioned, I didn't really think much of it at the time.

Four years ago, while I was researching the old U.S. Life-Saving Service for *Wreck Ashore*, I came across the terrible account of loss of the entire Pointe aux Barques Life-Saving Station crew save one during a rescue attempt.

While obviously it can't be proved, a little imagination would provide the answer to the strange encounter the yachtsmen had. The Pointe aux Barques crew perished in April 1879 and it was an April day when the sailor saw the strange rowing boat. The location for his sighting and the surfboat disaster are identical. Was it the life-saving crew returned again to save a vessel?[1]

The following story appeared in the *Detroit Post* for September 15,1884. The circumstances of the loss of the *Marine City* are correct. The mysterious light, however, is a bit less documented.

"A few years ago the steamer *Marine City*, plying between Detroit and Lake Huron ports, caught fire just off Harrisville and was run near shore when the passengers were nearly all rescued after a struggle in the water and the hull sank.[2]

"She had been at one time a fine craft and a favorite passenger boat. In one of my trips along that shore I chanced to fall in company with a dweller of that country and the conversation turned upon the mystery that followed the destruction of the old craft.

"'Have you heard of the phantom light which can be seen at midnight on the anniversary of the *Marine City*?' asked the intelligent old fisherman.

"'I never did; no, what is it?'

"'Come out here on the dock with me tonight at 12 o'clock and you will see.'

"I accepted the invitation and at the appointed hour we strolled out on the pier; and while we were on the way, 'There, look,' said he, and sure enough, as plain as the stars that twinkled in the heavens, a light, apparently a lantern, hovered above and around the old wreck.

"I confess I was somewhat startled, and rubbed my eyes to make sure it was no optical illusion. It moved about slowly as if carried by some unseen hand. Was it not some boatman moving about? No, 'cause it was not so dark or so far away but a small boat would have been seen and heard.

"I did not like to give it up so we engaged a boat and rowed up the shore toward the light. The crisp, evening air was as still as if hushed in a sleep, and as I bent over the oars with a vigorous will, I instinctively feathered them and handled them as noiselessly as if engaged in some midnight adventure requiring nerve and daring. Somehow the love of adventure does not seem to desert us as we creep out of our boyhood and enter the sedate period of manhood; and the desire to fathom the unfathomable is part of a man's nature. The old fisherman entered heartily into the spirit of the occasion and offered to relieve me at the oars.

"'You're a good 'un at the oar, but if your hand is not in you'll lame yourself, for it's a good mile up there.'

"Easing up a bit and pulling more cautiously, I glanced over my shoulder toward the light. It seemed to be receding, a sort of ignis fatuus; and again I doubled over the oars.[3] Soon we were at the old sunken hull, but the light had disappeared. We rowed around the burnt wreck resting in shallow water and looked down into its cold black depths, but could see no cause for phosphorescent lights. Then we rowed to shore and examined the banks – sand and gravel – nothing else; no swamp or rotten wood, nor stream of water near; in fact nothing, that I could discover, that would cause this will-o-the-wisp.

"'You believe men have souls that live after death?'

"'I most certainly do.'

"'Well, don't you believe souls have the power to talk to us one way or another?'

"'I am not so sure about that.'

"You have heard about friends dreaming about their friends being in danger and soon after get word that the danger was real and possibly their friends died at the very hour they were dreamed about. Now what would you call it?"

"Well, I should call it a communication with the spirit world that I don't care to have anything to do with until I have done with this world.'

"'Then you are a spiritualist, I see?'

"'Not if I know myself; unless in the sense that all professedly Christian people (whether really or professedly I do not say) are spiritualists to a certain extent. But what about that light? Are you getting into the theology of the light? What is it?'

"'Well sir, I'll tell you what I think it is. It was said that the *Marine City* was set on fire by one of the deckhands or firemen out of revenge for some real or imaginary wrong and that he was one of the few that was lost. And my opinion is if that is true, then he is doomed to punishment to bring that light here every night during the month in which the boat is lost, to light the others that were lost safely over the "dark river," and possibly as a warning to others that may be like tempted to murder or other wickedness. We can't tell what God's ways are, but we can see by the warnings all around us, and I believe this is one of God's beacon lights.'

"'Well, my friend, there is certainly no harm in the thought. I am at least ready to give it up as a mystery that I can't fathom – and here we are at the dock again.'"[4]

A popular Great Lakes writer wrote the following piece. It is reproduced with the stipulation that his name not be used.

"I got a good one of my own to tell, as long as you don't let it blow my reputation as a researcher and such. … Twas in August of 1983, and my folks and I were camped in the motor home at the Soo. The campgrounds just above Mission Point to be exact. It was pre-dawn, and like a good little boat-nut I got up long before the sun so I could shower and dress and be ready to take photos at first light. It was a clear night as I went into the shower facility, but when I came out about 20 minutes later, one of those famed Soo fogs was really setting in, and the visibility was dropping fast. From the shower room I saw two amber masthead lights going down river. I kept a close eye on them as they headed down the river and as I walked back to the motor home. They were just too close together to be a big laker, I guessed about the size of a 200- to 300-footer, perhaps a saltie, I figured. The fog was setting in so fast that the whole thing was gone by the time I got into the motor home and turned on the scanner. That was just in time to hear Soo Control closing the river. I figured that was good because the odd boat that I saw would be just around Mission Point and would have stopped there. When the fog lifted I could just walk down and see who it was. I spent the morning telling my brother about the strange boat and guessing who it may be. We speculated for hours about which boat it may be and I told him that as soon as the fog lifted, all bets would be settled because she'd be right in front of us. The fog held until just before noon then lifted rapidly. I walked down to the point and looked, but nothing was there. The *Bevercliffe Hall* was just above the rock pile downbound, and the *Herbert C. Jackson* was just below the point, upbound, and the *Mesabi Miner* was downbound with another 'footer' ahead of her, but nothing else. No salties, no tugs, nothing! I kept on the scanner all the rest of the day, but there was nothing smaller than the *Jackson* in that river all day … spooky, eh? I'll never forget those amber colored lamps on those two high masts, and I've been scratching my head about that one for many years since."[5]

Next to the famous Chicago-Mackinac Race sponsored by the Chicago Yacht Club, the Port Huron-Mackinac race is the most prestigious on the Great Lakes. Starting in 1925 with a dozen boats, it has grown to roughly 270 entrants ranging from 26 feet to more than 90 feet and 3,000 sailors. An estimated 75,000 people crowd Port Huron on the St. Clair River for the race festivities and to watch the start. The first boats usually leave around 9 a.m. on Saturday and the fastest will reach Mackinac Island Sunday evening. Other classes will wander in during the next several days.

Today there are two courses used: the traditional 235-mile shoreline track up the Michigan coastline or a 290-mile Southampton course, which angles to a race buoy five miles off Southampton, Ontario, then swings north to the finish line at Mackinac Island. The Southampton course is relatively new, the time-honored one going to Cove Island, at the end of the Bruce Peninsula, before turning for the island. The bigger boats take the east course and smaller ones the west. Despite the shortness of the race, it can be a great adventure, especially if "unusual" forces intervene. And therein lies the tale.

A few years ago I was sitting in the Pink Pony Bar on Mackinac Island late one afternoon. It was a miserable day with intermittent rain and drizzle, a good time for me to just nurse a beer and make a few story notes for a project I was working on. There were only a couple of other people around. It was late in the season and most of the Fudgies were long gone. There were still a few boats in the marina. During the season it was usually packed.[6]

Being bored, I started to talk with the guy sitting next to me. He said his name was Pete. He looked in his mid-60s, fit and tanned but could have been much older. There was nothing remarkable about him. After a while he mentioned that he had a sailboat in the marina and was just laying over a day or so before delivering it to the yard at Sturgeon Bay for the winter. In turn I related that I was doing some research for a book and he managed to pry out of me the topic: Lake Huron ghost stories. We went through the normal dance of "do you believe in that %&¢$#," etc.? After I waffled around a bit, we determined we both agreed that there were things we didn't understand. Moreover, we had both experienced things we couldn't explain either. A couple more beers flowed and eased the conversation. What follows is from my memory. I didn't take careful notes or have a tape recorder. To be honest, a lot of people seem to be intimidated by a tape recorder so using one isn't always possible.

Pete turned on his stool, looked at me and said, "I got one for you. You heard of the Port Huron-Mackinac race, right?" I said I did and while I never had the pleasure of sailing it, it looked like great sport. "Well," he said, "I've sailed it for a long time. Either in my own boat or crewed with friends."

Pete continued, "About 20, maybe more, years or so back I crewed on a friend's boat. There were eight or so of us onboard and we had trained all spring to get ready for the race. We thought we had an outside chance of wining best overall time and wanted to be prepared. Come race day we were rar'n to go, locked and cocked, as they say. She was a super boat, too, a big 60-foot baby and a real flyer. This was before all the multihull garbage you see today. Owner had money and enough sense to put a couple of professional crew on board to really drive her. The rest of us were more brawn than brains, but that is a lot of sailing, too. We started with pretty good wind, maybe 15 knots and up from the south. It gradually increased to 20 plus and shifted southwesterly, good for a fast run to the island. Of course we're running the Cove Island course.

"It was a great start. There were a couple hundred boats at least between the two courses. As the day wore on we separated out pretty good, as you would expect. We were a fast boat and, all things being equal, should leave most of the fleet behind. By late afternoon it turned squally with periods of rain and mist. The wind kept strong and we had to stay lively to get everything we could out of the boat. I don't doubt some of the fair-weather guys just reefed up and lay to but we hung in there. The waves were maybe 5, 6 feet and steep so the motion was really lively. It was one hand for the ship and one for yourself. But we didn't care. We had a race to win.

"Just after the weather closed in, a truly strange boat came up on our lee side. She was a real old-timer, a ketch with a couple of big wood sticks and everything. I remember her hull was jet black. I hadn't seen anything like her since I was a kid. They are beautiful boats, but a real bitch to maintain with all that wood. This one was a honey and seeing her flying through the waves was a sight to behold. I wish I had my old video camera! The odd thing was she looked like she was flying through the waves. He motion was unnatural. It was almost like the waves weren't affecting her the same way they were us.

"All night long the squalls kept coming in, winds maybe 30 knots or better. You could actually see them on the old radar we had, showing up as kind of a fuzzy green blur. It was a miserable night. Foul weather gear was the order of the day and I don't care how you button it up, water seeps down your back, into your boots, just miserable. A couple of the guys were heaving their guts out before morning. At some time or another everybody gets sick. There is no shame in it. Off and on during the night we saw the nav lights from the old-timer, but they were different. They didn't look like other nav lights. I can't describe it except to say they pulsed as if they were alive. She was running off our lee and keeping up with us, too. Strange reddish phosphorescence showed around her bow. Green is fairly common but none of us had ever seen red before.

"When daylight came the weather was still blowing and raining. Sometimes visibility dropped to a hundred yards or so in a rain shower then opened up to a mile or a little better. We kept booming right along. So did the old-timer. We tacked and she tacked, as if she were our shadow. There was no way she should be keeping up with us. No way at all. But somehow she was there.

"By midmorning the wind had picked up and the squalls grew more intense. We were thinking about throwing a reef in but kept looking at the old-timer with her wooden sticks and said, Damn if they can keep going without a reef, so can we. I mean we're a brand new boat. We have to be stronger than she is. I didn't even notice radar on the mast. Even the little guys got radar!

"So we both just keep booming along. Our VHF-FM radio dropped out of its mounting when we slammed into a particularly bad wave so we didn't know where any other boats were. The second radio wasn't working, either. Lots of static but no receive. For all we knew we could be leading the fleet. Can't let up now.

"All day it was one long battle. It was the race of a lifetime; a strong southwesterly wind keeping us on our toes, the boat

24

completely drenched with spray and rain, water running down the decks when we buried the bow, damn near everything below wet from the crew hustling around in foul weather gear and rain pouring in when the hatch was opened. It was far too rough to try to eat anything, but the sandwiches were stashed in a cooler. Off watch we only managed to snatch a few minutes' sleep in the rack before the loud bang of a wave woke us. It was some of the best sailing I've ever done!

"As the day wore on the old-timer slowly pulled ahead of us and I was able to finally get the name across her stern, *Witchcraft*. It was fitting because she was flying along like a witch anyway. Did I mention her sail number? No, it was 13! And the numbers weren't plain either, but kind of twisted if you know what I mean. I thought, boy this guy is tempting fate. And right above the numbers were a set of weird looking cat eyes, really strange looking. Sailors are usually a bit superstitious and this was definitely over the line. That wasn't the craziest thing, either. There was a broom lashed to the top of the main. Not the kind of broom you see in Kmart or you have at home but an old-fashioned one with the straw bundled around the end. From my Navy days I know subs used to tie a broom to the mast when coming into port as a way of announcing they swept the seas clear of enemy shipping, but I've never seen one on a sailboat mast. The crew working in the cockpit were all wearing black rain gear, too: jackets, trousers, boots and even their sou'westers! I haven't even seen black ones in the catalogs. And considering the foul weather, none were wearing a life jacket or a safety line. And that was stupid. The motion the boats were kicking up could easily have pitched a man overboard. What really made that crew so different wasn't the color of the rain gear. When I put the glasses on them they all appeared to be women! Today an all-woman crew isn't unusual, but back then it sure was. I don't remember any all-woman crew racing the Port Huron-Mac before.

"Throughout the day *Witchcraft* slowly drew ahead of us. We couldn't understand it. Here we have this old wooden boat beating a modern one with all the bells and whistles, designed specifically for speed. It didn't make any sense. No matter what we did, we couldn't catch her. Visibility was still garbage, open up to maybe a couple of miles then close down to a couple of hundred yards. It was damned frustrating!

"The odd thing was we never could get her on our radar. When she was sailing close aboard I figured she was under our sweep, our dish was two-thirds up the main so the sweep of our beam could have passed over her. Since she was wood, the return would be weak anyway. But as she pulled away we still never had her. I didn't notice a reflector, either. There weren't any other boats around either, but we had good land return, so we knew the set was working.

"By late Sunday Mackinac Island is coming up quick and *Witchcraft* is still a good piece ahead. For us the race is over. There is no way we are going to catch her. She charges across the line and 10 minutes or so later we cross. We were all angry. Being beaten by an old wood boat was embarrassing. We stowed our sails and motored into the marina. It was time to drown our sorrows right here in the Pink Pony. In all the activity of getting ready to moor, we lost track of *Witchcraft*. She wasn't in the marina. Maybe she continued on to St. Ignace and tied up there. But since she clearly was first to cross the line she ought to be at the island celebrating. When we stopped at the race committee to verify our time and finish, they had no record of her. Nothing, zero, zilch, nada! As far as the committee was concerned she didn't exist and never did.

"Now this really was spooky. What the hell was she, a ghost ship? I later found out no boat named *Witchcraft* was entered in the race. None of the race guys at Port Huron or Mackinac knew anything about her. You can believe me or not. I don't give a rip, but I was there, it was an experience. I can't explain it. We raced that damn boat up the length of Lake Huron and it didn't exist!"

I can't explain it, either. All I can do is relate the tale as best I remember it. The problem is, stories like this are impossible to verify. Is it just the ramblings of a gin-soaked old sailor making good speed for the funny farm, or a genuine experience of the unexplained? I have since found nothing to prove or disprove his story.[7]

One of the strangest of the Great Lakes ghost ships is the *Hunter Savidge*. The 117-foot, gaff-rigged, two-masted schooner is typical of the hundreds of small vessels that plied the lakes when sail was king. She was part of a small fleet of three schooners owned by lumberman John Muellerweiss Jr. When not used in the trade, she paid her keep by carrying whatever freight she could, wherever it could.

On August 20, 1899, the *Hunter Savidge* was sailing northeast of Pointe aux Barques, Lake Huron bound for Alpena. Aboard with Captain Fred Sharpsteen and his six-man crew was the captain's wife, Rosa, the owner's wife, Mary Muellerweiss, and her 6-year-old daughter, Etta. Mrs. Muellerweiss was not feeling well and it was

hoped that a lake trip would help her regain her health. The captain's wife went along to provide her company. The *Hunter Savidge* was running light having just delivered a cargo of coal to Sarnia, Ontario. The little wind that earlier wafted the schooner over Huron's calm waters had died out completely and she lay becalmed, rolling gently on the glassy surface. Her limp canvas sails hung lifeless from the yards.

Without warning the schooner was struck squarely by a powerful white squall. Blasted by the screaming wind, she dug her bow in and rolled completely over, finally ending up with her bow deep underwater and stern projecting above the surface. Within what seemed like only seconds, the deadly squall passed, leaving the devastated vessel dying in its wake. The broken schooner dangled at a 45-degree angle, seemingly ready to plunge for the bottom at any second. Captain Sharpsteen and four of his startled crew, all on deck when the squall hit, were tossed into the lake. Finding various pieces of floating wreckage, they desperately hung on until the steamer *Alex McVittie*, which witnessed the tragedy from several miles away but was unaffected by the squall, rushed to their rescue. One of the missing men was the captain's 16-year-old son, thought dragged to the bottom when he was unable to shed his heavy sea boots.

Also gone were both women and the child. Captain Sharpsteen believed that they were still below decks, caught in the stern cabin. He knew they could still be alive, breathing desperately in a trapped air bubble. It had happened before.

Captain Sharpsteen may have remembered years earlier when the schooner *Experiment* capsized on a sand bar at St. Joseph, Michigan, during a squall. Resting hull up, she was firmly anchored in the sand bottom by the short stubs of her shattered masts. The following day curious townspeople who climbed over the broken vessel were startled by frantic pounding coming from within the dead hull. Quickly chopping through bottom planking, they discovered the captain's wife and two children still alive. Their remarkable survival was attributed to an air bubble trapped inside when the schooner went over.

There was other precedence for the survival of people trapped below. On June 1, 1853, the schooner *G.R. Roberts* was sailing in Lake Michigan about eight miles northwest of Grand Haven when her crew was surprised to find a schooner floating nearly bottom up. When they climbed aboard to assess the chances of salvage, they were startled to hear desperate cries coming from inside the hull. Cutting through the thick planking, they soon released the captain, Andrew Bergh, and a passenger and part owner, Lukas A. Farnsworth. Both told their sad tale to the *Roberts'* crew. The schooner departed Michigan City on Sunday, May 29, bound for Grand Haven. At midnight Captain Bergh left the deck in charge of two sailors and went below. About two hours later, he was awakened by a loud noise on deck and he flew out of his berth, running for topside. Just then the schooner went over, topside becoming bottom side. Working his way into the cabin, he found Farnsworth and two crewmen. To keep their heads above black water, the four had to wedge into one of the narrow berths. By Monday the two sailors could no longer keep their grip and slipped into the water and drowned. Bergh and Farnsworth hung grimly on until rescue two days later.[8]

Another example was the schooner *New Connaut*. When a white squall knocked her over in Lake Erie in the fall of 1883, all on board, except an elderly woman passenger, were able to escape in the yawl. The survivors believed that the old woman had been knocked into the lake and drowned. But five days later, when the schooner was righted and partially pumped out, she walked out of the cabin unharmed, having survived in an air pocket. Captain Sharpsteen believed that his wife, Mrs. Muellerweiss, and her child were also trapped in his schooner. If he could just get through to them, he could save their lives.

Try as he may, he was unable to convince the captain of the *McVittie* to stay by the wreck and explore it. The *McVittie*'s master callously told him all were dead and it was foolish to waste time there. The best he would do was transfer the survivors to the steamer *H.E. Runnels*, would in turn drop them at Sand Beach where the U.S. Life-Saving Service crew could assist. The *McVittie* captain was utterly unwilling to do anything more. After all, he had a schedule to keep. He had wasted enough time already.

At Sand Beach, Captain Sharpsteen urgently tried to hire a diver to explore the still-floating wreck, but by the time he located one, it was night and the diver refused to make such a dangerous attempt in the dark. Sharpsteen did manage to charter the fish tug *Angler* to take him on a fruitless search for the missing schooner.

Although the life-saving crews from both Sand Beach and Pointe aux Barques looked hard for the schooner during the following days, they never found her. Local tugs also combed the lake with equally empty results. All the while, the desperate Captain Sharpsteen continued to hope for a miracle. It wasn't to be. The distraught captain patrolled the shore for months following the disaster but in vain. The *Hunter Savidge* with the two women and child was gone forever. Or was it?

In later years, sailors, plowing through the cold, clammy tendrils of a Lake Huron fog, claimed to have sighted the ghostly stern of the lost schooner. It was still floating, waiting forlornly for the rescue that never came. One minute it was there, and then it was gone, swallowed again by the hungry lake. In about 1987, David Trotter and other members of Undersea Research Associates discovered the wreck of the schooner in approximately 155 feet of water. The mystery of her location was solved but not the mystery of the wandering sightings of the dead ship.

The *Hunter Savidge* was not a virgin in terms of causing shipwreck. During a dark night on November 14, 1892, she rammed the two-masted, 95-foot wooden schooner *Minnie Davis* near Amherstburg, Ontario. The *Davis* sank, but no lives were lost.[9]

A Great Lakes "Flying Dutchman" story involves the lumber schooner *Jamestown*. Whether true or false is, of course, open to question, but it is nonetheless a great story. Those who might doubt the truth of the tale should realize that there was a schooner, *Three Brothers*, a 349-tonner built in Black River, Ohio, in 1873, and there were several vessels sailing under the name *Flying Cloud*. The following is directly quoted from the April 17, 1886, issue of the Ishpeming, Michigan, *Iron Agitator*:

"I'm telling you that the Great Lakes have their mysteries as well as the seas," said the captain of the schooner *Three Brothers* as he lay down the paper he had been perusing for the last half hour. 'Boy and man, I've sailed the lakes for the last 25 years and I've met with some things that have staggered me. Perhaps the strangest of all was the loss of the crew of the *Jamestown*.

"This affair took place in 1862, during the excitement and hurly-burly of war, and the circumstance was speedily forgotten under the press of other matters. At that time I was in a wheat carrier called the *Flying Cloud* and hailing from Chicago. The *Jamestown* belonged somewhere on the Ohio shore of Lake Erie – at Painesville, I think. She was in the lumber trade, making her runs between Saginaw and Toledo and Saginaw and Sandusky. On the night of the 21st of August in the year named as we were abreast of Alpena, on Lake Michigan, the wind died, but we scarcely had steerage way and the lake was almost as smooth as a mill pond. It was a warm, starlight night and the only sail in sight when night shut down was a propeller far to the east of us, evidently bound for Georgian Bay. What little wind there was and what we had for several hours was directly aft, or from the north, and any vessel beating up against it could not have made a mile an hour. Remember, now I have told you that at dusk, no vessel was in sight to the south of us.

"About 10 o'clock, with the wind so light that our booms were swinging inboard, when the schooner lifted now and then on a long swell and when everybody aboard except the mate, lookout and a man at the wheel had turned in, the voice of the lookout was heard shouting:

"'Port! Port! There's a schooner dead ahead of us! Over with her, heave! The man at the wheel pulled her over and her head went around slowly and next moment we rubbed alongside of a craft so close that any of us could have jumped aboard of her. I was on deck as she came abreast of us and I ran to the port side, followed there by three or four of the crew and called out to know what she was doing without a light in the rigging. She hadn't even a light in her binnacle and all aboard was dark and silent, with never a man showing his face. She had all sail set and as true as I sit here she was sailing dead in the wind's eye! She passed us slowly and majestically and though we hailed again and again, not a human being showed himself. She hadn't passed us more than two lengths before her head fell off to the northeast and she seemed to lose her way. I know we weren't making a mile and hour and so you may reason that what sailing was done was performed by the strange craft and that dead to windward."

"Well, sir, as she lay to after passing us the mate comes running up and sings out that everybody aboard of her must be asleep or dead and it seemed the proper thing to drop the yawl into the water and board her. Before doing so, however, we hailed her several times at the top of our voices without getting an answer. I took the boat and two men and pulled over to her. She was in ballast, with nary a rope trailing overboard and I had to get up by the chains. I took a lantern with me and one of the sailors climbed over the bows with me while the other held the yawl fast. We found everything as shipshape as you please, every rope coiled down and every halyard made fast in sailor fashion. There wasn't a sign of a struggle on deck and no more could you discover any evidence that the crew had left in a hurry. The yawl was missing but the curious thing about it was the tackles had been hauled up as if by somebody on board. This wouldn't have been the case, you know, if the boat had been lowered in a hurry and brought alongside.

"We made a dive into the forecastle but found no one. The men's bags were there and nothing had been taken. We visited the cabin, but with the same result. Clothing hung on the hooks and everything looked as if captain and mate had just stepped on deck. We examined the pantry, but there were no signs that food had been taken away. Here was a vessel on a calm sea with every sail set and nobody aboard and I found myself growing chicken-hearted, as we looked her over. Had she sprung a leak? I don't believe it because she had the buoyancy of a dry vessel, but we pulled off a hatch and descended. She was as dry as a bone.

"I had recognized the craft long before as the *Jamestown* and knew her captain to be a man named Charles Day. She carried six men before the mast and there was captain, mate and cook to make the supplement nine. When we had hunted from top to bottom without finding a soul aboard, I just felt my hair trying to stand up and a cold chill climbing up my spine. The man with me was completely unnerved and I had to cuss good and stout to keep him from running away.

"Here was a big chance for salvage, as you can see, and I called the other man aboard and we took in all sail. We then got her hawser over the bows, pulled her head around and took it aboard of the *Flying Cloud*. With any sort of decent weather we had a good show of getting her into Tawas or Port Austin. When it came to putting a man at her wheel, not any of my crew would go, no matter what promised. I had therefore decided to go myself in case a breeze sprang up, when what should come booming down upon us but a white squall. It caught us in a box and we escaped by the skin of our teeth. When we got time to draw breath and look around, the *Jamestown* had disappeared, the hawser having snapped, and she was not seen again by mortal eyes.

"I reported the case, of course, and it was unknown all around the lakes, but I'm telling you, sir, that the schooner not only passed out of sight forever but neither her nor a man of her crew has been heard from to this day. They were looked after by tugs and other craft and the shores were watched for months, but all in vain."[10]

Georgian Bay, hanging off the east side of Lake Huron, has often been called the Sixth Great Lake. This is, of course, ludicrous since there are only five Great Lakes, but that said, Georgian Bay is a very big body of water and well deserving of our respect. Under the right storm conditions it can also be extremely rough, and many good ships and crews have met their end on her.

The best known of the Georgian Bay wrecks is the propeller *Asia*, lost on September 14, 1882. While every shipwreck is unique, the *Asia* is a fine example of many of the old propellers lost through a combination of poor design, lax if not nonexistent government regulation, poor officer decision-making and good old fashioned "corporate" greed. For a change, this was Canadian greed as opposed to the much maligned U.S. greed.

The 136-foot *Asia* was built in 1873 at St. Catherines, Ontario, as a combination passenger and freight carrier. Her design was that of a Welland Canal propeller, long and narrow to maneuver through the small canal and connecting waterways. Her beam was only 28 feet, giving a real tendency to roll hard in a beam sea. Running the open lake in any but calm conditions was dangerous for the canal propellers. Originally the *Asia* carried freight to Canadian Pacific Railroad construction gangs on Lake Superior. The CPR was working to complete the first trans-Canadian rail link and prodigious amounts of various supplies were needed to be carried north to the wilderness of the Superior shore. Considering the reputation of Lake Superior for storm weather, the *Asia* was not a good choice for the trade. After a time, she shifted to general passenger and freight trade on Georgian Bay, a far more protected environment.

The *Asia* left Collingwood on September 12, calling at Owen Sound around midnight bound for French River and on to the Canadian Sault. By any stretch of the Plimsoll mark, she was overloaded with her holds stuffed and decks piled high with logging equipment, general freight, 14 horses, hay and other livestock and passengers. Barrels and boxes were stacked everywhere. The less

32

well-stowed the cargo, the easier and quicker it was to unload. Perhaps the reasoning ran, "Why spend all that time securing the cargo with cribbing and rope if we have to go through all the trouble of unsecuring it to unload?" "To hell with it. Just put it anywhere it fits." Many passengers had to camp out in passageways, public cabins, cargo holds and even the open deck. There was no other room for them. Although the *Asia* was equipped with 30 passenger cabins, all were filled or, in fact, overfilled. In total she carried an estimated 100 passengers and 25 crew. There were also 11 women and nine children among the crowd. It seems that the purser never left a list of the exact passenger names or even a head count. Such an omission wasn't uncommon for the times. Ominously, she was only supposed to carry 40 passengers and had merely 40 life jackets aboard.

Most of the cargo was intended for the northern lumber camps. The cutting began in the fall and went on all winter. There was considerable pressure on the *Asia* to deliver the greatest load of men and equipment possible. Come spring, the harvest was boomed off to the mills and the jacks hit town with a season's worth of money in their pockets. This partially explains why she was so heavily loaded.

After a quick stop to refuel with cordwood at Presqu'ile around 4 a.m., she continued north into an increasing westerly storm. The officers knew that a storm was coming; forecasting was sufficiently advanced to provide some notice of impending bad weather. Regardless of the official forecast, the wheelhouse barometer was very low. In today's slang, "It didn't take a rocket scientist" to see a real hell banger was coming. But Captain John Savage knew that he was expected to keep to his schedule and it didn't call for waiting out bad weather safe in port. The *Asia* would just pound her way through as she always did.

To this point the *Asia* was running in the lee of the Bruce Peninsula, a long finger of land jutting northwestward from the Canadian mainland. To the east of the Bruce is Georgian Bay and to the west, open Lake Huron. Once the *Asia* left the protection of the peninsula past Tobermory and came up to the Lucas Channel between the bay and lake, the full force of the storm would explode into her.

And blast her it did! At 9 a.m., the *Asia* was bucking hard into the cold steep waves. Slamming into wave after wave she started to spit caulking and open seams. Her clanking steam pumps spewed out the flooding water back into the lake as fast as they could, but could they keep up?

Wooden vessels always "work" in a seaway and *Asia* was being put to the test. Combers smashed into her deckhouse and rolled down the open decks, running in torrents down companionways into her innards. She rolled her guts out, too, accentuated by her narrow and less than seaworthy design, overloaded condition and poor cargo stowage. Passengers and likely crew were seasick everywhere. Animals whinnied with fear and tried to stay upright.

Sometime before noon the propeller was in truly desperate shape. The increasing storm threatened to tear her apart. Cargo was strewn everywhere and much was smashed. Correctly stowing and securing cargo is an art. Properly done, it will withstand virtually any storm. Unfortunately there were no cargo stowage artists on the *Asia*. Everything was mostly just heaped up, trusting to inertia to keep it from shifting. In the midst of the storm, inertia let them down.

If the *Asia* continued on her northerly course, it was only a matter of time before she was overwhelmed by wind and wave. Out of pure despair Captain Savage turned west toward Lonely Island. If he could haul up in its shelter, perhaps, just perhaps, the *Asia* could survive. He ordered cargo jettisoned. On the wildly heaving and rolling ship it was a very difficult order to follow, but at least most, if not all, of the horses were shoved over the side to their certain death.

The *Asia* wasn't going to make it. Caught in the trough of a monster wave, she pitched high up at the bow and sank stern first, allowing some lifeboats to float off and the deckhouse to break free of the hull. Passengers and crew leaped madly into the water, grabbing whatever flotsam available. There was no effort to launch lifeboats or noble nonsense about "women and children first." Panic reigned unchecked. Within minutes the *Asia* was gone, down to the cold and lonely bottom of Georgian Bay.

Desperate survivors hung on to hatch covers, deckhouse, tables, chairs, trucks, barrels, whatever floated and could keep them alive for just a few more minutes. The lake claimed each one as they dropped off into the deep, too tired and cold to hold on any longer.

By chance and certainly not design, 18 survivors ended up in a lifeboat, for a time at least. When a wave capsized it, many were lost. Others hung on the overturned boat until the waves calmed enough to right it. Only nine people scrambled aboard: two lumberjacks, the purser, a passenger, second and first mates, captain and two 17-year-olds, Christy Ann Morrison and Duncan Tinkiss. By chance, the first mate was Morrison's cousin. They had no oars or shelter. The boat was only a floating island without sustenance. Over the ensuing two days, all aboard died one by one, except the two teenagers. It was the bone-chilling, soul-sucking cold that did the trick. Each man in turn just drifted off to sleep and never woke up.

The lifeboat with its cargo of death finally drifted ashore near Byng Inlet on the east side of the bay. Christine and Duncan dragged the dead men from the boat and to the beach. Launching the boat again, they headed for what they thought was a nearby lighthouse, but with only a small branch for a paddle, they were forced ashore again. This time they curled up and slept on the cold and deserted beach. The next morning they tried again for the lighthouse but discovered it was only an old derrick. When all looked the blackest, an Indian couple came by in a small sailboat and took them to Parry Sound after Duncan bartered his gold watch for their help. Everything has a price in the north woods, even helping those in distress.

The propeller was the third ship named *Asia* to be claimed by the lakes. In 1855, a schooner so named sank in a collision with the propeller *Forest City* off Traverse City in Lake Michigan. Another schooner hit Spectacle Reef in northern Lake Huron, becoming a total loss. No lives were lost in either wreck.

Where the *Asia* actually sank is open to speculation. One theory claims she sank about 35 miles northwest of Parry Sound. Another holds she went down off the Limestone Islands and no further north than Byng Inlet. A third conjectures she struck a shoal a dozen miles off the Blackhill Islands. Her whereabouts remain a mystery.

At the inquest following the disaster, a coroner's jury condemned the *Asia* for "gross culpable negligence" and a laxity of safety provisions on board. Captain Savage drew special denunciation for his poor decisions. For example, she was carrying more passengers than permitted by her certificate. That the certificate had lapsed was even more damning. The public criticized the Board of Steamboat Inspection for general neglect, especially in allowing her to sail overloaded, and urged a complete survey of Georgian Bay, something that had never been done. There was always the chance that she struck an uncharted shoal. The *Asia* catastrophe did spawn a thorough survey of the bay, so some good came of the loss.

Regardless of where the wreckage of the dead *Asia* rests on the bottom of the bay, there are those sailors who claimed to have heard the propeller's distress whistle blowing hard and high as she battled thought the storm. They say she may be dead and gone, but when the northwest gales howl down from Lake Huron, the *Asia* is still out there … somewhere, still trying to make safe harbor with her crew of the lost on a voyage of the damned.

During a dark fall night in 1906, a party of hunters on Georgian Bay's White Cloud Island huddled together around a blazing campfire. As hot drinks doubtless spiked with a "touch of good Irish whiskey" warmed their chilled bones, stories of the day's hunt filled the air. Suddenly, something else also permeated the cold night sky. Frantic cries were plainly heard coming from somewhere out in the coal-black lake. "Help me," and, "God save us," echoed weakly over the tumbling waves. Although desperate to help, the hunters were powerless. The night was too dark and stormy to launch their small boat and the cries seemed to come from everywhere and yet nowhere. "Where were the yells coming from and where do we go?"

The following day the lake calmed and the men used their boat to search hard for the source of the night's wretched shrieks. They found nothing – not a trace of man or beast. Whatever was the source of the dreadful appeals was long gone.

When the story was repeated ashore, knowledgeable "old salts" just shook their heads, knowing full well that the hunters had experienced a re-creation of the terrible loss of the steamer *Jane Miller*. The *Miller* was a small coastal steamer built in Little Current on Manitoulin Island at the north end of Georgian Bay. Only 78 feet in length, she was 18 feet in beam and 210 tons. The steamer was no thing of beauty. Her lines were square rather than graceful, but for her designated role in life she was efficient enough, regularly handling passenger and freight traffic between Collingwood, Meaford, Owen Sound and Wiarton at the south end of the bay and in and out of all the ports on the east side of the Bruce Peninsula and Manitoulin Island.

Her captain was R.D. Port, the brother of the owner, Andrew Port. Ominously, Captain Port had the reputation of being a mariner who always pushed the limits. He was less likely to take shelter than "gut it out." Perhaps, he thought, "The old *Miller* can take it. She always has before."

The steamer's last trip started on the morning of November 25, 1881, when she departed Owen Sound for Meaford. There she loaded 30 tons of freight and passengers before turning west for Wiarton. Reportedly, the freight wasn't safely stowed below but just hastily piled on deck. Although a strong southwest gale punished the *Miller* all the way, she safely reached the mouth of Colpoys Bay where she loaded cordwood at Big Bay. Rather than burn relatively expensive hard coal, the *Miller*'s steam engine used cheap wood. Since wood took far more room than coal and provides much less energy, refueling was a constant chore. To provide ready supplies of wood not only for the *Miller* but also for a fleet of other steamers, many small wood docks were established along the Georgian Bay area. At 8:30 p.m., she pulled away from the fuel dock bound, she thought, for Wiarton, a dozen or so miles to the west. Heavily loaded with both cargo and passengers, as 28 souls had entrusted their fate to the small steamer, she pushed on, churning her way through the dark water. All during the long dark night the southwest storm blew hard and the *Miller* battled dead into it.

What happened to her is a mystery. The steamer simply never reached Wiarton, or any other location of the living. What little wreckage was discovered later was on White Cloud Island at the mouth of Colpoys Bay. And it was really very little: a flag staff, smashed lifeboat, oars and some of the crew's uniform caps. Although the area was extensively dragged with steel cables, the hull was never found.

Marine men speculated on numerous reasons for the loss. Perhaps the gale disabled her rudder, the cargo shifted, storm stress sprang a plank or the engines failed. In any of these cases the storm would have quickly overwhelmed her, sending her to the bottom and those aboard to a "better world."

The local paper editorialized that the *Miller* was overloaded and top heavy, claiming she carried no ballast. When blasted by the high winds, she just rolled over and sank, trapping passengers and crew within.

Although it was perhaps little realized, the cordwood carried by the *Miller* also served as ballast since it was stowed below, ready for access to the firebox. Wood as ballast is only marginally useful since it is light in comparison to normal ballast of iron or stone. To be effective, ballast must be stowed low and centered as well as very stable. By contrast, cordwood is somewhat higher and, of course, consumed as fed into the boiler fire. Without a doubt, the more wood she burned, the less stable she became until she finally rolled.

The wreck is still part of local lore. An official plaque commemorating the disaster is at Colpoy's Lookout Conservation Area on County Road 1 about 11 kilometers east of Wiarton.

But what did the hunters hear 25 years later? If old sailor superstitions concerning those waters where ships sank being haunted by the restless ghosts of crew and passengers are correct, then what happened was obvious. The *Miller* wreck re-created itself; the agony of an icy death was replayed again and again. The souls of those aboard the doomed vessel have had no rest.[12]

Great Lakes ships are normally named after people or places with some connection to the lake trade. A corporate president or port of call is often a good choice. Sometimes the choice is more whimsical, as evidenced by the old "poker fleet" in which the ships were named *Ace, King, Queen, Jack* and *Ten*. But corporate boys at the Cleveland Cliffs Iron Company office in Cleveland must have been nipping at the bottle of "Old Overcoat" when they stuck the tag *Kaliyuga* on their new freighter.

Supposedly, the name came from Kaialigmiut, an Eskimo village on Nelson's Island, Alaska. The remote village created an international sensation when it was discovered in 1884 due to its perceived advanced social character. Remember, this was still the Victorian Age, when courageous explorers were crashing through remote jungles and braving Arctic seas to discover the secrets of the world, filling the huge areas of the globe still labeled "unknown." It was only 16 years earlier that Stanley found Livingston in darkest Africa. Peary reaching the North Pole was still 22 years in the future. For generations, newspapers carried banner headlines trumpeting the successes and failures of the daring men prying loose the secrets of past civilizations and, with apologies to TV's "Star Trek," going where no white man has gone before.

So imagine the potential scene in the CCI office that fateful morning. The vice president looks at the president and says something like, "Frank, remember we have that new freighter over at Langell's yard ready to launch. What do you want to name it?"

The president looks over at the vice president and mutters, "Haven't got a clue. You have any ideas?"

Just then the secretary of the board, leaning back in his swivel chair with his feet resting on his desk, looks up from the newspaper and exclaims, "Hey, you guys read about this unknown Eskimo village they found up in Alaska? Paper says they had a real proper society with elected officials and taxes and all. Imagine that!"

The president looks over and asks, "What's the name of the place?"

The secretary replies, "Damned if I can pronounce it but it's spelled, K N A I A K H O T A G A. Maybe it's pronounced something like Kali Yuga."

38

The president smiles, pulls a bottle of "Old Overcoat" and three glasses from his lower right desk drawer and pours three fingers in each glass, handing one to each man. "Gentlemen, have a drink to the good ship *Kaliyuga*!" When the time came to formally launch her, a bottle of champagne smashed into the stem and the newly named *Kaliyuga* slid into Lake St. Clair.

The previous is, of course, all the wildest conjecture. But there certainly was a strong element of whimsy in the naming of the *Kaliyuga*. Unfortunately, there was a very dark side to the name also, but that in good time.

The Simon Langell shipyard at St. Clair, Michigan, built the 280-foot wood freighter in 1887. Cleveland Cliffs didn't contract for the ship prior to construction, but with the booming iron trade from Lake Superior to the Lesser Lakes mills, it needed more tonnage capacity, so purchased the hull.

From the very beginning the *Kaliyuga* wasn't a happy ship. Trouble and downright strange occurrences seemed to follow her like a sled dog smelling fresh meat. It is claimed that in August 1897 she ran into a pea soup fog while downbound on Lake Huron. Crewmen on the Texas deck, just aft of the wheelhouse, were shaken when they heard the barking, growling and eerie howling of what they took to be a large dog close aboard. The swirling gray mist prevented them from seeing where the alarming sounds were coming from. Since the ship was off Presque Isle and 15 miles out in the lake, the creature was clearly not on land. The incident provided lots of fodder for supernatural speculation, and doubtless a few men remembered the tales of the deadly Black Dog of Lake Erie.[13]

Two years later, an even eerier event happened to the ship. Steaming downbound in a fog on Lake Superior, one of the deckhands saw a twin of the *Kaliyuga* appear out of the mist and run alongside until the pair were a bare 30 feet apart. Standing at the rail looking directly at him was his double! Whatever he did, the doppelganger copied his action. It was just as if the crewman were looking in a mirror. The only difference was the eyes. The double's eyes seemed to radiate evil. When the crewman shouted, "Who are you," the double bent down and seemed to write something on a torn piece of cardboard. When finished, he slowly stood and held the cardboard up. It said, "Get off that ship!" Seconds later the ghost ship just faded into nothing. When the *Kaliyuga* reached Detroit, the crewman jumped ship and quickly signed aboard another freighter. He didn't mind sailing, but just not on what he saw as the cursed *Kaliyuga*.

Aside from such ghostly experiences, the ship had other problems. She could never seem to keep a proper schedule. While all ships are governed to a large extent by the weather, most are able to manage bad lake conditions with keeping a schedule. Balancing the needs of the ore docks, hunger of the steel mills for the right product and availability of ships, to haul it, isn't easy. A ship that can't do her part, for whatever reason, is more liability than asset. Changing captains made no difference. She just did what she wanted regardless of the wants of the Old Man.

The last trip for the *Kaliyuga* started in Marquette, Michigan, on October 19, 1905, when she loaded a cargo of rich Marquette Range iron ore. Captain Fred Tonkin was in command. Aboard was a crew of 16 men and a woman cook. When she left the loading dock the following day, the crew was amazed to see a dozen local Ojibway men and women dressed in ceremonial clothing standing on the shore near the harbor lighthouse watching the ship and mysteriously chanting. "What the hell was going on?" In all the trips they made to Marquette, the crew never saw the like of it before. Did the chanters know something of the fate of the *Kaliyuga*? Where they cursing her or wishing fair voyage?

The ship ran safely though Lake Superior's heavy seas and locked down the Sault without incident. Everything was as it should be. When she cleared Detour Light at the base of the St. Marys River, Lake Huron was rolling rough, but not unexpectedly so, and the *Kaliyuga* continued on south for Cleveland.

At 4 p.m. on Thursday, the captain of the steel steamer *Frontenac* sighted her off Presque Isle about half way to Port Huron. A storm had broken over the lake and waves were running very high. Rather than continue south, the *Kaliyuga* had turned and was heading bow into the northeast seas to lessen the impact of wind and wave.

Captain John Duddleson of the big steel steamer *L.C. Waldo* saw her around dusk still running eastward against wind and sea. She was now between Middle and Thunder Bay islands. It is speculated that her end came around 2 a.m. on Friday when the wind shifted to near hurricane force from the northwest. With the waves still running high from the east and the winds now blasting powerfully from the northwest, the old steamer could have been caught in conditions beyond her ability to survive. Perhaps she was blown into the wave trough and capsized or the seas broke her in two. Since the wreck has never been found, the answer is unknown.

When the *Kaliyuga* failed to arrive and there was no word of her anywhere, a search was made without result. She was just gone. Finally on October 26 the steamer *Lillie Smith* found her pilothouse and part of a cabin floating in Georgian Bay. Remains of some of the crew eventually came ashore south of Kincardine and Port Elgin on the Canadian side of the lake. Lake Huron gave up little of the cursed ship.

Confusion does reign over the name. As I illustrated in the beginning, one theory is the Eskimo village inspiration. Another says it was taken from an Eskimo village on Cook Inlet named Knaiakhotaga and translates as "vessel of the northern waters." Supposedly a member of the CCI office claimed it meant "Age of Iron."

There is a far more ominous explanation, however. It seems "Kali Yuga" also refers to the last era in the Hindu cycle of world ages. In the ancient text of the Vishnu Purana (part of the Hindu scriptures), time is divided into four ages. The first is the golden age, second a less peaceful age and third a violent and decadent time. The Kali Yuga is the fourth age, also called the "Age of Chaos," which comes just before oblivion. Certainly it was a very poor name for a ship.[14]

Regardless of her cursed career and horrible name, she has become one of Lake Huron's ghost ships, spectral vessels that appear for brief intervals only to vanish again into the past. Sailors running past Presque Isle in storm and gale have been startled to see the image of an old-time freighter valiantly fighting her way through the heaving seas. The steamer is clearly visible, bucking into the foaming swells then just fading away. Often the mournful blasts of her steam whistle desperately blowing distress signals can be heard riding above the wind. A sighting is usually taken to mean that the storm will peak soon.

The following story probably isn't true. Yet it is a fine yarn that appeared in the *New York Sun* on August 20, 1883, and was reprinted as fact in several newspapers in waterfront towns around the Great Lakes.

I say the story probably isn't true because there never was a schooner named the *Erie Board of Trade* and during my research I never found the name Jack Caster among the rosters of lake pilots. There is truth in this story, however. Its value lies in the intricate detail the storyteller uses to spin his yarn. For example, it is obvious that he personally knew the way sailors lived and worked on a Great Lakes sailing ship in 1883. He understood the tugs and pulls of the Niagara River on ships anchored off Black Rock, an old community long ago absorbed by Buffalo. He knew the way schooners tacked against the westerly trade winds when sailing from Buffalo to Chicago. And he was familiar with the practice of hiring tugboats to pull a string of sailing boats against the currents of the Detroit and St. Clair rivers while passing from Lake Erie to Lake Huron.

There was a schooner named the *Chicago Board of Trade* in those days, and I suspect our storyteller either knew this boat very well, or may have worked her decks. And who knows that a red-haired man named Scotty didn't die in an accidental fall from her mast?

The setting for this story was the waterfront at New York City. Several old "salties" were lounging in front of a ship chandler's store, telling ghost stories. One old man sitting on an anchor stock started his yarn:

"I saw a ghost once," he said. "I saw it as plain as I ever saw anything. The captain of the schooner I was on and the man in the waist both saw it, too. There wasn't a drop of liquor on board. It happened up on the lakes, and I reckon you know the captain. It was the talk of the docks the whole season."

"I know a Captain Jack Caster of Milan. He's the only fresh-water captain I'm acquainted with," answered the ship's chandler.

"He's the man," the old sailor said. "I heard him speak of you once. It was a little over 10 years ago. I was before the mast then. It was at the opening of the season and I was in Chicago. ..."

The storyteller told how he arrived on a canal boat and got a chance for better pay aboard a three-mast schooner, the *Erie Board of Trade*. "The *Erie Board of Trade* was as handsome a craft as ever floated on the lakes. She'd carry about 45,000 bushels of corn. Her model had as clean lines as a yacht. As I came down the dock with my bag under my arm, I had to stop and have a look at her. The old man saw me at it. He was proud of her, and I thought afterward that he rather took a fancy to me because I couldn't help showing I liked her looks."

The sailor said he remained aboard the schooner for two trips to Buffalo and back to Chicago, hauling grain east and returning with coal. He said the pay was good … two dollars and fifty cents a day … and everybody was fed well. "But the old man made it hot for us. There wasn't any watch below in the daytime and we were kept busy painting her up on the down trip and scrubbing the paint off again on the passage up." For this reason, most of the crew quit the ship at Chicago after a single trip and new people had to be hired.

"I'd seen worse times than what we'd had, and when I got my pay I asked the old man if he'd want anyone to help with the lines when the schooner was moved from the coal yard to the elevator. He said he reckoned he could keep me by if I wanted to stay, so I signed articles for the next trip right there."

Among the new men signed aboard for the second trip was a redheaded Scotsman appropriately nicknamed Scotty. "The captain took a dislike to him from the first. It was a rough time for Scotty all the way down. We were in Buffalo just 12 hours, and then we cleared for Cleveland to take on soft coal for Milwaukee. The tug gave us a short pull outside the breakwater and we had no more than got the canvas on to the schooner before the wind died out completely. Nothing would do but we must drop anchor, for the current, setting to Niagara River, was carrying us down toward Black Rick at three knots an hour.

"When we got things shipshape about docks, the old man called Scotty and two others aft and told them to scrape down the topmasts. Then he handed the boatswain's chairs to them." He said Scotty complained that the rope to his chair was worn. "The captain was mighty touchy because the tug had left him so, and he just jumped up and down and swore.

"Scotty climbed the main rigging pretty quick." But Scotty had no sooner rigged his chair to the supporting ropes and put his weight on it, and the chair broke away, plunging him to his death. "He fell all bunched up till he struck the cross-trees, and then he spread out like and fell flat on the deck, just forward of the cabin on the starboard side. I was kneeling beside him in a minute and so was the old man, too. Scotty opened his eyes and looked at us. Then in a whisper, he cursed the captain, and his wife and children and the ship and her owners. It was awful. While he was still talking, the blood bubbled over his lips and his head leaned over to one side. He was dead.

"It was three days before the schooner got to Cleveland. Some of the boys were for leaving her there, but most of us stayed by, because wages were down again. Going through the (Detroit and St. Clair) rivers there were four other schooners in the tow. We were next to the tug. Just at the big bend below Port Huron a squall struck us. It was too much for the tug, and some lubber cast off the towline without singing out first. We dropped our bower as quick as we could, but it was not before we'd drifted astern, carrying away the headgear of the schooner next to us and smashing in our own (life) boat. We were a skeary (sic) lot going up Lake Huron and no boat under the stern.

"There was a fair easterly wind on the lake and we got out of the river in the morning. We were standing across Saginaw Bay during the first watch that night. I had the second trick at the wheel. The stars were shining bright and clear, and not a cloud was in sight. In the northwest, a low dark streak showed where the land was. Every stitch of canvas was set and drawing, though the booms sagged and creaked as the vessel rolled lazily in the varying breeze.

"I had just sung out to the mate to strike eight bells when the captain climbed up the companionway and out on deck. He stepped over to the starboard rail and had a look around, and then the lookout began striking the bell. The last stroke of the bell seemed to die away with a swish. A bit of spray or something struck me in the face. I wiped it away, and then I saw something rise up slowly across the mainsail from the starboard side of the deck forward of the cabin. It was white and all bunched up. I glanced at the captain and saw he was staring at it, too.

"When it reached the gaff, near the throat halyards, it hovered over it an instant, and then struck the crosstrees. There it spread out and rolled over toward us. It was Scotty. His lips were working just as they were when he cursed the captain. As he straightened out, he seemed to stretch himself until he grasped the main topmast with one hand and the m'zzen with the other. Both (masts) were carried away like pipe-stems. The next I knew the ship was all in the wind. The squaresail yard was hanging in two pieces, the tophammer was swinging and the booms were jibing over.

"The old man fell in a dead faint on the quarter-deck, and the man in the waist dived down the forecastle so fast that he knocked over the last man of the other watch. If it hadn't been for the watch coming on deck just then, she'd have rolled the sticks out of her altogether.

"They got the head sails over, and I put the wheel up. In a minute it seemed we were laying our course again. The second mate was just beginning to curse me for going to sleep at the wheel, when the mate came along and glanced at the binnacle. He said the ship had laid a course on the other tack."

The storyteller said he left the ship as soon as it reached Chicago, which was a good thing to have done since he claimed the *Erie Board of Trade* sank on its next trip.[15]

CHAPTER 3

Lakeside Spirits

If you were a French voyageur, you called them "Les Cheneaux Iles." To an English fur trader they were the Cheneaux Islands and a modern vacationer might just say he was going to the "Snows." Regardless of the name, they are a remarkable and beautiful place.

The passel of 36 islands runs for roughly a dozen miles across the top of Lake Huron and is 30 miles or so northeast of Mackinac Island. Like all of the northern isles, they were spawned by the glaciers and literally carved out of the rock. Instead of being more traditional "island" shaped, however, they are long and lean. In fact "cheneaux" translates better as "gutters" than "channels," but both words reflect the linear shape of the islands, long and narrow.

The Snows were never well populated. Not by the Indians, French or English. It wasn't until the 1850s that lumbermen, homesteaders and small groups of sport fishermen started to arrive. The trees were soon harvested and the soil was too "thin" for good farming, but the fishing was exceptional. Local guides showed the tourists how to catch the local perch, black bass and pike. By the late 1800s and beyond, the islands were discovered by vacationers looking for an out-of-the-way place to build summer homes "up north." In the 1920s and into the 1930s, many homes dotted the islands and several good-sized resorts were active. The Les Cheneaux Club, Lakeside and Islington were particularly noted. Folks from Chicago, Detroit, Cincinnati and Pittsburgh were especially common, either as resort tourists or owners of the island cottages. Neither homes nor resorts were on the scale of Mackinac Island in size or luxury, although they were certainly fine establishments. The first Chris-Craft dealership in Michigan was in Hessel in the heart of the islands. While the local folks appreciated the sleek lines and style of the boats, what they really liked was their pure speed! They could outrun any other boat. Throughout Prohibition Chris-Craft boats proved their value by running booze deliveries between the bootlegger's stash and customers at resorts and private homes.

The Snows honor the old Chris-Craft connection by hosting a marvelous wooden boat show every August in Hessel. More than 170 entries grace the Hessel waterfront, each trying to outshine the next, but most attendees haven't got a clue as to the "rest of the story."

Vacationers are still part of the Snow scene with kayaking particularly popular. The islands offer a long hundred miles of winding and sheltered channels, all well-protected water for the painted log paddlers to enjoy.

Certainly the old voyageurs had the greatest influence in the early use of the islands. The voyageur route ran from Montreal, up the Ottawa River and French River into northeastern Lake Huron. From there it was up the North Channel to St. Marys River. They could continue up the river to Lake Superior and Fort William or other posts or follow the north shore of Lake Huron to Les Cheneaux to Mackinac Island and on through the Straits to Lake Michigan and points west. The route reversed for the return. These old voyageur routes were the Interstate highways of the 17th and 18th centuries and their large canoes the 18-wheelers of the day.

There are two recurring Les Cheneaux ghost tales. The first involves a rumrunning Chris-Craft and the good old days of Prohibition. As the story goes, one night in the fall a boat carrying a load of booze was flying along the islands headed for one of the big resorts. Chasing along behind at a slightly slower speed was the county sheriff in a boat confiscated from another rumrunner. Since the first boat refused to stop, the sheriff started firing at it with his World War I surplus BAR (Browning Automatic Rifle), a powerful automatic firing .30-caliber high velocity slugs. Hitting anything other than sky and water while firing from a bouncing speedboat is pure chance. Hitting another bouncing speedboat from a bouncing speedboat is the purest of chance. Hitting the fuel tank such that raw gasoline pours onto the hot manifold and igniting it into a sea of fire is fortune beyond understanding, but that's what happened. In moments the rumrunner was ablaze and seconds later exploded with a shattering roar, gasoline and booze forming together in a

spectacular fireball. There were no survivors and just a small amount of floating debris. Local rumor claimed that the sheriff was not doing his duty in trying to enforce Prohibition but rather trying to stop the boat because the rumrunner "stiffed" him on the expected payoff! Bribing the forces of law and order to allow the booze to flow was commonplace.

The noble defender of the law later disappeared from the local scene. Whether he fled for reasons of personal "health" or was given a brand new pair of cement overshoes in reward for destroying the delivery isn't known. The lawman could still be on the bottom of Lake Huron. Cement shoes tended to keep one in place. Certainly the owners of both booze and boat were not happy campers. Neither were the thirsty folks waiting for a shipment that never arrived.

Regardless of the exact circumstance in years after, on the anniversary of the explosion, a brief bright flash of fire could be seen in the exact spot of the disaster. It only appears for a few seconds and all is black again. In recent years, the phenomenon has been only infrequently observed. It is a Snow version of the famous "flaming ship" vision of salt-water fame.

The second ghost story is far older. For several generations after tourists discovered the area and houses and resorts were built on the lonely rocky sentinels, there were stories of strange canoes seen paddling through the islands on foggy nights. They weren't the small variety commonly made by the local natives, but big ones, perhaps 30 feet long and paddled by maybe a dozen men. The bearded paddlers wore cloth caps and sung chant-like songs in gutter French. A string of four or five of the big canoes would slide out of a fog bank and be visible just briefly before fading into another patch of gray mist. Seeing the canoes always meant bad weather was coming, usually within a day or so.

Rumrunners and voyageurs, Les Cheneaux Islands are indeed a very different place.[1]

"It was the most incredible damn thing I have ever seen. I still can't be sure if I saw it at all, but here goes. The girl was standing there plain as day, with a pair of legs that went on forever. Her headlights damn near burst out of a red corset kind of thing with ribbons hanging off it. Long black hair hung down to her bare shoulders. But her face, she was drop dead beautiful … very pale but absolutely stunning! She gave me a slight smile and she held out her arms for me. Unable to stop myself, as if I was in some kind of trance, I stepped forward and …"

Sometimes ghost stories are a long time coming together. They can be like a puzzle, especially the ones that are more involved than the simple, "I heard someone walking up the stairs when no one was there" variety. You catch a piece here and another edge there. Years pass before the final bit drops in that makes it all make sense. The following is a good example of the really complicated kind of ghost story.

This tale came to me in dribs and drabs over perhaps 20 years. A long time ago, I spent a lot of time interviewing an old-time steamer captain, a fellow who sailed for nearly 50 years starting in the late 1930s. We talked mostly about his experiences on the lakes, but toward the end he mentioned that his uncle was a sailor, too. I asked if he had any unique experiences and, since I was doing some research on Great Lakes crime, I was curious if he related any stories of illegal activities around the turn of the century when the uncle was doing much of his sailing.

The captain looked at me for a long moment and asked if I had ever heard of the Lime Island Market. I said I was familiar with Lime Island, that it was an old coaling station and later oiling point for the freighters running the St. Marys River. He laughed, saying that wasn't all it was.

He said that his uncle told him about it, but only on the promise that he would never let his father know who he learned it from. His old man was too straight-laced and would be very angry if he learned how the son knew about the "market."

By now I had run out of cassette tapes for my recorder so what follows is from my interview notes, and I couldn't "note" as fast as the old-timer could talk.

"You're right, boy, Lime Island was the refueling stop for steamers. That dock was piled high with coal and when ships started burning oil, the company added a couple of tanks and we filled with that, too! Used to take us maybe four hours to take on a load. Whether up or downbound, didn't make any difference.

"If you been doing your homework you know about the houses. I guess it is more correct to call 'em brothels, common in the big ports. The flats in Buffalo were about the worst, but Chicago and Detroit were pretty bad, too. The police didn't give a hoot for sailors, so if they went to get a girl and got rolled and even murdered, no one really cared. All the places were paying the cops off every week anyway. Some of the saloons were just as bad. A few of the really low ones would slip a 'Mickey' into a sailor's drink, roll him and drop the body through a trap door and into the river. They got rid of the evidence quickly and cleanly.

"Well, it seems that an enterprising gal named Ida built a house on the back side of Lime Island. Nice place, about a 10-minute walk from the dock along a little path through the woods. Seems she used to be a doxie in Port Huron, I think, so she knew the trade well. Knew some of the captains, too, so she let 'em know she was there. She made a lot of friends among her customers in Port Huron, so it didn't take too long for her to build up a nice steady trade. To obscure the business, she called it 'Ida's Market,' so that everyone could say they were just going to the market for a minute. All the men got a joke out of that. Of course, she always paid off the coal agent on the island so she never had any trouble from him. In a couple of years she added on to the house and hired a couple of gals from back home to come on up and work for her. So she became the madam and retired, so to speak.

"My uncle said that before too long she had a real nice setup. The front room had a good sized bar and well stocked, too. The old red-eye wasn't nearly as bad as sold in some places and, while it was more expensive than some dump in Port Huron, it wasn't bad. But again, it was better grade, too.

"An upright piano was in the corner and a huge black fellow made the ivories sing. He knew all the popular tunes and he was the strong arm if one was needed. Surprisingly, most of the men were well behaved. It was rare for the big black to toss a man out the door, but when he tossed, you stayed tossed!

"A kitchen was off to the side and a small parlor with heavy drapes blocking it from the main room. The girls often hung out there when they needed a break.

"There were a number of very small houses out back. They weren't shacks either, almost like little dollhouses. Each girl had one to entertain in. They weren't much, a bed, a chair and room for clothes, a little potbelly stove, that kind of thing. That was really unusual since in the cities they always worked from the big house. That way, the madam could control 'em and make sure that they didn't run off or anything. I guess on that island there wasn't anywhere to go. When business was slow the gals lived in those little houses.

"My uncle said that some of the girls came down from the Sault, either U.S. or Canadian. It didn't make any difference in those days. Nobody cared who crossed the border or how. The gals worked the season then went back home for the winter with a pile of cash in their purses. A number ended up marrying sailors they met from the boats. I'm not sure who got the better deal with that. I do know that my uncle's wife, Annabelle, came from the Sault, so maybe he found her at Ida's. I always remembered her as a real fine looker!

"The place was popular with a lot of boats, but not all. If the coal company boys in Cleveland knew she was back there, they would have shut her down in a minute. The company was owned by a bunch of them holier-than-thou folks and they wouldn't have taken to the service she was providing. Again, the manager on the island knew, but he was getting a take, too. Not every captain knew about her. My uncle guessed that maybe only 10 or 20 percent of the boats running the river. She didn't want the biggest operation, just one that would give her and the girls a good living.

"Anyway, one trip my uncle's boat moors up and starts to get a load of bunker and he gets the urge, so to speak. I think he was mate at the time. So he and a couple of the deckhands haul off down the path to the market. It was late afternoon and when he arrived the house was very quiet. This was odd. When he rapped at the front door with the big brass anchor knocker there was no answer. Sensing something was wrong he slowly pushed it open and entered. He said he would remember the horror for the rest of his days. Ida was sprawled across the floor face up in a pool of blood. It looked like her throat was slit ear to ear. The big black piano player slumped on the stool leaning forward into the music stand with an axe blade buried in his back. One of the girls was sitting in the corner, her back against the wall and head leaning over at a crazy angle, evidently from a broken neck. My uncle and his men quickly checked the houses out back and found three more dead girls, all lying in bed with their necks slit. It looked like they were dead for perhaps a day. Ida always kept the cash in a small strong box behind the bar. It was gone.

"My uncle was a take charge kind of guy so he quickly brought his men back to the boat where they closed themselves off with the captain and coal manager. After a while the deckhands were let go after being sworn to secrecy. Clearly, if they said anything at all, trouble would be the result. My uncle, captain and manager decided there was nothing they could do. Whoever committed the murders and robbery was long gone. As things stood though, somebody else with less discretion would eventually find the bodies and then all hell would break loose. With little other choice, the three men went back to the house, buried the victims and torched the buildings. It wouldn't be long before the woods grew over everything, hiding both Ida's Market and the terrible crime.

"Well, that's the story my uncle told me. I don't know if he ever let my aunt know what happened. My guess is that he didn't. I know she talked about going up to the Sault to visit friends, but he always managed to find a reason she couldn't go just then. I think he didn't want her to know what happened.

"When I was sailing, we used to stop at Lime Island for bunkers, too, and one day I walked around the back side just to see what I could find. It was a miserable hike. The island is lousy with poison ivy and you really have to be careful. Anyway, I did find several burned foundations that were old. I certainly don't know if they were the ones my uncle knew, but I was in the right area so I suppose they were."[2]

This is an interesting piece of secondhand information. There was no way I could verify it and the times I was on Lime Island I was not able to find the foundations. As the old captain said, there was poison ivy everywhere and the brush was very thick. In the end, I just filed away his interview.

A couple years ago I came across a kayaker with a very strange ghost story. Like many folks with firsthand experiences, he was very willing to relate it, but completely unwilling to attach his name to it. In the real world he works as a lawyer for a big-city firm and his professional standing is critical to him. Getting involved with a spook isn't career enhancing.

52

In the late 1990s, the Michigan Department of Natural Resources developed a water trail along the St. Marys River running from Detour Point, past Lime Island and on to the Sault. Several of the old fuel station buildings have been rehabilitated into shelters for trail users. The kayaker I spoke with disdained the cabins and instead worked his way around the backside of the island looking for a wilderness campsite. The DNR discourages such use, but their presence is limited, so finding a good place isn't hard. The kayaker found a fine spot and came ashore. After dragging his kayak safely on the beach, he carried his tent and gear to a small grass clearing well hidden by the trees. After setting up camp he explored his surroundings. It was then he saw a building tucked away in the trees 50 or so yards from the water.

It looked occupied. A red lantern hung from a hook to the left of the large wood door. He thought that was odd. Maybe the red light didn't attract the bugs?

Thinking that he might as well check in with his neighbors, he walked to the house, up the steps to the long wood porch and rapped the big brass door knocker. It was very distinctive, shaped like an anchor and clearly custom made. After a minute the door opened and a tall woman wearing a long dress with a high ruffled collar greeted him. "Hello, sailor. Are you looking for a little relaxation?"

He thought what an odd thing to say. And that dress was right out of the "Gay Nineties." He guessed that she was in her late 30s and very good looking. Her hair was wrapped around her head in a bun with a couple of large pins holding it together. Her skin was very pale but lips full and red. She looked like an old-fashioned Gibson girl.

He stammered out that he was only going to be camping for the night and wanted to make sure it was all right with her. She looked him in the eye and said, "Most sailors don't spend that long, but why don't you come in and have a drink?" He thought, "Why not," and followed her inside.

My lord, he thought, this place looks like a Hollywood bordello! The bar, overstuffed chairs, fringed oil lamps, Persian rugs and even an upright piano with a big black guy in striped trousers, red suspenders and white shirt sitting at it. What is this place?

The woman appeared at his elbow with a shot glass of amber fluid. "Drink up sailor, it's good for you," she said. He took a tentative sip. Whiskey, and not bad stuff either. He took another deeper drink and then upended the glass. His throat burned with the pure fire of it, but he'd been paddling long enough for it to really feel good.

"Marybelle is the only girl I have today. The others went up to the Sault to go shopping. You know how girls have to go shopping," she said with a laugh. "You look like an honest fellow, so you can pay me when you are finished. It'll be the usual $2."

She clapped her hands and a girl walked into the room from behind a set of drapes. But what a girl! The kayaker remembered, "It was the most incredible damn thing I have ever seen. I still can't be sure if I did see it at all, but here goes. The girl was standing there plain as day, with a pair of legs that went on forever. Her headlights damn near burst out of a red corset kind of thing with ribbons hanging off it. Long black hair hung down to her bare shoulders. But her face, she was drop dead beautiful … very pale but absolutely stunning! She gave me a slight smile and held out her arms for me. Unable to stop myself, as if I was in some kind of trance, I stepped forward and she wrapped her arms around me. Looking up at me with her big blue eyes, she asked where I had been and why I hadn't stopped by in so long. I don't remember what I said, something about work taking me away for a while. She said it didn't matter, she was happy I was back and she had something special for me."

The girl took the kayaker by the arm and led him out the back door to a small cottage set in the trees. He thought it almost looked like a dollhouse. How strange!

Once inside they did what "comes naturally." For the kayaker, it was better and longer than he ever had. The little bed springs squeaked and squealed as they had never before. Afterwards they talked, about everything and nothing. Then they rolled again and perhaps even a third time before he fell asleep exhausted beyond memory.

He awoke the next morning with sun peeking through the leaves above. He wasn't in the bed or even his own sleeping bag, but sprawled out on the ground. Getting stiffly to his feet, he shook his dazed head to remember what happened and how he came to spend the night on the forest floor.

Slowly, it all came back to him: the house in the trees, the woman in the long dress and Marybelle. He remembered Marybelle most of all. He ran over to where the big house was and found nothing. It was gone, except for a very weathered brass doorknocker shaped like an anchor lying in the leaves. He picked it up and wandered back to where he woke up, but there was nothing there either, just a shallow indentation in the weeds and undergrowth where he slept.

He walked back to his camp. Everything was just as he left it. As he slowly brewed up a pot of coffee and made breakfast, he thought about the night before. Did he dream the whole thing? But what about the doorknocker?

Whether all this is true or not is basically pure conjecture. With the exception of the fact of the Lime Island fueling dock, the rest of the tale is essentially not provable. It is all up to the reader, but there is that brass doorknocker shaped like an anchor.

St. Joseph Island may not have a ghostly trader and his hidden pot of gold like nearby Drummond Island, but the lonely island is still rich in "things that go bang in the night." And several ghosts do prowl the gentle shores. First, there is the matter of a little history.

For a time, the British maintained a post on the island known as Fort St. Joseph. When established in 1796, it stood bravely as the westernmost outpost in the British North American Empire. To the east was civilization according to the British. To the north and west nothing but "heathen" Indians and traitorous Americans, and as far as the English were concerned, there wasn't much difference between them. The British had been comfortably occupying Fort Mackinac, but were forced to leave by the provisions of the Jay Treaty ending the Revolutionary War. Soon, more Indians were coming to trade at St. Joseph than ever went to Mackinac Island, at least until the Americans had their factories fully operational, when Mackinac assumed its dominant role again.

St. Joseph Island's early European history is linked closely to the fur trade, the North West Company establishing a post there in 1792. When the English took over the French North American Empire, they assumed old trade routes, too. St. Joseph Island was in a good strategic location at the south end of the St. Marys River and could help protect English Canada from potential American attack.

The island, about 28 miles long and 15 miles wide, is the most western of the Manitoulin chain and lies in the river separating lakes Superior and Huron. Originally called Anipich by the Ojibway, meaning "place of the hardwoods and trees," it was renamed St. Joseph by the old Jesuits to honor the patron saint of a church they were building there. The Jesuits always were a pushy bunch, naming places according to their whims and ignoring local tribal names. Fort St. Joseph was built on the southeast shore. Not only was it a military establishment but also a critical link in the fur trade route from the upper lakes to Montreal.

When the War of 1812 erupted between the British and Americans, it was Fort St. Joseph's chance to strike a blow for Crown and Empire. Her commander didn't miss his chance to make history. As soon as he could he mustered his small force of regulars, voyageurs and Ojibway, gained a lukewarm approval from his apprehensive and moribund superiors, and struck out for the mighty American fortress at Mackinac Island. Captain Charles Roberts' "army" wasn't much to look at, 40 or so soldiers from the Tenth Royal Veteran Battalion, 180 undisciplined voyageurs and 300 rowdy Indians. The soldiers should have been his solid corps, but they were mostly old broken-down drunkards, good for nothing but garrison duty. About all they could really do was wear the famous red coats and, at best, not fall over in formation. Half the voyageurs had no muskets and the loyalty of the natives was questionable. Commandeering a vessel from the North West Company, he transported his army to the backside of Mackinac Island and landed without being seen. Viewed from the front, the fort was very imposing, high walls and cannon overlooking the harbor on the south side, just as it is today. But armies rarely come by the front door if they can help it and Captain Roberts was quite happy to knock down the rear door.

On July 17, at a place forever more called "British Landing," Roberts landed his men and marched to the high ground behind the fort. He dragged only a single small field gun with him, but it would be enough to do the job. The American commander, Lieutenant Hanks, was unaware that war had even been declared. The messenger coming north from Detroit carrying the official notice of hostilities became scared of possibly being captured by the Indians and returned without delivering the vital message. One cowardly messenger meant the loss of Fort Mackinac! When Hanks noticed some natives leaving the island and the absence of more British traders than normal, he sent a spy to see what the British at St. Joseph were up to, but the scout was caught by the British and unable to report back. When the British were in position behind the fort and ready to attack, Roberts demanded that Hanks immediately surrender. Outnumbered and unable to respond to the fire of a single cannon, Hanks had no choice but to haul down the colors and the British marched into Fort Mackinac. The Americans were paroled and sent to Detroit. Hanks' days in the Army were numbered. Although he would die by enemy fire, it wasn't a glorious death. According to legend, he had his head shot off by a cannon ball fired from the Canadian side of the Detroit River as he was sleeping peacefully in a house.

The impact of the fall of Mackinac, the most important American fortress in the Northwest, was felt quickly. It was one of the reasons that General Hull surrendered Detroit a month later. Of course, the fact that that Hull was a miserable coward and inept military leader didn't help the American cause or his own place in history. By contrast, his nephew Isaac Hull, captain of the USS *Constitution,* provided the nation with a dramatic victory over the vaunted British Navy when he defeated the HMS *Guerriere* on August 19, 1812.

An American attempt to recapture Fort Mackinac in 1814 failed wretchedly. On the way to Mackinac, the Americans stopped at the British fort at St. Joseph Island, now abandoned since they had the much better Mackinac. There was little left of Fort St. Joseph, the British having burned it to the ground once it became redundant. Nonetheless, the Americans determined that the fortifications were never very much: a blockhouse, some barracks, bake house, powder magazine, commissary store, stockade and a small pier was all the infrastructure ever built. Continuing on to Mackinac, the Americans tried to replicate the British plan, landing at the rear of the island and quickly marching inland to the heights overlooking position. Once ashore and marching south, they stumbled into a British ambush resulting in the death of Major Holmes, one of the key American leaders. Lacking leadership, the Americans were soon driven off the island. Major Holmes' body was placed in a crude coffin carved out of a tree trunk and taken by ship to Detroit for burial. The story goes, however, that the coffin wasn't carried on the boat but rather was towed along behind, merrily bobbing in the wake as the schooner made its way down Lake Huron. An alternative tale claims that when his body was exhumed in Detroit in 1834 as a new church was being built, six cannonballs were discovered in his coffin. This would suggest that the coffin was carried on the ship but heavily weighted to assure that it would sink if British capture was imminent and it was tossed overboard. What value the dead major had to the British was never explained.

St. Joseph Island was also famous as the home of the man with two families, shocking puritanical visitors to the area. The man was Major William Kingdom Rains. As an officer in the Royal Regiment of Artillery, he fought under the Duke of Wellington in the Peninsula War as well as other campaigns. After retiring he moved to St. Joseph Island in 1837 with the intention of establishing his own fiefdom. It didn't work out, but a fascinating love triangle did develop since, when he came to the island, he brought his wife, Frances, their two children and her spinster sister, Eliza. In seems that some time after their arrival on St. Joseph, a bout of mutual love evolved between the major and his wife's sister, which was solved by the good (and he must have been very good) major establishing two separate households and giving his name to all the resulting children. The locale he settled is still called Rain's Point and is just east of the old fort. Both women were very well educated and, in today's term, "home-schooled" their children since there was no school on the island. When early steamers puffed their way up and down the St. Marys River, a traveler always pointed out the Rains ranch and told the "risqué" tale of the polygamous arrangement. Straitlaced female passengers always tittered and showed indignation over his "illicit" activity.

Today Fort St. Joseph National Historic Site commemorates the old post and operates as a historic, natural and archaeological site. Parks Canada has erected a modern interpretive center depicting the island's military, Indian and fur trading past. Although the government operates the site, all the attractions aren't officially provided. One former worker remembers two specific ghosts at the old fort. Neither is harmful or in any way disruptive. Both tend to be more active in the early season when the park first opens and fewer visitors are underfoot.

The first ghost is called "Rouge Pierre" after the red sash he wears around his waist. He seems to be the spirit of an old French voyageur and is seen swaggering about on the beach. He has a short dark beard and wears a long stocking cap and buckskin coat. He periodically takes a swig of something from a dark round bottle held in his left hand, presumably brandy. Sometimes he appears to be singing and the faint strains of

"Alouette, gentille Alouette
Alouette je te plumerai
Alouette, gentille Alouette
Alouette je te plumerai"

can be heard above the lapping waves of the river. Reports of "Rouge Pierre" usually occur at dusk, on unusually still and quiet evenings.

The other spirit appears to be that of a sleeping soldier seen slumped up against the nonexistent wall at the old barracks foundation. To him, of course, the wall is still there and it's a "bloody fine place to catch a nap in the summer sun." He wears a red coat and his musket is resting on his shoulder. This apparition is more common than Rouge Pierre and usually more solid appearing. More than one visitor has commented about the realistic "costumed interpreter."

Rain's Point may also have its own spirits. A camper staying there years ago reported being kept awake all night by the rattle of pots and pans and loud yelling. Considering it's the place that Major Rains balanced two households for two sisters and the resulting children, perhaps such domestic sounds are to be expected.[3]

On "dark and stormy nights" (how else can a ghost story start?) some folks claim that the ghost of an old trader still wanders the lonely shore of Drummond Island. Illuminated only by the flash of lightning, the hunched and withered figure stumbles along the stony beach carrying a shovel and a heavy iron pot. The apparition is only seen briefly before winking into the darkness and efforts to follow have always been unsuccessful. Why follow the ghost, you ask? Supposedly the iron pot is filled to the brim with gold and the ghost is hurrying to bury it in a safe place where no one but he will ever find it.

The tale goes back to the days when the British occupied Drummond Island. The old trader lived in a house on the little island on the north end, opposite the government wharf. After a time he became insane, aka bonkers, off his rocker, unhinged, nuts. Perhaps he sampled too much of the rotgut whiskey that traders typically fed to the local natives. While he was crazy, he wasn't dangerous, so he was just left alone. One day he walked out of his house carrying his money in a big iron pot and wandered off into the bushes at the south end of the island. When he returned after a couple of hours he was empty-handed. Questioned later, he claimed that he buried his "treasure" and no one could convince him to say where.

Even before the trader went on to the "Great Trading Post in the Sky," soldiers from the British fort looked for his hoard. Apparently none was successful. If anyone found it, he was remarkably quiet about the discovery. No one even questioned where the gold may have come from and how a demented trader on a small island in the backwater of British North America acquired it. In every legend there is usually a germ of fact … somewhere, and so there is in the tale of the old trader.

There is a story in the autumn of 1815 about General Monk, the Assistant Deputy Commissary who had accompanied the British forces on their withdrawal from Mackinac to Drummond Island. "From extreme anxiety to provide for the pressing wants of the troops and Indians, the poor fellow was broken down from overwork to the point of insanity." In addition to his general commissary duties, a difficult job under the best of circumstances, he was also charged with safeguarding the Army Chest. The "chest" was the quantity of money used to pay for supplies when written drafts (checks) were unacceptable and often also included payroll funds. It was typically a large amount of money and in the early days was literally a chest. Doubtless the poor man lived in constant fear of thieves. Under the circumstances isn't it possible the man, pushed into insanity by the pressure of the responsibilities, secretly buried the chest as a way of safeguarding it?

While the official records don't mention a crazy commissary officer burying the gold, they do affirm that the commissary department occupied the little island. Monk also built himself a house on the island, reputedly a better one than the other officers had. So all the elements of the tale are true: the crazy commissary officer (trader), gold (the army chest) and island house. All that remains is for a lucky soul to follow the ghost to the secret spot and dig up the booty. So far it hasn't happened.

The British Army occupied Drummond Island from 1812 to 1828 when it was surrendered to America under terms of the Treaty of Ghent ending the War of 1812. During this period the British maintained an Army garrison as well as Indian Department there. That a garrison even ended up on Drummond is a bit confusing. According to the treaty, both nations agreed to restore all territory seized during the war, which meant that the British had to leave Mackinac Island. The obvious place to go back to was St. Joseph Island just west of Drummond Island. It was relatively fertile and offered a good location to protect the eastern entrance to the St. Marys River. However, the boundary survey between British North America, aka Canada, and the United States was incomplete, inaccurate and confusing, so the British thought St. Joseph Island was likely on the American side of the border. Rather than move to St. Joseph only to have to move again when the Boundary Commission finished its work, they decided to relocate to an island they were certain was on their side of the boundary, Drummond Island. The island was barren and too rocky for farming but ideally situated in relation to the entrance of the St. Marys River and the

Straits of Mackinac. When the Boundary Commission finally finished arguing amongst themselves, it was decided that Drummond was American and St. Joseph British. Since by then there was little need to guard the border against the Americans, and the Indian wars had ceased, the British, military, civil authority and civilian, relocated to Penetanguishene on Georgian Bay, 185 miles to the southeast.[4]

Some stories are just creepy. There isn't any obvious supernatural connection; neither ghosts or monsters stalk the tale, but there is still a spine-chilling element pushing to the macabre. Perhaps even a little touch of Stephen King.

In seems that in October 1919 a young boy on Drummond Island was out duck hunting. He had his dogs with him as well as an old shotgun. As he slowly made his way from his home to the shore, his thoughts likely were on a nice fat duck or two for the family pot. Life wasn't easy on the island and a fresh duck was a nice treat for the entire family. There would be no ducks today but instead a grisly surprise. Sticking up out of the beach sand was a woman's withered hand and arm. The dogs running on ahead found it first and were busy sniffing at it and pawing at the sand when the boy arrived to see what the attraction was.

The boy ran home and breathlessly reported his ghastly discovery to his father. Quickly grabbing a shovel, his father headed for the spot, sending his son off to get other men from the village with their shovels. They would all meet at the beach.

The men carefully dug the sand from around the body soon realizing that it was only half there. Everything from below the waist was missing! None of the men recognized the woman. She was "far gone" and identification would be difficult. The village had no formal undertaker, but there was a woman who usually "laid out" the dead. After she looked at the remains, she recognized the dress as well as a special brooch. The jewelry was carefully removed and taken to the woman believed to be the victim's daughter who immediately identified it as her mother's. The boy who found her was actually her grandson.

Given this knowledge, the group hiked to the graveyard where the woman had been buried three months before. Under the watchful eyes of the county sheriff, the men dug up her coffin and lifted it from deep in the grave to the grass. The lid was carefully pried open and everyone peered in to see for themselves. It was empty!

What happened? Why wasn't the woman in her coffin where she belonged? Was she ever in it? If not, why not? How did she get to the beach? What happened to the lower half of the body? Was there a grave robber in their midst? Could it be a case of premature burial? Did she awaken in her coffin while still above ground and wander away in a dazed state only to "die" a second time on the lonely beach? Did the lid close when she climbed out and when the pallbearers carried it to the grave they failed to realize that it was empty? Could animals have devoured the lower half, dragging the bones off into the woods while wind-driven sand buried the upper half? There were many questions but not a single answer. The mystery remains unsolved.[5]

"My grandfather always used to tell this story when we visited his camp. The camp was up near Bayfield, Ontario, on the south end of Lake Huron. We just called it camp, but over the years it grew fairly large. The main house eventually grew into a regular sized home and there was a big barn, boathouse by the lake and some smaller buildings dating from when the family first got the property back in the late 1800s. Every summer my brother and half a dozen cousins, as well as I, went up there for a couple of weeks in July. It was always a lot of fun, swimming, fishing and just fooling around in the woods. Grandfather had a sauna right down by the lake and we would fire it up as hot as we could, bake for a while, then run and jump in the lake. I swear I could hear a sizzle when we hit the cold lake water!

"The last night of our summer stay he always had a big bonfire down on the beach and we cooked hot dogs and marshmallows. Grandfather used the occasion to tell some great ghost stories once we finished eating.

"Our favorite was the one we called 'the dripping' ghosts. It wasn't all that much of a story, but we liked it. Maybe it was because it supposedly happened right on the beach where we had the fire. The atmosphere was right, too: the dying red embers of driftwood, flickering shadows from the trees and people moving, the dark and whispering lake - it was all very spooky.

"Anyway, grandfather said, way back in the 1890s, when his father fished and cut wood in the area, there was a big storm on the lake. The ship *Nassau* was caught out in it and after a terrible battle with the waves, sank off Bayfield. The whole crew perished in the storm. Some tried to escape in the lifeboat, but they were lost, too. Many of their bodies were found washed up on the very beach we were standing on. The story goes that a year to the day after the wreck, his father was walking along the shore at night when he heard yells and screams coming from the lake. It was too dark for him to see anything, but he could hear the cries for help. A few minutes later he saw a lifeboat heading for shore. In a little bit it slid right up on the beach.

"Half a dozen rough-looking guys climbed out of the boat. Great-grandfather ran up to them and asked what happened, but got no answer, just cold stares from lifeless eyes.

"Great-grandfather had a cabin in the woods, just up from the beach. In fact it is still there. It's the building we all used to stay in, kind of a bunkhouse today.

"These guys are soaking wet, drenched to the bone. Great-grandfather tells the men to follow him to his cabin to warm up and get some hot coffee. So the little band starts out with great grandfather in the lead with an oil lantern to light the way and the men following silently behind. Every time he looked back they were all there but answered none of his questions. Finally they reach the cabin, but when he turns around to tell them to go in, there is no one behind him! A few seconds before they were all there. Then they just went 'poof.' Great-grandfather ran back along the trail to the lake and searched the beach, but found nothing. Even the boat was gone.

"It was only after great grandfather thought about it that he realized the date and the earlier loss of the steamer *Nassau* exactly a year before. He figured that he had seen the ghosts of the crew trying to reach safety. The following year, great-grandfather was going from the cabin down to the lake for water when he met the crew coming up again. They walked right past him like he wasn't there. The ghost crew went nearly up to the cabin door before vanishing before his eyes. He always said that every year they would come back and do the same thing. Grandfather said his father once took him down to see the ghosts. As they watched from the side of the trail the crew marched silently past then disappeared. When his mother found out about their adventure, she was really mad and made his father promise never to take him again."

Author's note: When I checked on this story, I discovered there was no *Nassau* lost in Lake Huron; however, there was a wooden lumber hooker *Nashua* wrecked on October 4, 1892, off Bayfield, Ontario. She was downbound for Toledo when she foundered in a gale, taking all aboard down with her. Is it logical to assume that over the span of several generations, *Nashua* became corrupted into *Nassau* and became the basis for this story?[6]

About five miles north of Port Sanilac, on Michigan's thumb, is the small town of Forester and another ghost, Minnie Quay. Forester used to be a busy lumber town, but when the trees went, so did the people and today it is primarily composed of summer cottages.

The story goes that Minnie was a girl of nearly 15 when she fell in love with a handsome young sailor. It was love at first sight for Minnie. Whether he felt the same about her is unknown, but being a sailor, he likely "kept his options open." Regardless, Minnie was certainly his main squeeze in Forester.

To facilitate the loading of lumber, Forester had a long pier stretching out into Lake Huron. The activity on the pier made it a center of community focus. Although long abandoned, the old pilings are still visible today.

It was said that the love affair was carried on against her parents' wishes and everyone in town knew that it was "wrong." Minnie was too good a girl for a lowly sailor. In any case, he later drowned in a storm in the spring of 1876. Despondent over his untimely death and perhaps too filled with nonsense from Romeo and Juliet about young love, Minnie was said to have waved good-bye to some street loafers in front of a local general store, then calmly walked off the end of the pier and drowned herself in the dark cold water of Lake Huron.

Apparently, even in death, she never found her sailor man or peace, either. Today it is claimed that her ghost stalks the lakeshore, still searching for her long lost love. It is even said that she has been seen in the water, waving and trying to lure other young girls to an early death in the icy water.

It is also claimed that the old Quay house is haunted, perhaps by Minnie's spirit. The lake is a cold and miserable place to hang out, so coming ashore in favor of a nice warm and dry house makes paranormal sense. The tale continues that her parents sealed off her old bedroom after her death and never used it again. Reportedly the room was only discovered in the 1970s when a false wall was revealed.[7]

There are many weird stories of the dead trying to communicate with the living. The strangest tale of all perhaps is that of an old captain's wooden leg. The tale goes something like this. Around the latter part of the last century, perhaps in the mid-1880s, there was a peg-legged lake captain on Lake Huron. He mastered a ship that sailed between Port Huron and Alpena.

One terrible night the captain and his ship were caught in a powerful storm. In the midst of the tempest a rogue wave swept over the vessel and washed him into the lake where he disappeared. His body was never recovered. Somehow though, the peg leg came loose and washed ashore. Since the captain's initials were carved into the wood, it was eventually returned to the grieving widow and son. She in turn had a rack made and the leg was proudly displayed over their fireplace mantle. What else would you do with your husband's wooden leg?

For a year the peg leg rested peacefully in its place of honor. Exactly a year later another big storm blew up. In the middle of the night, the young son heard a strange rattling noise. The boy took a candle and went to investigate. He could find nothing amiss in the house, all the windows were tight and doors locked. When he glanced at the fireplace, however, he noticed that the peg leg was shivering, moving rapidly back and forth. For three or four minutes, the bizarre movement persisted. The son could see no reason for it. He reluctantly concluded it was his father's spirit borne on the wind of the storm. The son went into his mother's room and related what he had seen. She said she had been dreaming of her husband and concluded it was his spirit coming to summon her to the world beyond. Within several days, the woman was dead. The peg leg was buried with his mother, the son feeling that if the leg had been the father's method of contacting his wife, it should go with her.[8]

One Indian legend old Lake Huron sailors were well aware of, and perhaps the more superstitious of them had reason to fear, was that of the infamous Sacred Rock. The rock, about 10 feet in diameter and 5 feet high, is near the water's edge approximately 6 miles north of Rogers City.

The tearing glaciers that so sculptured the whole Great Lakes region doubtlessly dragged down the Sacred Rock, composed of Engadine-dolomite, from Lake Superior country. To the north of the rock are the famous sliding banks, fully 80 feet high. There are numerous springs in the area causing the soil, made up mostly clay and sand, to constantly shift giving the impression that the banks are "sliding" into the lake.

The old rock was always a place of special importance to the natives. Passing travelers often left special offerings of tobacco, pipes or other expressions of veneration to appease the Great Manitou. Sometimes dogs were even sacrificed on its cold surface, the fresh blood staining the sides dark red.

Legend claims that the rock now marks the ancient boundary between the hunting grounds of two tribes. The chief of one was said to be especially aggressive, always violating the border resulting in trouble and sometimes even bloodshed. The other chief always retaliated in kind, causing a "tit for tat" war of domain. At last, the two chiefs met at the exact spot the rock now rests to settle their differences. Both argued invidiously, threatening a terrible war if the other didn't give in to his demands. Disgusted with their selfish behavior, the Great Spirit, Kitchi Manitou, who was traveling on Lake Superior at the time, seized a nearby rock and with a mighty heave threw it down, smashing into pulp both offending men. The shock of the impact was so terrific that the nearby hills began to shake and slide, starting the phenomenon continuing to this day. The rock therefore became a unique place of significance and worship.

In another version, the two chiefs were fighting on the rock when the Great Manitou sent a powerful bolt of lightning crashing into them, sending both quarrelers into the underworld. It is said that when rain washes the rock, the red blood of the slain chiefs can still be seen.[9]

The John A. Saloon in downtown Alpena has its own protective spirit beyond that found in the bottles on the back bar. The current owners believe that it is Agnes Lau, the wife of the original owner, John A. Lau. When the harbor was clogged with tall ships and the jacks and sailors swaggered through town with money heavy in their pockets and a hankering for a shot of redeye and a "pretty waiter girl," Alpena was a rip roarin' place. And the John A. was in the middle of all the action. Some folks will tell you that Alpena has gone downhill ever since those wild days of yesteryear.

Life for a woman was hard back then. Agnes gave birth to two children but "took sick" soon after and fled to Detroit for better care.

It was a fruitless effort. She died in Detroit at age 30 after a long illness, her Detroit relations tending her until the very end. Agnes' body was returned to Alpena and buried in the local cemetery. Since John was a saloonkeeper, an occupation that in the eyes of many community busybodies made him unfit as a parent, the children were sent to a Detroit convent.

John died at age 58 and was also laid to rest in the local graveyard.

When the current owners took over the old saloon in 1987 the new owner's wife could sense a presence in the old place. She felt that they weren't alone. Someone else was always there, keeping a close eye on things. When restoration started in 1991, the feeling grew stronger. There was nothing ominous, just a feeling that someone was watching them … or watching over them.

Finally, the owners brought in a spirit medium to see what was going on. The medium reportedly knew nothing of the building or of the Laus but was able to sense some very remarkable things. She detected a small woman with dark hair sitting at a window and gazing out on nearby Lake Huron. That the place where the woman was sitting was blank wall and had no window was immaterial; the medium "knew" she was sitting there. It turns out that during an earlier renovation the window was covered over. It was now invisible to the public, but the medium "saw" it.

The restaurant manager is a fan of Agnes' and believes that the spirit is a real judge of good employees, pulling hair and knocking over trays of those she doesn't like. Having things thrown at them and food dishes overturned can particularly harass staff and customers who claim too vocally that they don't believe Agnes is around. There are also unexplained blasts of cold air, strange smells and even a vibrating toilet! Perhaps a male customer failed to put the seat down?

Some believe spirits are loose at the Besser Natural Area 14 miles to the north of Alpena. Local philanthropist (aka lumber baron or concrete mogul) Jesse Besser once owned the land and its pine forest and later donated it to the state in 1966. Located on an especially picturesque stretch of Lake Huron, over time it will only become more treasured. Besser, of course, cut it over for his lumber business, so it wasn't exactly an example of unspoiled Michigan old growth forest.

However, back in the late 1800s, the small village of Bell with about 100 people was in the area. Serving the local lumber interest, it included a one-room schoolhouse, sawmill and saloon complete with "a stable of working girls" and several cabins. When the trees were harvested, the reason for Bell was gone, too. Today, other than a desolate chimney or two still reaching skyward, everything is gone.

A small cemetery in the vicinity is home to the remains of roughly 30 people, some Bell residents who checked out early as well as nameless sailors washed up on Lake Huron's lonely shore. The remains of several Native Americans are also said to be interned in the area.[10]

The region isn't always a quiet one. Hikers have reported seeing strange dark mists moving about the old graveyard. Following the nature trail through Bell, they claimed to hear the rough melody of dance hall music drifting on the wind as though lumberjacks were kicking up their caked boots on a riotous Saturday night. And

perhaps they are. We just can't see them. Perhaps Bell is a window into the past.

Alpena is also home to a phantom train. It seems that a set of railroad tracks were torn out some years ago and ever since people have claimed to see a train still high-balling down the old right of way. It is always at night and the old engine light is either white or sometimes even pink. While white is a good "manly" light for a train, pink is a color not normally associated with railroad men. One is reminded of the old Monty Python skit and the ballad, "I'm a lumberjack!" What else can you make of a "pink" headlight on a ghost train?

During the heyday of logging and sailing, Saginaw, Michigan, was one of those towns where lumberjacks and sailors both mixed and "mixed it up." The city had its fair share of spirits, most bottled but some more vaporous. The following is an example of what happens when the dead collide with the living.

"A GHOST STORY – How a Saginaw Family Were Visited by 'That Strange Man' – A Mysterious Affair – A Gun Fired and A Wounded Man Groaned – He Could Not Be Found

"For several months past, a family living on what is known as 'Big Ditch' on Mason street in Saginaw City have been troubled with what they supposed to be home breakers or meddlesome persons. Accordingly, a few weeks since, the head of the family loaded his shotgun pretty heavily and one night stationed himself a short distance from his house in the corner of his yard, and awaited his usual visitors. At about midnight he noticed a man, or what he supposed to be his living tormenter, prowling around the door and, taking accurate aim, fired and, as he supposed, slightly wounding him.

"Immediately upon the discharge of the gun, the man groaned somewhat and on running to the spot to clutch his intruder, the shootist, to his great surprise, saw him vanish. It now seems that the family, as the neighborhood gossip says, has been troubled for several months past almost beyond endurance, and more especially during the past two weeks. In the evening when any of the family are reading, there will be mysterious figures pass between the reader's eyes and the book, and the light will go out and the fire in the stove will really smother and go out. And not only are they troubled this way in the house, but when any of the family go out in the evening they are preceded through the yard by a ghostly pedestrian. In addition to these maneuverings [sic], the family at midnight are aroused and worried by mysterious rapping's [sic] and rumbling noises. The inmates of the house and also the neighbors positively assert the house is haunted, as the visits of this strange man are altogether too numerous. We understand a party of gentlemen, by invitation of the owner of the house, intend spending a night there, when we expect to hear more in regard to these strange doings."[12]

The city of Port Huron sits at the bottom of Lake Huron, right where the lake empties into the St. Clair River to begin the long flow to Lake Erie. It is an old-time shipping community that still manages to hold on to some of its nautical history. It even manages to call itself "the Marine Capital of the Great Lakes." Of course, while this is pure local boosterism without a shred of veracity, it is a good marketing ploy and doubtless most of the snide complaints come from folks who didn't think of it first. Remember the old slogan, "perception is reality."

Port Huron has its fair share of local spooks, although most seem to keep a low profile. A local restaurant (nameless to avoid undue attention) boasts what is thought to be the spirit of the fellow who owned it in the 1930s. Local lore says that he was murdered in the basement, likely in connection with his bootlegging activities. Sarnia, Ontario, was just across the river and a flood of illegal hooch poured from the land of the maple leaf to the United States daily. Perhaps the owner crossed a smuggler or, for that matter, a notoriously corrupt Prohibition Bureau agent. Regardless, he was rubbed out in the basement. In past years a waitress was closing up late at night when she clearly heard her name called out from the kitchen, but it was empty. Her friend working with her heard the voice, too. They were the only two humans in the place. "If we both heard it and no one else was here, what then?" Doors open and close and lights flicker on and off on their own volition. Perhaps the "owner" is checking things out.[13]

The long retired lightship *Huron* is a wonderful attraction nestled into a mooring directly on the river. Built in 1920, the *Huron* served as a relief lightship for Lake Michigan, "hanging out" at North Manitou Shoals and Grays Reef until being permanently stationed at Corsica Shoals, six miles off Port Huron in 1935. She faithfully held her station until retirement in 1970. Refurbished by a dedicated group of volunteers, she opened as museum ship in 1974.

Duty on a lightship is miserable by any standard. One lightship captain once stated, "If it wasn't for the shame of it, I would rather be in the state prison." The ship is designed to hold station in the worst of storm and gale, rolling and pitching with every wave. Their sea-keeping ability is excellent, but the effect on the crews is terrible. You were either a lightship sailor or not. Most men were not.

The *Huron* may be long out of service, but she still has a crew aboard. Most of them are all volunteers, there strictly for the pleasure of keeping the old ship alive. But apparently there are a few folks not with both feet firmly on the decks, sailors from years gone by, still serving aboard her. Ships seem to have a soul of their own. They may be built of steel or wood and pushed along by refined decayed dinosaur carcasses or natural or synthetic fiber, but they nonetheless have a soul, a spirit. Old-time sailors often talked to "their" ships as old friends. Experienced captains learned to "feel" their spirits and intrinsically understand what they could and couldn't do. "Things" do happen on the old *Huron*. Hatches close by themselves, lights flicker on and off, the sound of footsteps on empty decks, all common to ships active or retired. Just ask any real sailor about things experienced at night during a lonely watch. If he is honest, he will tell you about the "other" crew … the ones who never leave their ship.[14]

Harsens Island is a strange place. It really doesn't fit into today's fast-paced society and that's its charm. Located 20 miles or so north of Detroit at the outflow of the St. Clair River into Lake St. Clair, it is rich with history. Most of the island is owned by the state of Michigan and used for various waterfowl sanctuaries. When you think of the problems with Canada geese fouling parks, swimming pools and so forth and making absolute pests of themselves, think of Harsens Island bird sanctuaries. The remainder of the island is mostly occupied by small cottages. Roughly 1,000 people live on the island year-round and a horde of others arrives in the summer. Getting to the island is relatively easy with ferry service running from Algonac on the mainland.

The St. Clair River is an extremely busy shipping route and the main channel cuts close to the island making it a great place to grab a camera and photograph the "boats." Remember, on the Great Lakes anything floating is a boat. A 16-foot aluminum skiff or a 1,000-foot freighter are both called boats. It's a tradition that strips away a lot of "pretension."

The area made up by Harsens Island, the St. Clair Flats and the mainland part of Clay Township is one of the largest fresh-water deltas in the world. Several major waterways wind through the lowlands: St. Clair River, the North, South and Middle and Sni Bora channels among them. A host of smaller byways, channels, cuts and bays, including the Big and Little Musacmoot, Goose, Baltimore, Fisher and Maybury, dredged and natural channels and canals all add confusion to the region. There are so many waterways, navigable and not, that some folks call it the "Venice of America." On a dark and foggy night, you half expect to see some guy in a striped shirt and big silly hat poling a gondola along while warbling off key about a long lost dish of spaghetti or something.

The area was frequented by early French missionaries and voyageurs who called it the "great green meadows." The earliest inhabitants were, of course, Native Americans. The confluence of the Indians and French provided the critical link for the area's first industry – fur trading. Starting in 1615, French traders were eagerly hauling away bundles of prime furs brought in by the local natives. When French fortunes ebbed low following the disaster of the French and Indian War, the British took over control of the area. Later it was the U.S. flag flying over the "great green meadows."

Harsens Island was named after Jacob Harsen, a gunsmith and trader who arrived about 1778. He supposedly purchased the island from the local Indians for a keg of whiskey and string of beads. His son-in-law and his family accompanied him and, as legend goes, they were the first European settlers between Mackinac and Detroit.

The island gained an early moral if not legal start on Prohibition when Harvey Stewart started a distillery there in the early 1800s. Reportedly it was one of the first distilleries in the state. The firewater produced was used to trade with the Indians for furs and wild game, a common practice of very dubious ethics.

When lake shipping began in earnest, the North Channel was the preferred route, but a sandbar at the outlet prevented most boats from completing the trip. To solve the problem, a minor industry developed around transshipping cargos. The boats anchored in nearby Anchor Bay (where else?) and unloaded the bulk of their cargo to smaller boats to reduce draft. Drawing less water, the bigger boats slid over the sandbar to deeper water where they reloaded their cargo. It was grossly inefficient but at the time the only viable solution.

Some farming was done on the higher areas of Harsen and nearby Dickinson islands, but it was comparatively little. By 1840, enterprising men were building boats on the island, an activity that continued up until the Civil War.

As lake shipping grew, boats became larger and drew more water. The encumbrance of the shallow bar and channels of the St. Clair River could no longer be tolerated by the growing nation. In 1856, the federal government dredged a 6,000-foot-long ship channel past the worst of the hazards. The channel was constantly improved in the years following as needs dictated.

One of the benefits of the new channel was to provide access to the island for large passenger steamers running from Port Huron and Detroit. Harsen's was only 20 miles north of Detroit, an easy excursion run. But the visitors needed places to stay and things to do, so a number of resort hotels quickly developed along the South Channel. The White Star Steamship Line made 13 stops in the Flats alone, plus others along the route coming and going. Round-trip fare between Detroit and Port Huron was a whopping 50 cents. The most famous steamer to run the route was the 311-foot sidewheer *Tashmoo*, starting in 1900. The sidewheeler was rated to carry up to 4,000 passengers at a time but rarely exceeded 2,600 to provide better passenger comfort. The *Tashmoo* was also tied in with Tashmoo Park, a popular entertainment site on the island featuring a large dance pavilion, casino and other amusement. Today, the old park is part of Tashmoo Marina. Until she ended her trips in 1936, the popular sidewheeler was called the "Queen of the

St. Clair" or "glass hack" in recognition of the huge number of windows she sported.

Although the public loved the *Tashmoo,* old-timers on the river didn't much like her. In fact they predicted her loss. First off, she was a sidewheeler and sailors didn't like them at all. While they were fast, sailors questioned how seaworthy they really were. She was also named after an Indian and many thought that gave her an unlucky star. The steamer's tale is best related in the first chapter of this book.

When Prohibition rolled around, Harsens Island was in a perfect location to capitalize on the tremendous opportunities, as were its people. The United States made an honest drink illegal, but Canada had distilleries running full blast. And Canada was just across the channel, within "spittin' distance," as it were. The Harsen's Island resorts were filled with people wanting a drink and the local folks were eager to provide for their needs. It was claimed that virtually everyone became a rumrunner. Regardless of how hard the local, state and federal authorities tried to catch them, they never did. The multitude of channels, marshes, cuts, streams and canals made for a smuggler's paradise. It is also said that the local cops didn't really bother to try, the state cops tried very little and the feds were utterly lost!

Between the resorts and prohibition, it was good times for Harsens Island. But it didn't last. When Prohibition was finally repealed, it was the height of the Depression and money for "resorting" was in short supply.

When the *Tashmoo* wrecked in 1936 everything just died. Several of the resorts burned to the ground (funny how that happens when business takes a downturn), leaving only smoking mounds of memories. Today, the lone survivor is the Idle Hour Yacht Club. It is this remarkable relic from Harsen's Island's colorful past that we are concerned with.

The Idle Hour Yacht Club was built in 1891 by Charles Coulter and sold four years later for use as a fishing and hunting club. Originally called the Riverside Hotel, it was described as a "small but cheerful and home-like hostelry, where popular prices and first-class cooking prevail in a rare combination." All was quiet until World War II exploded on the local scene. The Coast Guard, unlike military services, did not conduct consolidated basic training at major bases but rather farmed the job out to existing bases or took over other facilities for the purpose. In 1942-43, the Coast Guard used the old hotel for recruit training, housing roughly 200 men in it. When the Coast Guard sailed away as the war emergency ended, the facility eventually became a restaurant until closing in the early 1980s.

But you can't keep a good place boarded up forever and in 1988 local businessman Ken Baker purchased it. After considerable renovation, he transformed it into today's Idle Hour Yacht Club. Its 48 rental rooms are mostly occupied by club members on a yearly lease basis, proving a cozy home away from home. As you will see, it is a spirited old place.[15]

The ghosts in the Idle Hour Yacht Club are anything but "idle." Although some members maintain that there are only three, Annabelle, George and Jacob, the plethora of stories would suggest that many more spirits call the old club home, too.

The building has been altered many times since it first opened as the Riverside Hotel. On the generally accepted theory that ghosts become active when things are changed, the club is in constant spiritual turmoil. Today, the lower floor has a large barroom, a ballroom, kitchen and several private apartments. Additional guest rooms are upstairs. Some are spacious and luxurious, really small suites, while others are less so. Club members use the apartments as weekend retreats from a hectic world. And, indeed, the Idle Hour is a "world of its own."

The building has a majestic view of the East Channel of the St. Clair River. The big freighters slide silently past the old hotel, perhaps several hundred yards distant. During the summer a host of private craft zoom up and down the waterway, too.

Most of the club members seem reconciled to the many spirits that they share the building with, having a live-and-let-live attitude (or perhaps a live-and-let-die attitude is more accurate). Some experience their own "close encounters."

Generally the ghosts are friendly, even a bit playful, but strangely usually not of the prank-playing poltergeist variety. Objects don't disappear only to reappear days later in another location, although lights sometimes do mysteriously turn on and off. Neither are the spirits especially quiet. It isn't unusual for members occupying upstairs rooms to be awakened by loud crashes and thumps right outside their doors. When they check, no one is around, at least no "living" person! After a while, people get used to such bizarre activity and tend to just ignore it.

The litany of ghostly happenings is near endless.

The ballroom and barroom are hot spots of activity. Numerous digital photographs showing strange white cloudy movements and glowing orbs have been taken in the middle of various party functions. The spirits must be exceptionally sociable and always ready for a good time. Unless they see the photographs later, dancers aren't even aware that they are sharing the floor with cavorting specters.

The old jukebox in the bar has been known to play itself without anyone (or at least any one visible) dropping coins in or even being plugged in to the electric outlet. Sometimes the pages of the playbook inside the glass front flip by themselves. The jukebox spirit is partial to old Gene Autry cowboy songs and doesn't like Elvis recordings. It's safe to say, Elvis isn't hiding out in the old Idle Hour Yacht Club.

While photographs capture the bizarre clouds, some encounters are far more substantive.

Before one banquet, a member was walking into the small hallway between the stairs and club when she encountered a beautiful woman in a white formal evening gown. Her blonde hair was cut in pageboy style and a sparkling diamond necklace glittered around her slender throat. The member didn't know the stranger, but the woman in white knew her and spoke glowingly of the fine work done on some recent club projects. The two women spoke for some time about current club events and affairs. The blonde also mentioned that she and her husband used to spend a lot of time at the club but had been unable to do so recently. After a time the two women parted company, the member heading upstairs and blonde into the crowded banquet hall. Mere minutes later the member wanted to point her out to a friend but searched in vain. She was gone! No one remembered seeing her, either. Was she ever there at all?

On one occasion a member was hosting her sister and her daughter in her large second-floor suite. The daughter suffered from Down syndrome and although in her 20s had the mind of a 4-year-old child. While the sisters were talking in the living room, the daughter was in the bedroom and supposed to be falling asleep. The adults could hear the child talking away a storm but to whom they couldn't imagine. Finally, the mother entered and asked whom she was speaking with. The daughter replied, "Annabelle." The mother settled her daughter down and left the room, telling her sister that she claimed to be talking to an imaginary friend called "Annabelle." The member said nothing but when the daughter again began to talk, went in and sternly said, "Leave her alone. Do you hear me? Leave her alone. She needs to get her sleep!" Afterward, she explained to her sister that Annabelle was one of the ghosts. Annabelle apparently listened, since the daughter was quiet and soon dropped off asleep.

One of the ghosts is George, aka "Leisure Suit George," since he is usually appears wearing a lime green leisure suit. Some members conjecture that he lives in the attic but is seen all over the building. A long-time club member claimed to have frequent conversations with him but never revealed what their "spirited" discussions involved.

There are numerous explanations for George. The most popular goes something like this. George was the hotel manager. The man he hired as a handy man began paying undue attention to George's comely wife. The attention was shared. At some point George caught the pair during a session of mutual attention reciprocity. George must have been a very forgiving soul or else so deeply in love with his wife that he couldn't bear to toss her out on her derriere as the faithless wench deserved. A short time later she and her "handy" lover rowed out on Muscamoot Bay during a dense fog and never returned. Perhaps they ran off together or even drowned. Sharing too much "attention" in a small rowboat can lead to an unstable relationship. Perhaps they are together forever drifting along the bottom of the quiet bay. George was inconsolable when his wife didn't return, and when he "checked into the big hotel in the sky" returned to the Idle Hour as a ghost in the hope that his miscreant spouse would someday return, too. How he acquired the green leisure suit is unknown, although there are those who believe that seeing it is enough justification for any woman to flee in terror.

The south wing of the building is newer, likely constructed in the early 1920s. Today it holds a number of small suites, but when built it housed a new kitchen featuring a huge walk-in cooler. Several psychics claim that the area adjacent to the cooler and the cooler itself are charged with evil energy. A couple of the investigators even refused to enter the cooler. The malicious feeling was too intense for them to handle. Other investigators who dared enter became short of breath and nauseous inside the old cold box and had to be helped out.

The hall running past the old kitchen and cooler has its own spirits. The strong smell of perfume is sometimes overwhelming and women's voices echo faintly down the hall when no one is present. Recently a male guest, who had never been at the club before, was staying in the room opposite the cooler. In the middle of the night he was overcome with the heavy aroma of lilac perfume. Claiming that he couldn't breathe, he fled to a friend's room for the night. Since the fellow was a real "macho man," afraid of nothing, his fragrance flight was ridiculed by his friends.

Another of the rooms is a kids' game room, complete with TV, toys and tables. In every respect it is a normal room, except that the happy sounds of children's voices sometimes are heard when the room is empty.

One of the club officers maintains a small suite at the extreme south end of the building. On several occasions she has been awakened when icy hands grab her ankles and slowly begin to drag her down toward the foot of the bed. Only when she violently shakes her legs is the grip released. It is also not uncommon for loud knocking to be heard at the door, but when opened, the hallway, of course, is empty. Sometimes the covers on the bed will slowly pull away as if by unseen hands. Every once in a while she will be reading in bed when the bed covers move as if a cat jumped onto them. The invisible creature will start to walk around leaving a clear imprint on the covers.

Although the building is usually filled with club members enjoying themselves to the accompaniment of the clack of the pool table, clink of drink glasses and chatter of conversation, in the early spring or fall when most of the members are gone for the season the club can be very quiet. It is during these rare spells of tranquility that the sound of old-time music resonates softly throughout the ballroom and bar areas. Sometimes it sounds like an Al Jolson tune; other occasions it's more like a raucous ragtime melody. Where is the music coming from? Could it be that "old" members are back and enjoying "their" club, too?

A woman's rest room is at the south end of the ballroom. A few years back, one of the members heard a woman yelling for help, something about being trapped and unable to get out. None of it made any sense but she hurried through the ballroom searching for the source of the yelling. It was coming from the woman's rest room. As she walked closer she noticed that the door, which opened inward, was bending back and forth, just as if someone was outside pulling it shut as the woman inside was trying to pull it open. When the member reached the door, she asked what the trouble was. The woman inside screamed that she was trapped, the door wouldn't open. The member grabbed the doorknob, turning it easily and the door opening effortlessly. The excited woman inside shot out! A guest at the club, she ran out the front entrance vowing never to return, yelling about "infantile pranks and someone holding the door shut." There was no lock on the door and it wasn't warped in any way. Was one of the ghosts playing a joke on an unwanted visitor?

A set of wide stairs leads from the old lobby on the first floor to guest rooms on the second. The area at the head of the stairs on the second floor is notorious as being a cold spot that seems to "live" there winter and summer. It can be a boiling hot day in mid-August, but that one little area of space is frigid. The building isn't air conditioned, so the handy excuse of being too near a vent duct isn't available. One day several residents were standing in the hall and talking when an icy blast moved up the hall hitting each person in turn. One man remembered that it was just like a wave sweeping over you, or a ghostly presence moving quickly down the hall.

The bedroom opposite the cold spot area had its own run-in with the unexplained. It seems that four members were sitting and chatting away when a strange black vapor appeared, shooting around on the floor between them like a playful puppy. After perhaps half a minute of frantic activity, "poof," it disappeared.

The building is marked by three towers, one at each end and at the center. All contain small suites. The rooms in the center and north tower are friendly and comfortable. The south tower is decidedly different. Investigating psychics claim that a strong and unhappy presence occupies the room. Some folks refuse to sleep there. It is also a magnet for flies. There is no discernable reason for the strange attraction, but the pests come in droves.

About the middle of the second floor is the old bridal suite. It's big and airy, with lots of room to romp and play, as would be expected on a wedding night. The room also faces the river and provides a wonderful view. Doubtless many brides (and grooms, too) spent their happiest time in the room. One bride may still be there. On several occasions, club members on the lawn in front of the building have seen a woman wearing white standing in the window looking out. Not only was she a stranger to them all, the room was locked, preventing entry. Who was she?

This writer was present when another very unusual event happened at the suite. I was speaking to the current owner about the old ghost stories, and as he shut the door the lock came off in his hand. The two screws holding the handle and locking mechanism together were completely unbolted! It had just been replaced the day before. Even stranger, the locking mechanism between the door and into the jam couldn't be extracted. Normally, it should slide out easily. Regardless of how much force we applied,

it wouldn't move. It was as if something were holding it in place. We both left to get a set of tools, but on return the slide opened effortlessly.

Just down a room or so from the Bridal Suite is another member's room and the site of one more "unusual" occurrence. It seems that the member and his wife were in the bar enjoying a few adult beverages and friendly conversation. When the hour grew late, the wife decided to call it a night and went up to their room to go to sleep. Her husband was having too much fun to cut the evening off and stayed in the bar. After donning her nightgown and doing the multitude of things women do before "retiring," she climbed into bed and settled down into her side, facing away from the door. At his point she realized that she forgot to turn the light off, but just then the hall door opened and someone walked into the room. Thinking that it was her husband back from the bar, she asked him to turn off the lights. The switch was located near the door and out of her view. Although there was no audible reply, the lights flicked off nearly immediately. In a couple of minutes or so she felt the familiar movement and creak of the bed as her husband climbed in and snuggled in beside her. Comforted by his presence, she was asleep within minutes. A couple of hours later she was suddenly awakened when the hall door banged open and the lights snapped on. It was her husband back from the bar and none too steady on his feet. Wait a minute. If this was her husband, who (or what) crawled into bed with her a couple of hours earlier?

The next room down the hall was never known for any paranormal activity but yet is the site of infamous "black spirits." Much as digital photographs in the ballroom have captured strange white cloudlike images flitting around the room, black ones were photographed in the bedroom.

Another new wing projecting west (to the rear of the building) was added in the 1960s to increase the hotel capacity. Some of the rooms are complete with baths while others use communal units at the end of the hall. It seems that one member arose in the middle of the night with a strong need for the john. As he ambled down the hall, he noticed a man walking behind him also heading for the john. Thinking it odd that both had the same need at the same time, he turned to make a comment only to find the hall empty. The second man had vanished.

Tales of supernatural happenings continue. Recently, two new members, both female, took a room on the second floor on a quiet Sunday night. They were the only guests staying over. Everyone else went home to be ready for the Monday work grind. All night long they heard women laughing and giggling in the hallway just outside their door. When they investigated, the hall was empty but the lights flickered on and off without apparent cause. Again, they were the only ones in the building, so what were they hearing?

Before a Commodore's Ball, the highlight of the club social season, a waitress was carefully placing the napkins on the dining tables. When she finished and turned to check her work, all were sideways from how she set them. Not deterred, she changed them all back again. Again she turned to check and again she found them turned around. This was too much and she ran yelling into the bar demanding that someone deal with the ghosts. Finally, one of the club officers went in to the dining room and yelled out, "Okay. We have a big party tonight and need everything done right, so quit playing around." Incredibly, they did. Ghostly ministrations ceased for the night. The napkins stayed as they were placed.

The experience of being followed by a something isn't unusual anywhere in the building. Sometimes the interloper is visible, but more likely it is just an overwhelming feeling of someone else, another presence just behind your back.

It seems that in the 1980s a husband and wife visited the club to look it over prior to applying for membership. Their high school aged daughter was with them. As the parents discussed membership with the club manager, the daughter grew bored and wandered to the second floor where she met another girl a few years older. The older girl wore a white uniform with a red stripe and said that she was the upstairs waitress. She was going to college and this was just a summer job. The two girls had much in common and conversed for some time before the high school student broke it off when she heard her parents calling for her. When she met them downstairs, she mentioned speaking with the waitress. While her parents thought nothing of it, the manager was amazed. He had no "upstairs waitress" nor any college girl working for him. Quickly summoning other staff, the entire building was searched, but no trace of the waitress was ever found. When the story got around, though, some of the old-timers remembered the tragic tale of a young girl who did work as the upstairs waitress when the club ran as a hotel in the 1960s. She died when her car ran off the road and into the water while returning home after a late night at work. Her description matched perfectly. Was she back at work at the hotel or just visiting?

There is evidence of at least one ghost that enjoys playing pool. During the off season, a group of members returned to the club after enjoying drinks at the Sans Souci bar only to discover the lights on in the barroom. Curious, since they made certain everything was locked up when they left, they walked up to the door to see if it was open. It was still locked tight, but "someone" was standing by the pool table. The figure was indistinct and only remained an instant before fading into nothing, but everyone agreed it was there.

I visited the Idle Hour in March 2006 and while I saw no ghosts (they never appear on demand), I did have a bizarre experience. I stayed in a small room on the second floor painted entirely in bordello red. All it needed was a mirror on the ceiling to fit into the infamous Mustang Ranch outside of Las Vegas. Evidently the decorator wanted to recall the hotel's reputation during the Roaring '20s for providing guests with every needed service. Although it makes no sense, during the wee hours of the night I heard a constant barrage of the word "wool." It was repeated again and again, loudly and softly, with a high pitch and low, in tones demanding and pleading. The voice was close, then distant. As I said, it made no sense at all.

The Idle Hour Yacht Club isn't the only place on the island with ghostly residents. The Old Club, another of the turn-of-the-century "hunt clubs," is reported to have the ghost of a tall black man. The specter is seen sitting in a particular chair. If the chair is moved, it always finds its way back to its proper place.[16]

The great island that marks Huron's North Channel is called Manitoulin, named by the Indians to honor Kitche Manitou or the Great Spirit. Manitoulin is filled with legends and traditions. At more than 1,000 square miles in size, the Canadian Island is five times larger than any other in the Great Lakes. Manitoulin is also the world's largest island within a lake. The Ojibway, Ottawa and Potawatomi, all tribes of the Algonquin family, believe Kitche Manitou lives deep in the island's interior, a place far beyond the reach of mere mortals.

A 300-foot bluff is topped by "Dreamer's Rock," a sacred spot on nearby Birch Island for young braves to come and experience a spiritual voyage while fasting and praying for a vision. Dreamer's Rock attracted vision-seekers for centuries, who fast for days, awaiting spiritual direction. It was claimed that the dreams provided both insight and the true path for the rest of their lives. If they dreamed that they were hunters, warriors or farmers, so they became. Their dreams said it would be so and so it was.

The rock itself is smooth with a flat top, just the right size and shape to hold a person sleeping on his side. The seekers remained for days, drinking only water and protected by a mere blanket against the cold nights as they waited for the visions to come. One of the famous seekers was the Ojibway chief Shawonoswe. Long before Europeans came to the New World, the chief, then a young brave, came humbly to the rock to gain insight to his future. No visions came. The spirits ignored the young man and left him barren of dreams. His friends all had visions, but not him. Deeply ashamed, he still became a great warrior, unafraid of the weapons of his enemies.

Many years later, as an honored chief of his people, he came again to the rock to seek the visions denied him as a youngster. Now the spirits smiled on him. A great thunderbird appeared before him, placing Shawonoswe on his back and taking him across the deep and dark waters of Lake Huron to a mountain called Nehahupkung. Climbing down from the great bird, the chief walked to the edge of a cliff. Before him, standing on a cloud, was a strange figure holding a bowl of water.

The chief asked, "Who are you?" The figure replied, "I am your creator" and told the chief to walk off the cliff toward him and look deeply into the water. While the chief was afraid, he knew better than to ignore the orders of the creator, so he did as he was bid.

Stepping off into thin air, he found that he did not fall, but instead it was like walking on deep moss. Walking toward the creator, he stared hard into the water. He was rewarded with the sight of animals and, even more remarkable, he could understand their talk and even read their minds. The creator intoned, "The animals are your relatives. You should not abuse them." Ominously, he also saw men dressed in dark robes with hair on their faces. The infamous Jesuits would not come for centuries yet, but it was an evil future for his people. Looking deeper into the bowl, he saw that wherever the robed men went, the land was swallowed up and his people perished. Terrible wars ravaged the land and wreaked havoc on his tribe. It was a future of death and destruction brought by the terrible robed and bearded men.

The creator also gave the chief rules to live by, much as the Christian Ten Commandments. When Shawonoswe returned to his people, he became even a greater chief and instructed them in the will of the creator. Every year following Shawonoswe's return, the guidance of the creator was celebrated in spring and fall. A large cedar pole erected as a kind of totem was used as a gathering place for the Indians. Many years later, when the French voyageurs and the infamous Jesuits finally arrived, it was said that they found the tribe gathered around the cedar pole and that they were kind, innocent and tender with each other.

Indian legend also accounts for the word *Mindemoya,* the name of both the lake and the community. According to one story, Nanabush, the infamous trickster, was running with his grandmother on his shoulder but tripped and fell, sending her flying through the air, landing on her hands and knees in the center of a large lake. She magically turned into an island, and the lake was named after her: Mindemoya, "the old woman." The nearby community of Mindemoya took its name from the lake.

Northeast of Lake Mindemoya is a cliff standing 540 feet above Lake Huron. It was believed that the great god Manitou lived on the top with his wives. Since no human being dared set foot within this sanctum, it was treated as a place of many mysteries. Natives worshiped and supposedly offered sacrifices to appease the anger of their gods in the cliff's dark shadow.

Nanabush didn't always get away scot-free from his pranks. According to legend, long ago women of the village did their chores along the riverbanks. Of course, their babies went everywhere with them usually wrapped in sphagnum moss in their cradleboards. Often cradleboards were tied to the branches of nearby trees, while others were leaned against large rocks or at the base of trees.

Nanabush sometimes played tricks on the women by coming along and spinning the cradleboards hanging from the branches or knocking others to the ground while the women were busy with their chores. The babies would cry as a result and the ruckus pleased the trouble-making Nanabush greatly.

But the mothers had their revenge. One day, they caught Nanabush at his childish pranks and chased after him, beating him with sticks and stones. To avoid getting caught, he slid down a steep rock face. As he slid, he skinned his rear end on the sharp stone and some of the flesh clung to the rock. Through magic, these slices of skin became lichen, still visible on the rocks.

Just to the north of Little Current is Great La Cloche Island, home of the ancient Ojibway holy relic known as Bell Rock. For centuries, perhaps stretching to a thousand years, the Chippewa believed that it sang with the clear powerful voice of the gods. When hit with stone or tomahawk, it resounded with a bell-like ring audible for miles. They regularly provided it with offerings of tobacco to appease the gods.

When French voyageurs began visiting the area, they stopped at the strange rock to strike it with their axes just to hear the clear tones so reminiscent of a church bell. They claimed that it could be heard for 40 miles. It was said to be more than 6 feet tall and it took four men holding hands to reach around it.

The rock was also used as a warning signal. If the dreaded Iroquois were sighted, Ojibway braves pounded the rock to summon their warriors. But one dark night, the Iroquois slinked in unseen and attacked the Ojibway village, murdering many people. Only a few Ojibway survived to escape into the dark forest. The Iroquois settled by the sacred rock but, according to legend, strangely could not make it ring. No matter how hard, where or with what they struck it, no sound came forth. After a time, the Iroquois fell ill with a terrible skin disease and in three short days they were wiped out, their disfigured and bloated bodies littering the primal forest floor. After a time, the Ojibway returned and unceremoniously buried their dead enemies in a mass grave. Such was the fate of those defilers of the Ojibway. The rock was again safe from interlopers and when struck gave forth the previous rich tones.

At some point in the 20th century, the rock split into three pieces. Some folks claimed that it was the result of a lightning strike. Others said that a wandering Jesuit priest blessed it and the split was the result of driving the devil out. It could have just crumbled from sadness at the death of the old ways before the relentless grind of European gods. Although two of the pieces are mute, the third is said to still ring true when struck. In honor of the rock, Ojibway still leave occasional offerings of tobacco.[17]

Europeans have also made their mark on the island, in fact and myth. A good example is the ghost of Danny Dodge. There are many versions to the story, but one that seems reasonably accurate goes something like this.

Danny was the son of John Dodge, one of the founders of the Dodge automobile fortune. Dodge owned a large hunting lodge at Maple Point and Danny spent most of his summers growing up on the island learning to love the woods, water and slower pace of life, so different from the frantic hustle and bustle of the Motor City. He also fell in love with an "island girl," 19-year-old Lorraine MacDonald, a Gore Bay telephone operator. However, both families opposed the match: the Dodges, since they looked at Lorraine as a gold digger after the family fortune; the MacDonalds, likely thinking that she would be happier with one of her own kind. What could the two possibly have in common? They came from different worlds. Regardless of the objections, Danny and Lorraine were married in August 1938 in lower Michigan at what is now Rochester Hills. They returned to the Dodge Manitoulin Lodge to honeymoon.

Apparently bored one day, Danny wandered out to the garage where he discovered a box of dynamite complete with blasting caps and fuses. Having nothing better to do, he crimped a fuse to a cap, stuck the cap in the stick, lit the fuse and threw it through the door outside where it gave a satisfying explosion. Happy with his success, he assembled another charge and lit it. However, just as he was preparing to toss it through the door, his new wife and several friends arrived outside to see what the earlier blast was about. Since he couldn't throw his stick through the door without injuring them, he tried to toss it through an open window on the opposite side of garage. His aim was off. The stick hit the frame and bounced back inside where it exploded with devastating results for Danny and his guests. Apparently the idea of just pulling the fuse out never occurred to him!

While all the people were injured, Danny was the worst. Reputedly he was near death. He needed immediate medical attention to have a chance to live. To avoid a trip over the rough island roads, Lorraine and her two friends, all injured, loaded an unconscious Danny into the lodge speedboat and headed out to cross the North Channel for the town of Little Current and the nearest medical aid. Unfortunately, the lake was roiled by 4-foot waves making it a very rough trip.

About halfway to Little Current, Danny apparently regained consciousness and stood up in the wildly rocking boat only to be tossed out and into the water. Although the boat quickly turned around in an effort to save him, he disappeared beneath the waves.

Since it was a bare 13 days into the marriage, there were accusations of murder, that Lorraine had managed to "do in" her husband to gain his money. No criminal charges were ever filed, but it took a civil trial to finally straighten out the legal affairs. Eventually she received a settlement of more than a million dollars and the Manitoulin Island lodge.

Apparently, though, Danny's spirit is restless since it is claimed that he periodically haunts his old lodge, now a bed-and-breakfast inn. Is the ghost somehow looking to implicate his killers or is he just in a place he always considered home? Danny clearly marched to the beat of a different drum than did the offspring of other early automobile tycoons. His spirit seems to continue to hear the same offbeat drummer. As long as his ghost stays away from playing with dynamite, there shouldn't be a problem.[18]

Many ships and aircraft have vanished off Manitoulin Island. Some publications even call the area the "Great Lakes Triangle" in recognition of the numerous losses. Some were easily explained and others are far more mysterious. There is even a story about the crew of the old *Griffon* being found on the island. Estimates of the losses range as high as a couple of hundred ships and perhaps three dozen aircraft. One of the planes is a Beechcraft UC-43B Staggerwing lost in August 1943. At the time, President Franklin Roosevelt (known as the "bad" Roosevelt) was vacationing on the island. To make sure that the President had the latest official dispatches and news, the Army provided daily mail flights from Selfridge Air Base just north of Detroit. While taking off from a local bay on the return flight, an electrical fire broke out aboard and the plane crashed, sinking in 90 feet of water. The two-man crew was saved. In recent years, the wreckage was located and parts recovered for a local museum.

A particularly colorful story links Manitoulin Island to a couple of headless haunts. The tale, in its full glory, is best told in the book

Drummond Island, the Story of the British Occupation 1815-1828, by Samuel F. Cook:

"The intrepid fisherman who sails nearby or ventures to land on the shore of the Great Manitoulin Island after sunset, is appalled and his blood is curdled by the sight of two headless soldiers who walk to and fro, clad in the red coats and other regimentals of the early part of this country.

"And stranger still, when nights are dark and cold, and the belated fisherman, lured by a firelight on the shore, thinking that friendly greeting and warmth await him there, runs his boat on the beach and hastens to the blazing logs piled high a short distance away, he finds there no fisher comrade belated like himself, but instead the two headless soldiers sitting on a log in the glow, and warming themselves by the blaze made furious by the night wind. With chattering teeth, with hair erect and eyes starting from their sockets, he runs to his boat and puts out into the night regardless of the dangers of the deep, so that he may but be far away from the uncanny guardsmen of that lonely shore. And afterward, being jeered by his acquaintances for his superstition and cowardice, he goes to the same spot by daylight, he finds the selfsame pile of logs deeply charred by fire, but not then burning. Nor does he see any trace of the two headless redcoats.

"It was in midwinter, so the tradition runs, that two soldiers of the King deserted from the post at Drummond Island. They were evidently homesick. They longed for the scenes of old England. They could no longer endure the hardships, the rigors, the lonesomeness of that little village in the northern wilds. An officer would have more ample pay, and wife and children with him, and would have some traces of home life and enjoyment, from all of which the private soldier was cut off, he being condemned to the monotony of fatigue duty and rest, without opportunity for enjoyable recreation. They might perchance have made their way to Mackinaw (sic) Island and thus been freed from military restraint; but this was not their choice. They evidently set out for home. Their hearts longed for the lands beyond the rising sun. The shores and bays of Lake Huron were frozen over, and over the bridge thus made for them across the unsalted sea, they would make their way to the farther shore of Georgian Bay, and thence eastward to the scenes for which they yearned.

"But the post commander was wrathful when he learned of their unannounced departure, and stormed as only a Briton or a fisherwoman can storm, with swaggering bluster and volubility of oaths. Then he sat down and wrote. In his anger he had sworn to have the men or their lives. He had murder in his heart. When he arose from his desk, an orderly took the sheet on which had written and nailed it on the door of the barracks. It made an offer of $20 each for the heads of the two deserters if found dead, and the same for their bodies if found alive. There were whisperings about the post, but there were none who dared to express their thoughts. In the Indian camp there seemed greater quietness than usual; but before the day had passed two swift snow-shoes runners were noticed to leave the post as if on an urgent errand. A night passed. A day – a short winter day – slipped away, more quickly closed to the denizens of Drummond post by the high ridge which towered on the west of the town, and under the shadow of which they were hid. Another long night settled down, dragged its weary length across the northern ice and snow, and at length was driven far away from the clear depths of Georgian Bay. For since the days are shorter in those regions, their glorified brightness is such that it makes amends for the brevity.

"The post commandant had not yet taken his morning coffee when in walked two Indian athletes covered with frost, their breaths coming quickly, and their eyes eager and ferocious. Advancing to the center of the room, each unfastened from his girdle a human head that had dangled there, and placing it on the table, demanded the reward for the two deserters.

"The commissary was quickly summoned, and soon the bearers of the heads were washing away all thought of the blood they had treacherously spilled for money, in copious libations of the King's rum; rum, the main reliance of the British in those days for the accomplishment of their most nefarious ends; rum, with which they made slaves and brutes of the Indians; rum under whose influence they plotted massacres and murders, and by the aid of which these were accomplished.

"The Indian runners, as the tale is told, following hard after the deserters who, all unaccustomed to travel over the ice and snow, had made their way with difficulty, came up with them on the Great Manitoulin Island. But they did not warn them of their danger. Like beasts of prey, they skulked out of sight until a favorable moment should appear. Weary and cold, the soldiers gathered material for a fire. High they piled the logs and loud was the crackling of the frozen wood. The flames leaped high. Higher yet they piled the wood, and having eaten their scanty supper, sat them down before the fire with no thought of impending danger.

However in the darkness two red men watched their every motion; even their every breath. Lulled by the warmth and dulled by their weariness, the soldiers dozed. Perchance they are dozing yet, for they never wakened in this world. Stealthily from behind came the swift swish of the tomahawks as they cleft the air, falling upon necks conveniently bending forward. The deed was done. The two heads were fastened by the scalp locks to their girdles, and back they hastened, eager for their money and their rum.

"The headless trunks remained sitting on the log and warming themselves by the fire which made the night lurid with its glare. And ever since, unburied, they wander in those shores, seeking the heads which there they lost while sleeping; and when the nights are cold, the fire burns brightly, and they sit and warm them there."

This was not the first time Indians had been sent after fugitives or returned with such grisly proof of their success. One summer five soldiers deserted and Indians were sent to track them down. A couple of days later the braves returned with five heads in a burlap bag. Doubtless further desertions were discouraged.[19]

One supernatural tale involves an Ojibway chief who, much as contemporary folk "die" and see the great white light only to be yanked back to their bodies to resume living, experienced the same "almost made it to heaven" experience. In the mid-1840s when this story was collected, Ojibway in the Lake Huron area believed that when they died their souls would travel westward and they told their friends to make certain that they placed items in their grave such as bows and arrows, eating utensils, a blanket and other things they needed for the journey. The Ojibway believed that the souls of the items buried with the dead would be of great value to them as they journeyed in the spirit land. Just as "real" implements were needed in life, "spirit" ones were required in death. The dead were also to be buried with their heads to the west to help the departed determine the direction to travel to the "Land of the Sleeping Sun." Some of the Ojibway adopted a custom more common among the Blackfoot, burying the dead in the ground and erecting a small house over the grave. These diminutive death houses can be seen today in many Ojibway cemeteries. Death was celebrated with dishes of food brought into the "Grand Medicine Lodge" for the departed spirits.

The story involves a chief named Gitci Gauzini. After a few days of illness, he apparently died. He had been a great hunter and earlier told his friends that when he died he wanted his fine and trusty rifle buried with him to help on his journey west. Several friends suspected that he wasn't truly dead and prevented his immediate burial. Listening to their concerns, his widow stood a lonely vigil for four long days watching for any sign of life. At the end of the fourth day, he suddenly revived, telling a remarkable story.

He said that he had truly died and his ghost traveled on the broad trail of the dead toward the west, passing over Great Plains of luxuriant grass and beautiful trees accompanied by the delightful sound of songbirds. At last he reached the top of a hill and looked down on the city of the dead, far across a nebulous chasm, partially veiled in vapor and brilliant with glittering lakes and streams. He saw vast herds of deer, moose and other game, which were fearless and walked along his path with him. Since he didn't have his gun he turned to return to his grave and retrieve it. When he started back, he ran into a stream of men, women and children heading west to the city of the dead. They were all heavily burdened with guns, pipes, iron kettles, bows and arrows, blankets and presents from friends. All were complaining of the difficulty of carrying so much. One overloaded man offered the chief his gun, which he refused. He wanted his own fine rifle, not another man's castoff.

When the chief finally reached the place of his death, he suddenly became trapped in a ring of fire. No matter where he turned flames surrounded him. Desperately he leaped through the inferno only to awake from his death state.

When he related his experience, he told his people they should no longer put so many extra items in the grave with the dead. Carrying them only slowed the traveler's journey to the west. He told them to only put objects into the grave that the deceased was especially fond of or asked for. Such advice was only possible because of Chief Gitci Gauzini's ghostly journey and return from the city of the dead.[20]

Just to the northwest of Parry Sound on Georgian Bay is an especially rugged set of islands, known simply as the McCoy Islands. Surrounded by reefs, rocks and shoals, it is a very dangerous area for boaters. Big McCoy Island is said to be the site of the ghost of an old trader known to history only as McCoy. His reputation was a vile and black one with claims that he swindled both Indian and white man alike. No man would call him friend. Life had a way of evening the score with such misbegotten characters and McCoy didn't escape his just reward. Late one dark September night, someone, identity unknown, dealt with McCoy in a very permanent and appropriate fashion. The next time a customer came to his lonely cabin, he found McCoy stone cold dead. No one mourned his demise. The old miscreant never cheated anyone again unless it was the devil in the very bowels of hell.

Supposedly every September, when the moon is full, two unearthly screams can be heard echoing from the depths of the island woods. Some say it's McCoy protesting his murder; others that it's the trader celebrating beating the devil in some unholy deal.[21]

Just south of Parry Sound, on the eastern shore of Georgian Bay, is a lovely old vacation cottage. Built in 1890 and tucked neatly into the lakeshore, it's a wonderfully restful place to spend a weekend, a week or forever.

The wilderness cottage is also home to the restless and mysterious ghost of a young woman. As far as is known, the apparition was first sighted in the summer of 1980. The owner had guests in for the weekend and one of them, a young woman schoolteacher, clearly saw the ghost clothed in an old-fashioned long white dress and wide-brimmed hat, disappear into the woods behind the house. The image was very detailed and there was no doubt in the teacher's mind that it was a spirit manifestation.

Some years later, another house guest, a Ph.D in engineering, without an ounce of imagination in his soul, saw the same ghost.

The engineer, standing outside as the owner closed the cabin door, was startled to see the pale figure of the woman watching intently from a window. It vanished when he called attention to it.

The owner, his wife or their two children have never seen the young woman and have been unable to find any clue to the reason for the haunting or who the spirit is. Previous owners of the cottage deny any knowledge of it. Instead of being scared or even uncomfortable with their supernatural guest, the family is very accepting of it. During storms, they say it provides a calming influence over the old house. No matter how hard the wind blows or how close the lightning bolts strike, there is never a feeling of danger.

Is the young woman a kind of guardian spirit, watching over "her" cottage, protecting it from harm? Was she a victim of shipwreck, perhaps a soul lost on one of the many Georgian Bay disasters? Or is she a wandering spirit who has just found shelter in the friendly old cottage?[22]

Collingwood, Ontario, is a medium-sized city at the south end of Georgian Bay. A long-time shipbuilding center, it had one of the largest dry docks on the Great Lakes. Once upon a time, the yard at Collingwood spat out lakers one after another almost like sausage. It also has its share of spook stories.

One of the tales involves an Erie Indian chief and a maiden from the local Petun tribe. As in all such stories, there are variations. The prevailing one has the chief and maid becoming lovers, angering the girl's brothers. Consorting with a non-Petun was unacceptable.

The brothers attacked the interloping chief, dispatching him with a few heavy tomahawk blows and tossing his body over a cliff where it dutifully thumped on the rocks far below. The maid witnessed the murder and, as a result, withdrew into a form of mental shock. Not only was her lover dead, she watched her own brothers viciously kill him. Some days later the brothers discovered that their sister was missing. After days of searching she was found deep in a local cave, her cold and lifeless body resting alongside that of her lover chief. She had dragged his broken remains into the makeshift mausoleum and, without the will to live, she just laid down and died. Afterwards local legend held that their ghosts haunt the area in and around the cave. They were always seen together. Denied time together while alive, they would pursue a life together in death.

A variation of the story claims that the pair was caught together (in very compromising circumstances perhaps) by the brothers and, to protect the maid's honor, they promptly hurled the chief over the cliff to his death. The girl broke away and leaped off the cliff after her lost lover. Today the cliff is known as "Lovers' Leap" in recognition. Supposedly, too, the spirits of the pair haunt a nearby cave.

While the original and variation are good stories, on reflection I don't think there is an area on the Great Lakes with high cliffs that doesn't have an associated tale about Indian maidens (often a princess) jumping off to their deaths for various and sundry reasons. There are a hell of a lot of "lovers' leaps" out there.[23]

Northwest of Collingwood, still on the shores of Georgian Bay, is the little town of Port Severn, another old maritime community. It, too, has its share of resident ghosts. One is even located in the Muskoka Tourism Information Center. The center occupies an old farmhouse moved from its original location some years ago to fill the new mission. The ghost, known locally as "Uncle Tom," stayed with the house when it was relocated. Why the spirit still hangs around is unknown, as is the history of Uncle Tom.[24]

Just across the bay from Port Severn is the historic naval base at Penetanguishene.

Following the disastrous British defeat on Lake Erie by Commodore Oliver Hazard Perry in 1813, there was a clear requirement for a new British naval base in the upper Great Lakes.

It needed to be in a secure location, unlikely to attract undue American attention, somewhere out of the way, with deep water and good shelter.

As early as 1793, Englishman Sir John Graves Simcoe noted the strategic importance of Penetanguishene Bay as a potential site for a naval base. The steep-sided, deep-water bay would be an ideal spot for the protection and maintenance of ships and could serve as a vital transport link from York (Toronto) to the northwest communities. By 1817, the British Navy, anxious to patrol and protect the upper Great Lakes against a future American attack, started construction in earnest.

The base soon became home to a fleet of more than 20 vessels, supplying British posts to the northwest and housing more than 70 personnel, including officers and their families, sailors, civilian workers and soldiers.

When relations with the Americans eventually improved, the British gradually decreased their naval commitment for the defense of Canada. In 1828, a large army force was moved from Drummond Island when that territory was finally ceded to the Americans. Many soldiers and settlers made their new homes at Penetanguishene, joining the small military contingent already there. By 1834, the Navy moved out and the base was now fully an army one, maintaining daily drill and garrison routines.

Now called "Discovery Harbour" (likely because no one could spell or pronounce Penetanguishene the same way twice), it has been restored to the 1840 period, complete with reproduction schooners and replica historic structures, including wharf, sailors' barracks, dock yard, assistant surgeon's house and other buildings. Guides in period costume show visitors around the complex. Some people suggest that not all the guides are "on the payroll," at least not the current payroll.

The story goes that on New Year's Day 1839, Private James Drury froze to death in the kitchen at the rear of one of the buildings. Circumstances around the incident are a bit murky. For example, one would suppose, regardless of the outside conditions, that the kitchen of all places would have been warm. It is assumed that Drury was potted with enough rotgut booze to make him "immobile" and therefore subject to freezing.

Supposedly curators claim that he is the source of strange activity. Wine glasses vanish, unusual noises are heard in the building and beds are "dented" as if someone is sitting on them. Is the potted private the cause?

There could be other spirits about the complex. The cemetery is filled with victims of the wilderness environment. Many succumbed to disease, others to accident and at least one to pure fear. The earliest soldiers sent to Penetanguishene trekked over the muddy ruts of the Penetanguishene Road, which ran from Penetanguishene to the head of Kempenfelt Bay on Lake Simcoe. The term "road" is really a misnomer. It was really just a glorified Indian trail. Even by the times, it was a miserable and difficult journey running through the deep and dark heart of the Canadian north woods. It was on this route in June 1831 that two brothers, Privates John and Samuel Mc Garraty of the 79th Regiment, died in very strange circumstances. According to legend, while traveling, one brother become ill and was left in the care of the other. When their comrades eventually returned with help, both were found stone cold dead. Fever apparently claimed the one originally ill, but the sheer terror of being alone in the woods claimed the other. How would such a fearful spirit react to being confined in a small coffin buried deep in the dank and dark dirt? It would seem to be a prime candidate to go "a-wandering."[25]

Sailors have always been a rowdy lot and sometimes they even were tossed into the local clink to sleep it off. Doubtless the old jailhouse in Goderich, Ontario, had its fair share of sailing inmates. Perhaps it is even a sailor's ghost haunting the joint.

This unique and imposing octagonal building officially was the Huron County Gaol and is now a National Historic Site. The building also housed the County Courts and Council Chambers, as well as serving as goal and House of Refuge. Think of it as a kind of government "mall." The government could make the law, try you for breaking it and toss you in the clink, all under the same roof.

It served as the Huron County Gaol from its opening in 1842 until 1972 when all inmates were transferred to newer regional facilities. Executions were also performed at the gaol, one inmate hanging in 1869 and another in 1911. Hanging was always a "hit or miss" affair, at least in terms of how it affected the prisoner, beyond the fact that he always ended up dead. Death by hanging could be very quick or very, very slow, depending on the skill of the executioner and method used. It the old days, the prisoner stood on something, perhaps a wagon bed, had a noose thrown around his neck and on signal the wagon was driven off leaving the prisoner dangling in midair. His death came via strangulation and it could take some time, as he kicked desperately and clawed at the noose before finally expiring. The Navy was a little more efficient, literally "stringing" the prisoner up, using a rope through a bock made fast to a spar and hauling away on command until the victim was suspended high off the deck. Later executioners became a bit more skilled, using a proper gallows with a trap door and a noose with the knot placed just behind the ear to give a quicker death. The prisoner had to be positioned over the trap door and legs and arms bound to prevent any unseemly kicking. On command, the trap was sprung and the miscreant launched into eternity. Eventually, tables were carefully developed based on the prisoner's weight to determine the exact length of the drop before the noose "caught." Too short and the prisoner would strangle to death. Too long and the head popped off like an overripe pimple. Being executed by hanging had a number of names, too. In the States it was sometimes called doing the "Texas Two-Step" or the "10-toed tap dance." As old Billy Shakespeare said, "A rose by any other name is still a rose," or words to that effect. Call it what you want, the result is still the same.

A spiral staircase leads to the old cells on the upper floor of the Huron gaol. Windowless, they are not much bigger than closets. The jail was built according to period principles of prison reform, with the objectives of rehabilitating and reforming prisoners, not coddling them in accordance with today's psychobabble. At the time, the goal was hailed as a model of humanitarian prison design. In the 1860s, the original external walls were removed to provide more exercise space. Over the years the jail was also used as a refuge for the poor and insane.

The nearby jailer's house, sometimes pompously called the "governor's house," built in 1900, is large, gracious and airy. Stones from one of the prison courtyard walls were removed to make room for it.

A place filled with as much aberrant history as the old gaol should certainly have a few ghosts wandering about and if the stories are true, spirits are very active. Some investigators claim that the old jail and governor's house are both haunted. Supposedly misty apparitions of former prisoners have been sighted floating about in the cells, still bound in by the ancient iron bars. It well could be the specters of the two murders still "hanging around" the jail. Cold drafts and the feeling of being watched are common complaints from tourists (not the ghosts; although, come to think of it, with all the "paranormal investigation teams" out there today, perhaps the ghosts would like a little privacy). The nearby governor's house has its own set of specters. Cold spots, moving shadows and disembodied steps all give rise to the claim of shades still stalking the old house.[26]

Deep in the southeast corner of Georgian Bay is an island with the intriguing name of Giant's Tomb. With a moniker like that, it has to have a story behind it and indeed it does. Like many of the area's place names, it goes back into the dim mists of Indian legend.

According to the story, a Huron god named Kitchikewana roamed the area creating havoc. He was a giant of a god, taller than today's CN tower in Toronto. His head was adorned with a headdress of thousands of bird feathers and he had a robe made from 600 beaver pelts. A necklace of tree stumps dangled from his massive neck. It today's parlance, he was big man in those parts.

He was also always angry and never pleasant company for the other gods. One of them came up with the suggestion that, if he had a girlfriend, she could calm him down. We all know behind every good man there is always a better woman, so why wouldn't the same be true for the gods?

The other gods told Kitchikewana to find a girlfriend. As luck would have it, there was one girl in a local tribe that he really liked. Her name was Wanakita. Slowly screwing up his courage, he prepared to ask her to be his girl. But he waited too long. When he finally posed the question, she said she was already in love with a warrior from her tribe. The big angry god could take a hike. Telling a god to "buzz off" isn't a good idea!

Enraged with her answer as well as his own senseless delay, he dug his massive fingers into the ground and threw great clumps of earth into the air. Wherever they fell, land formed, thus making the reputed 30,000 islands of Georgian Bay. The five-finger marks where he tore the earth out of the ground became five bays: Midland, Penetang, Hog, Sturgeon and Matchedash bays. With his huge heart broken forever by Wanakita, he laid down and fell asleep forever.

The sleeping form of Kitchikewewana morphed into the island called Giant's Tomb. The silver birch on nearby Beausoliel Island is a result of the giant's temper tantrum. When he was throwing around the land that became islands, he accidentally killed poor Wahsoona, the daughter of a local chief. The silver birch is in her memory.[27]

Mackinac Island

Mackinac Island is a veritable paradise for ghost hunters. By all accounts spirited specters should be everywhere. Strangely though, they are largely unknown. It seems only until very recently the haunted side of the island has remained hidden, but whether deliberately or through simple omission is unknown.

By the way, Mackinac Island is always pronounced by popular acclaim, Mackinaw. Pronouncing it Mackinac identifies the visitor as an illiterate bumpkin of dubious parentage and lacking of social grace. Or even worse, a FUDGIE![1]

Mackinac Island is likely the most historic location in the entire Great Lakes region.

Ojibway tradition holds that Mackinac Island is a sacred place populated by the "first people" and home to Gitche Manitou, the Great Spirit. Situated at the confluence of lakes Huron and Michigan, it was a gathering place for the tribes and a sacred location where offerings were made to Gitche Manitou. The tribes also interned their chiefs on the island to honor the Great Spirit.

It was said that Indians traveling the Straits region compared the shape of the island to a turtle's back and called it Michilimackinac, Land of the Great Turtle, thus the name. To see the turtle you need to approach the island in a canoe, low in the water. Once the Europeans arrived in numbers, the Indians believed that Gitche Manitou fled Mackinac to live in the northern lights. Since the Norwegians believed the northern lights to be the flash of light off the armor of the Valkyries collecting the bodies of slain Viking heroes, there is an obvious mythology conflict. Personally, I prefer the Valkyries.[2]

The island's strategic location was attractive for the Europeans, too. Perhaps the first non-Indian to see the island was Jean Nicolet, a French-Canadian courieur de bois who arrived in 1634 on an upper lakes exploring trip. Mackinac Island soon became a center for the upper Great Lakes fur trade. For a century and a half, through French, British and American occupation, the island was the key point for the industry. Indian-trapped beaver, muskrat, otter and fox pelts were bartered for European trade goods on Market Street. Everything came through Mackinac, even the furs coming down from the great rendezvous at Grand Portage, Minnesota, on the western shore of Lake Superior. By the 1820s, the island was the key post in the vast American Fur Trading Company empire of John Jacob Astor. At one time Astor was reputedly the richest man in America, the result of a fortune founded in part on Mackinac Island fur and the upper Great Lakes trade.

Early missionaries also saw the importance of the island. Jesuit Father Jacques Marquette operated a mission there for his Huron followers in 1671. Protestant missionaries came afterwards and were equally energetic in saving heathen souls and building a political power base.

In addition, Mackinac was a place of military conflict. Once the British won the French and Indian War in 1763, they took over the upper Great Lakes region from the French and occupied the fort at the northern tip of Michigan's southern peninsula at today's Mackinaw City. In 1780, they decided to relocate it to the island. The island was far more secure than the mainland location and, considering the growing threat from the Americans and increasing hostility of the Indians, an improved defensive position was important. By 1781, the fort was newly constructed on the bluff above the harbor, a position it still occupies.

Following the American Revolution, the British Army garrison moved to St. Joseph Island in the St. Marys River, 44 miles or so to the east. The War of 1812 was a debacle for the American Army stationed at Mackinac Island. The British commander at St. Joseph Island knew that the war started before the American commander at Mackinac, and being an energetic soldier, he promptly attacked, landing his force on the back of the Island. He quickly marched to a spot of high ground overlooking the fort, compelling its surrender. Thinking that if it worked for the British, it should work for us, the American Army attempted to duplicate the back door approach two years later. However, the British were alert and forced a battle in the area of the present day Wawashkamo Golf Course, causing the Americans to withdraw with numerous casualties. The treaty ending the war required the British to turn the island and fort back to the United States.

For a time the island was also a center of commercial fishing. Rich stocks of lake trout and whitefish were just offshore and Indian and European fishermen harvested them regularly. By the 1830s, fishing was a major industry and began to replace fur as the economic engine of the island. Its heyday was comparatively brief, crashing before the turn of the century. Increased competition, rapid rail service to the Straits area and overfishing all played a role in the end of commercial fishing on the island.

The village of Mackinac was incorporated in 1817 and in 1818 it was the territorial seat for the territorial county of Michilimackinac, which encompassed most of what is now Michigan. In the years after the American Revolution, Fort Mackinac housed the government for the entire northern frontier.

After the Civil War, Mackinac Island started to become a popular destination for vacationers from the big cities. Quick to take a cue, island businessmen switched to a tourist-based economy. They had little choice: Fur was dead, fishing dying and living off a small military base unsupportable. If the city folk wanted a gentrified north woods vacation, let's give it to them. The customer is always right.

In 1875, Congress created Mackinac Island National Park, the second national park after Yellowstone. The commander of the fort was "doubly hated" as the park superintendent, which meant that the soldiers became the defacto park maintenance staff. While the Army Department in Washington objected to such a flagrant misuse of the military, Congress declined to change its mind. When the Army finally abandoned the fort in 1895, it spelled the end of the national park. Congress, of course, refused to spend money to maintain it as a park without being able to purloin the operating money from the Army. After a bit of political arm-twisting by Michigan political leaders, Congress transferred the land to Michigan for use as a state park. In due course, Mackinac Island became the first state park in Michigan. Some folks felt that had Congress not conveyed the land to the state, unscrupulous land developers of the ilk of the notorious timber barons would have slurped it up. Others took a different view. The island was essentially worthless. It had no mineral resources or timber of any note. There was no valuable economic activity based there, so all it was good for was a park. Let the tourists have it.

When the rush to Mackinac by vacationers was in full swing, the rich started to build opulent Victorian summer homes on the island, especially along west and east bluffs. Many of the cottages nearer town have been converted to wonderful bed-and-breakfast inns. Railroad barons, corporate lawyers, lumber pirates, meat packers and others soon had a summer home "up north."

Local carriage drivers also saw "gold in them thar tourist folk" and soon were offering tours of the island as well as generic wagons and the like. In 1896, local operators petitioned the town to prohibit those newfangled horseless carriages that were scaring their horses. Doubtlessly they realized the potential for the motorized devices to eat into what was (and still is) a very lucrative business. Why put up with all the problems of horses if you can just hop in your "merry Oldsmobile and drive around the island?" By the mid-1920s, the carriage operators banded together into an "association" to better monopolize and control the trade. The same monopoly still exists.

Today roughly 83 percent of the island is owned by the Michigan State Park Commission, which started in 1917. It has done a wonderful job of protecting this jewel of the Great Lakes.

While the island is much different today than it was in the old days, it is also still in many ways the same. Most visitors will arrive by water as in the distant past, although now by a constant stream of ferries running from Mackinaw City or St. Ignace. In the old days, large excursion and passenger steamers from Buffalo, Detroit, Cleveland and Chicago stopped regularly at the island. A few tourists today also arrive by small plane into the island's airstrip. During the winter when Lake Huron gets "hard," islanders will establish an ice road to the mainland for snowmobiles. To keep folks from wandering off into the white void when blowing snow destroys visibility, islanders drill holes in the ice and plant old Christmas trees as rough highway markers. There are only 500 to 600 year-round residents on the island.

Since automobiles are banned, transportation is by foot, bicycle or horse-drawn carriage. Since there are roughly 700 horses on the island during the summer season, the opportunity to experience the "good old days" is great. (Translation – watch where you step.)

In the old days, when the island was one of the country's great Victorian resorts, visitors danced to Strauss waltzes, enjoyed Sousa marches, ate flopping fresh whitefish and ambled slowly along the Grand Hotel porch. Today, visitors are much more plebian, with far less emphasis on style than on buying the island's infamous fudge and enjoying the "ambiance" of a place where time is perceived to have stood still.

Regardless of what the island is like today, the overwhelming history, the conflict and activities that occurred everywhere have left an indelible mark. Indians, French, British and Americans have all ruled the island amid conflict and combat. Voyageurs, fur traders, Jesuit and Protestant missionaries, soldiers, fishermen, sailors, rich men and poor men, students working for a summer and folks seeking respite from big city pollution all boiled together on Mackinac. It surely must be one of the most ghost-ridden places in the Great Lakes.

Bed-and-breakfast inns seem to be a hotbed for spirits and Mackinac Island's are no different. Perhaps it is the result of the physical changes necessary to convert an old home into a B&B that disrupts the ghosts. Or perhaps it is human activity generated by the guests that "stir the pot" and get the specters moving. Regardless, humans are not the only occupants of some (perhaps many?) of the island B&Bs.

Small Point Cottage, like many of the early vacation homes on the island, was built in the late 1800s. Originally located along the picturesque shore of the East Bluff, it was later moved to its present location just east of the Mission Point Resort. Today, it is a wonderful B&B offering a unique Mackinac Island experience. The house has a magnificent porch with a tremendous view of Lake Huron, while a grove of cedars provides shelter and privacy.

Apparently the house long had a haunted reputation, but that did not dissuade the teacher who purchased it in 1971. He would be working at the small island school and needed a home big enough for his large family. It was one of the very few that fit his requirements. After the family moved in, they ran smack into poltergeist activity. Objects left one place would become "lost," only to reappear elsewhere later. Footsteps were heard upstairs when no one was there. Some people familiar with the house and its haunts believe that the spirit is that of a young girl who once lived there a long time ago. Others claim it's a small boy and they dubbed him "Aaron," for want of a better name. Whether male or female, the spirit is mischievous and easygoing.

Perhaps more than one spirit occupies the house. Before it became a B&B, a young boy staying in the house as an overnight guest told an unusual tale at breakfast the next morning. He claimed that he was scared during the night when he awoke to see a man in his room. The strange man was sitting in a non-existent chair and floating in air. A large smile was on the man's face. The boy woke his younger brother in the next bed and both watched until the floating man slowly vanished.

Since the house converted to a graceful B&B, it's claimed that the occasional supernatural activity still occurs.[3]

Pine Cottage is another B&B with a contingent of permanent guests. A large house built in 1890 with 42 rooms spread over three floors, it sits part way up Brogan Lane in the heart of downtown.

There have been many strange ghostly occurrences in the house. At one point the owner was playing cards with some friends before the season started. The card players heard the front door swing open and heavy steps on the front stairs. When the owner yelled, asking who it was, he received no answer. A quick check of the house showed it to be empty. So who (or what) came through the door?

Shortly after purchasing the house from the old Moral Rearmament group that ran a religious retreat and college on the island for a few years, the new owner went upstairs to select a bedroom for himself. When he opened one of the bedroom doors, a woman ghost rushed out of a closet and directly for him. He later remembered that her hair was up in an old-fashioned bun and her eyes glowed red. Worse, she only had an upper half! Everything below the waist was missing. Perhaps even stranger, she literally knocked him over. For a ghost to have such substance is nearly unheard of. The speeding spirit sped right out the window!

Ghostly action tended to be more prevalent in the fall of the year, but all of it was benign, not threatening in any way. One child remembered waking up to see what he thought was his grandmother in a long dress standing by his bed. When he asked her in the morning why she was there, she said it was just to tuck the child in. What she didn't tell him was that she wasn't in his room at all. She didn't want to scare him, thus her "white lie." Guests will also sometimes encounter very cold spots on very warm nights. Others have commented that it felt like someone was trying to push them out of bed at night. The doorbell occasionally rings, but no one is there. Or are guests arriving that simply can't be seen?

Some of the sightings have focused on a little blonde-haired girl, a spirit several folks claimed to have encountered in the house. Once the owner's wife was in her bedroom when she heard a child screaming in the hallway. Quickly opening the door, she saw a little girl standing in the hall and crying. Instantly the child ran down the hall and vanished. Another time a woman found the child in the kitchen. When she approached the girl, she ran through the wall and disappeared. Once the cook found her crying in the hall outside his bathroom. When he asked what was wrong, she replied, "Mommy, I want to go home." When he reached to comfort her, she went "poof." In another instance a passerby came to the door to ask the owner if they were aware their little girl was in the attic. He saw her standing at a window, crying. There is a rumor that a woman was murdered in the house in 1942. Perhaps this is linked to some of the bizarre activities.[4]

The Chateau Lorraine also has the ghost of a little girl; perhaps the same one ventures from house to house. The Chateau Lorraine girl has been known to play melancholy tunes on a baby Steinway grand piano. The Steinway was purchased from the Grand Hotel in the 1990s and was used in the film "Somewhere in Time" starring Christopher Reeve and Jane Seymour.[5]

The Bailey House is said to have its own shade. Objects fall off shelves and counters, doors open and close on their own. The sound of boxes sliding across the attic floor has also been reported. Some say the ghostly figure of a woman is seen looking into guest rooms.[6]

The ghost of Shamus McNally is said to keep watch over the McNally Cottage Bed and Breakfast on Main Street. Michael McNally built the house in 1889. Shamus was his son. The story goes that a woman guest was suffering from a stomach ailment, awoke late at night and was unable to fall back to sleep. Suffering alone with her sickness, she suddenly felt a hand on her shoulder. When she turned to look, she saw a small old man standing behind her. She felt no fear, only a sense of relief and calm. She returned to bed and slept soundly. The next morning at breakfast she noticed a photograph of Shamus McNally on the wall and realized that he was her "guardian angel."[7]

The term "Mackinac Island hotel" and the name Grand Hotel are nearly synonymous. To many visitors, the Grand Hotel is the feature most remembered about the island, whether they are fortunate enough to be guests there or not.

The characteristic most striking to visitors, especially first-timers, is the massive front porch. Stretching 660 feet, it is reputedly the longest in the world. Three railroad companies, The Michigan Central, Grand Rapids and Indiana, and Detroit and Cleveland Steamship Navigation Company joined forces to build the Grand. Construction started in 1886 and it opened the following year. Built of Michigan white pine, popular history claims the hotel was finished in a mere four months.

The hotel's present 385 guest rooms are all unique, with no two decorated alike. Five U.S. presidents have visited the Grand: Harry Truman, John Kennedy, Gerald Ford, George H.W. Bush and Bill Clinton. Two movies were also shot at the hotel, "This Time For Keeps" with Esther Williams and Jimmy Durante in 1949, and "Somewhere In Time," starring Christopher Reeve, Jane Seymour and Christopher Plummer in 1979. Ten years later, the U.S. Department of the Interior designated the hotel a National Historic Landmark.

Any hotel with the rich history of the Grand is bound to have some ghost stories attached to it. The Grand certainly has its fair share of them. The shame is, I suspect, that many went unrecorded and are forever lost.

One tale claims that the builders unearthed many skeletons while digging the building's foundation. Whose bones they are is unstated, but the likelihood is certainly Indian. Could they be part of the spirit disturbance?[8]

A few years ago an employee at the hotel during the winter was working on one of the floors when he kept hearing doors opening and closing, people talking and footsteps walking up and down the cold and empty halls. Since he was the only person on the floor at the time, he beat a hasty retreat, discretion being the better part of valor.[9]

The Chippewa Hotel has long been a fixture on the Mackinac Island waterfront. Built in 1902, the hotel is the home of the famous Pink Pony Bar and Grill, a favorite watering hole for yachters, boaters and general Fudgies alike. The hotel provides special Victorian style and elegance to all visitors.

It is certainly fitting that the hotel have a ghost and apparently it does. As the story goes, an employee was painting rooms during the off-season when he heard strange noises in the hallway. It sounded like a whole troupe of people were walking around, stomping and yelling. When he looked, of course, no one was there. After he felt a cold spot move through him, he'd had enough, running down the stairs and into the welcoming street. Whatever was going on, he didn't want any part of it.

Mission Point Resort has a long and colorful history and its own string of spirits. In the 1820s, a Protestant minister established a mission and church to serve the local Indian community in the area now occupied by the resort, thus the name "Mission Point." In the 1950s, Frank Buchman's Moral Rearmament organization, a group dedicated to purity and honesty in a world evangelical movement, constructed a massive conference and educational center at the point, including a theater, meeting rooms, dining halls, guest rooms and a sound stage for the production of organizational propaganda films. At the time of construction in 1958, the production sound stage was the second largest in the world. Universal Studios used it in 1979 during the filming of parts of "Somewhere in Time." The film cast and crew all lived in the facility (then called the Inn on Mackinac) during their island sojourn. The main lobby is certainly one of the most exceptional buildings featured on the island. Supported by huge trusses, the peak soars to 36 feet high and resembles a giant tepee.

In 1966, Moral Rearmament fled Mackinac Island and established a new facility in Switzerland. Doubtless the death of fearless leader Frank Buchman affected organizational focus and leadership. The property was deeded to Mackinac College, a new educational institution striving not only for a traditional educational focus but also to develop programs in statesmanship and leadership with a "one world" bent. The college was a miserable failure, attracting 150 students for 700 slots.

In 1970, televangelist Rex Humbard purchased the college and attempted to make it into a religious retreat and educational institute. After a couple of years, it also failed and Humbard remade it into a vacation resort. Bowing to the pressure of continued failure, it was sold in 1977 to a Dallas firm, becoming the Mackinac Hotel and Conference Center.

The present Mission Point Resort came into being in 1987. The name, capturing the island's past with its present, touches historic Mackinac Island in a way other hotels didn't. The popular resort is a wonderful and very successful addition to the island.

One ghost tale involves a fellow named Harvey who supposedly broke up with his girlfriend and, as a result, committed suicide by leaping off the buff behind Mission Point, smashing himself to a lifeless pulp on the rocks below. Evidently he didn't subscribe to the notion of there being a lot of fish in the lake. If you lose one girl, just go get another. Harvey was said to have been a student at the long defunct Mackinac Island College. For reasons that are not determined, he apparently now makes his home in the resort carpenter shop. Workers sweep up a pile of sawdust only to have it scattered around the shop when they turn their backs. Tools left one place will vanish and reappear somewhere else. Sometimes they never reappear. The carpenters just blame it all on Harvey.[10]

The theater seems to be another hot spot for ghosts. Various folk claim to have seen images of soldiers walking around outside the building. There is no threat. They just walk in peace and slowly fade away.

The Old Mission House was at one time the center of missionary efforts directed at the Indian population, especially as they came to trade furs and receive treaty payments. Today, it is part of Mackinac Island State Park and used to house employees. It is heavily renovated from the mission days. Legend claims that native children who contracted tuberculosis were kept in a makeshift hospital in the basement under the impression that the cold and damp air would help them recover. Of course, today we know the treatment is the opposite of what was good for them. Death was common under such sad circumstances. There are reports from park workers of ghosts of Indian children in the basement and two floors above. The spirits seem especially active at night.[11]

The Geary House on Market Street is the site of an offbeat ghost tale. It seems that the town fish inspector, Matthew Geary, lived in the house in the 1870s. Fishing was an important local industry and assuring the quality of the catch was critical for market acceptance. When Geary went on to the great fish market in the sky, it was not unexpected, since he was elderly. A coffin was duly brought in to the parlor, Geary dressed in his best suit and dropped into it. After the wake, it was carried out to the hearse and the procession headed up the hill to the Catholic cemetery, the mourners dutifully trooping along behind. After just a minute or so, one of the women realized that she had left her gloves in the parlor and hurried back to get them. When she opened the front door, there was Geary's ghost coming down the stairs from the second floor. You could say he was trying to catch up with his own funeral.[12]

Marquette Park, just below the south wall of the fort, is home to a bronze statue of the old Jesuit missionary Jacques Marquette. A duplicate of the statue is in a small park in Marquette, Michigan. Back when the fort was an active installation, the soldiers built a vegetable garden in this area. It is claimed that during the construction of the park, workers unearthed the remains of more than 1,000 people. Although the number is likely a great exaggeration, the claims of seeing their ghosts strolling through the park aren't. The best guess is that the site was an old Indian burial ground.

St. Cloud Dormitory is said to be haunted by the ghost of a little girl and perhaps that of an old man, too. A few folks think the man may have killed her. Regardless, the girl bangs on the pipes, making an unholy racket and her presence is said to be most powerful in room 33. Some folks claim to have been touched by her icy hands. One man had the sheets fly off his bed and end up in a heap in the middle of the floor, supposedly the result of the little ghost yanking them away.[13]

Dating from 1781, the fort is said to be rife with wandering spirits. Certainly any place with the rich and tragic history of Fort Mackinac should have a direct pipeline to the world beyond.

It is claimed that the children of a former post commander still wander around the hill quarters. Park workers have heard the sounds of children playing when the fort is closed, and some visitors report seeing "marvelous little costumed reenactors." "Where did you get those great children? They are just charming."

There is a rumor that a skeleton was found in the prisoner pit in the guardhouse. Some visitors claim to get chills in the building and encounter unexplained cold spots, the presumption being that the victim is still under lock and key.[14]

The post hospital is another haunted area. Various visitors claim to have seen the faint forms of soldiers resting on the ward cots. Others assert a weak antiseptic smell. Some just say the room gives them "the creeps."

The post cemetery behind the fort contains 84 graves: 63 are soldiers, 15 family of soldiers and six civilians with a government connection such as sheriff, customs inspector and so forth. Although the cause of death isn't always available, most seem to have "taken the last roll call" through disease or accident, especially drowning. It is a collection of potential ghosts just made for walking and at least one seems to be doing so.

The cemetery is located in a small wooded glade just up Garrison Road, a half-mile north of the fort. A low white picket fence marks the graveyard boundary. It's an eerily quiet location, a fitting place for the dead to rest and a perfect setting for a wandering ghost or two.

Supposedly, a weeping woman can be heard and sometimes seen near the graves of two young children, son Josiah Hamilton Cowles (died September 4, 1884) and daughter Isabel Hitchcock Cowles (died December 12, 1888) of Lt. C. D. Cowles and his wife. Josiah was 13 months old and Isabel 6 months when they "passed." The loss of one child is terrible; the loss of two is devastating. The Cowles children aren't the only young buried in the cemetery. Just a headstone away are Frank M. (died October 7, 1865) and William A. (died December 11, 1862) Marshall, aged 2 years and 3 months and 2 years, 4 months, respectively. Their parents, Sergeant William and Matilda Marshall, would have been just as distraught as the Cowles. Could the mysterious weeping woman be Matilda? The grave of J. Russell Mills (died August 30, 1869), son of post surgeon Hiram B. Mills and wife, Alida B., is proximate to the Cowles and Marshall graves. Could Alida be the female apparition? The remains of six other children also rest in the old burying ground and as each was a loved member of their family, the potential for a still grieving mother can't be discounted.

The cemetery also holds the remains of these two soldiers: Corporal Hugh Flinn (died December 5, 1828) and Private James Brown (died February 1, 1830). While the details surrounding both are at best murky, their deaths add to the legend of Mackinac Island and to the questions: Why exactly did Brown kill Flinn, where and how, and where was Brown hanged?[15]

In 1829, Brown, Company G, 5th U.S. Infantry, became mixed up in an argument with his squad leader, Corporal Flinn. Continuing to dwell on the argument, Brown became so mad that he shot and killed Flinn in the company mess hall. The Army lost no time in trying and convicting Brown of the murder. After a legal dispute over the original court-martial, he was promptly tried again with the same result – death by hanging. On February 1, 1830, Private Brown was marched out to a scaffold, the noose dropped around his neck and on command, stretched appropriately. The location on the island where the execution took place is unknown. The best guess would be the middle of the parade field.

There is a claim that the original post cemetery was where the small horse corral is now located behind the fort. When the cemetery was moved to the present location, not all of the original inhabitants were included. Some bodies are supposed to still be under the corral.

There are two other cemeteries on the island: St. Anne's Catholic Cemetery adjoining the post cemetery to the west and a Protestant cemetery adjoining to the west. They, too, are said to have their own spirits and stories. St. Anne's holds the remains of former Michigan Governor G. Mennen Williams, known to legions of Michiganians as "Soapy" Williams.

Allegations are made that the sound of rifle fire can be heard on the old Rifle Range trail. Qualification firing was a common and repetitive activity for the soldiers at the fort. The specter of a soldier carrying a rifle is also reported in the area.

Wawashkamo Golf Course, the site of the battle between British and American forces in the War of 1812, is said to have spirits of dead soldiers still wandering about the battlefield. When golfers yell "fore," do the ghosts duck out of the way?

"I've never believed in ghosts, I mean I'm just not the sort to buy into the whole haunting nonsense. Or at least I wasn't. Things that go bump in the night don't bother me, never have. I don't go looking for old graveyards to wander through at midnight on Halloween. I know what's dead is dead. People just don't come back from the grave.

"A few years ago my wife and I were staying at the Grand Hotel on Mackinac Island. We are Grand Hotel junkies, just love the place. The old-time ambiance, tremendous service, wonderful guest accommodations and excellent food make the hotel the best in the world as far as we are concerned.

"We try to stay at the Grand several times a year. We're retired and I did well enough in the insurance game for us to pretty much do whatever we want to in terms of travel. So, we end up at the Grand fairly frequently.

"Our favorite times are late spring and early fall. The island isn't completely run over with herds of damn fudgies and usually

the weather is pretty good. And we can often get an off high-season rate. I do try to save a buck when I can.

"At the end of the day, it's my habit to grab a scotch and wander out to the porch and find a chair on the west end. It's the quiet end away from the carriage road and I just take a seat and admire the view. It really is a special place. I am almost always alone; few guests walk so far down the porch.

"On our last stay I met a really interesting man. He said he was a retired doctor, but never said anything more about it so I guess he was a G.P. (general practitioner.) Most specialists always make it a point to rattle on and on about what they do. I once sat next to an OB/GYN (obstetrician-gynecologist) at a dinner party. Talk about a disgusting conversationalist. At least he wasn't a damn proctologist!

"My porch mate wore a straw hat I later found out was called a 'boater,' and a white linen suit with a kind of small rolled lapels. His clothing looked a little bit out of date, but I thought, what the hell, it takes all kinds to make the world go around. He looked trim and fit and I judged his age at about 65. Both his hair and clipped Van Dyke beard were gray.

"The thing was, he was never there when I arrived. For a few minutes I always had my corner to myself. After a while I noticed, really 'felt' would be a better word – someone else around me only to discover he was in his chair. I never saw him arrive.

"Anyway, every day for nearly a week the same thing happened. I arrive, then he appears, but I never saw him do it. It was a bit unnerving.

"We talked about the old days on the island. After a few days, I noticed I was talking in the past tense and he in the present. For example, I mentioned how nice the garden looked and spoke about planning for a new walking path or bed of flowers. I mentioned I noticed the Governor's mansion had a new coat of paint and he countered about seeing the Young children playing in the yard. Later when I did some reading about the history of the mansion, I realized what he was talking about.

"He really knew his history, too, going into the details of the Grand's construction that weren't in any of the history books I ever read, and I thought I'd read everything I could find about the island. He knew the crew foremen by their first names, their wives and children. It was remarkable.

"We would chat for a half hour or so, then I would excuse myself and go inside to collect my wife for dinner.

"A few days into our nightly conversation my wife came out to the porch to fetch me for dinner. When I saw her approaching, I said good night to my newfound friend and walked away to meet my wife. When I reached her, she asked who I had been talking to. I started to tell her and turned to point him out, but he was already gone. Strange, I thought, but I just turned back and went inside for dinner.

"Several days passed. My wife and I enjoyed ourselves as usual. Rented a couple of horses and rode around the island, played a round of golf and even walked down Fudge Street, something we rarely do.

"On Friday evening, the last night of our stay, I wandered out to 'my' chair on the porch to drink in the scenery for the last time. After a few minutes my friend arrived as usual, just suddenly appearing. This time it was very, very different.

"He was sitting at his regular chair, but he was there, but yet not there. I could see the chair through him!

"He didn't miss a beat though, greeting me as if nothing was different. Now let me tell you, I was a bit rattled since I finally figured out he was a ghost. For the last week I had been having nightly conversations with a ghost! As I said earlier, I don't scare easily, but I was scared now.

"Just as I normally did, I said hello then asked why he was so thin tonight. He chuckled at my little joke and muttered something about ectoplasm being affected by the weather or something like that.

"Feeling bolder, I asked what was going on. I told him I didn't believe in ghosts, but since clearly he was one, I was wrong.

"He smiled and told me ghosts were very real and the island was filled with them. Some were more powerful than others in that they had the ability to make themselves visible, sometimes to many people at the same time, sometimes to just a single person. This explained why my wife didn't see him the other day.

"When I asked who he was, he just said it wasn't important. His mortal remains are up on the hill and marked by a stone, but family members never visit anymore. After I pushed a little harder, he related that he had been a doctor on the island for a long time and watched the place change dramatically.

"As a young man he watched the Grand being built and spent as much time as he could speaking with the contractors. When the hotel finally opened in 1887, he was on scene for the festivities. He mentioned that he never missed a chance for a visit to the old place.

"He said, like my wife and me, the hotel was his favorite place, and during the 'season' he often spent time sitting in his chair admiring the view. Rarely is he ever disturbed, as usually he isn't visible. Guests come and go but never see him. Sometimes a guest will just catch a glimpse of 'something' that doesn't belong, perhaps a wisp of mist or fleeting shadow, but when they look again there is nothing. He said every few years, though, someone actually sees him. Why they do is a mystery, but he thinks it is because of the mutual admiration for the Grand. Because he and I were on the same wavelength, so to speak, he was visible to me. Why my wife didn't see him is unknown. Perhaps my scotch helped!

"Throughout our conversation he kind of flickered in and out, varying in visibility. When dinnertime came, I said goodbye and that I hoped to see him again on our next stay. He said he couldn't promise anything about being seen, but he would always be there waiting."[16]

Just past Mission Point Resort and Conference Center, at the point where the Lake Shore Road comes very close to Lake Huron, is a tall bluff on the land side. On old island maps it's marked as "Robertson's Folly." Newer maps seem to ignore this fascinating part of the old island's legends.

The fact that the story can't be absolutely confirmed isn't a reason to ignore it, especially since certain parts are verifiable. British Captain Daniel Robertson was the commander at Fort Mackinac, serving from 1782-1787. An experienced soldier, he joined the army in 1754, campaigning in North America during the French and Indian War. He was said to be popular with his men as well as Indian allies. Assuming he entered the army at age 15, not an unusual age for the time, and assuming he met his Indian princess immediately on arrival at Fort Mackinac, he would have married her at age 43 or older. But I am getting ahead of the story.

There are two versions of this tale. In the first, the good captain falls in love with a beautiful young Indian princess. Her father, the chief refuses to allow Robertson to marry her since he promised her to a warrior of his choosing. That she loved the English captain and hated her father's choice of a husband was immaterial. After all, father always knows best.

Robertson marries her secretly and installs her in a small summer house he built in the area, now called Robertson's Folly. Their home was right on the edge of a tall cliff with a magnificent view of Lake Huron. For a while they lived undetected and happily.

However, one day the warrior she was promised to discovered the little house and, finding the princess alone, murdered her with a quick slash of his hunting knife, her blood splashing wide over the rough floor. If he couldn't have her, no English soldier could. At the very moment of the murder, when her blood spurted red, Robertson walked in the door. Seeing what happened, he leaped at the Indian in boiling vengeance. The two men locked together in mortal combat, fighting from inside to out and slowly wrestling toward the cliff. Before either was aware of the danger, they plunged together over the edge to their deaths on the rocks below.

The second version is quite a bit different. Robertson is described as a "gay young English officer" who always had a sharp eye for the ladies. He was strolling in the fields behind the fort, smoking his favorite pipe, when he spied a young woman crossing his path. He guessed she was about 19, dressed very simply with long black hair running down her back. When she turned to look at him, he was immediately smitten by her lustrous black eyes and haunting smile. Robertson thought her to be the most beautiful woman he ever saw. He tried to catch up with her, but she quickened her pace, disappearing around a curve in the road before he could reach her.

That night all he did was speak about her in the officer's quarters. He said she was not an Indian, and since no ship had stopped in weeks, she couldn't be a recent arrival. Who was she? Consumed with desire, he hardly slept that night and inquiries in the village the following day came up empty. No one knew who the mystery woman was.

The following evening, Robertson was again walking behind the fort smoking his pipe. Again he saw the woman on the same path and about 30 yards ahead. He called out to her, "Mademoiselle, I beg your pardon." She turned back and looked directly at him, her face radiating smiles, then turned and again quickened her pace. Robertson walked faster, but when he gained no ground on his quarry, started to run. She still kept the distance, again disappearing behind a curve in the road.

This time the captain took action, returning to the fort and calling out his fellow officers as well as the garrison to hunt down and find the woman. The men looked everywhere, searching the surrounding woods, fields, beaches and paths, but she was gone, vanishing into thin air. The soldiers must have thought she was just a figment of Robertson's imagination. He had been on Mackinac Island too long!

Two days passed and, while his brother officers forgot about his mystery woman, he didn't. In fact, he was in love with her. The first glance of her lustrous eyes and radiant smile was enough to capture his heart forever. They hadn't seen her wonderful beauty as he had.

That evening he again went on his lonely walk behind the fort, but now took the path toward the steep bluffs to the east. It was here that he had lost her before. Maybe he would see her once more, but this time, he would not lose her. Suddenly she was there, sitting on the large rock at the edge of the cliff, gazing out over the blue emptiness of the lake. Since she was trapped between the cliff and him, escape was impossible. He would find out who she was now.

As he carefully approached his elusive maiden, gravel crunched under his boot and she turned quickly around. He said, "Pretty maiden, why do you attempt to elude me? Who are you?" She made no answer, but stood and retreated several steps toward the cliff. "Do not fear me," said Robertson, "I am commander of the garrison at the fort here. No harm shall come to you, but do pray tell me who you are and how you came to be on this island."

She said nothing, but again stepped backward toward the cliff, stopping a mere 3 feet from it. Afraid that she could stumble and fall to her death, he said, "My dear young lady, I see you fear me and I will leave you, but for heaven's sake, do pray tell me your name and where you reside. Not a hair of your head shall be harmed, but Captain Robertson, your devoted servant, will go through fire and water to your commands. Once more my dear girl, do speak to me, if but a word before we part."

While delivering this speech, the captain made a step toward her, causing the girl to move right to the edge of the cliff. The slightest loss of balance and she would fall.

To stop such a calamity, Robertson quickly sprang forward to grab her and pull her to safety. Just as he grasped her arm, she pulled away from him, throwing herself off the cliff. Off balance, he followed her, both striking the rocks far below and dying instantly.

When he didn't return to duty, a search party was dispatched from the fort. It found him dead among the rocks. But it found no one else. The body of the mysterious woman was gone. Was it ever there? Was she just his imagination or a ghost sent to lure him to his death? Some folk claim that he drank too much of the good French brandy the fur traders brought over from Montreal and just imagined the young woman. Others felt she was indeed real, but couldn't explain what happened to her.

The captain's body was said to be buried in a small knoll in the middle of the island. His soldiers and brother officers mourned Robertson for his social qualities and gentlemanly bearing. Perhaps in death he joined the elusive young woman he loved.[17]

"Okay. You want a Mackinac Island story. Here's one for you. About eight or nine years ago several friends and I took the boat up to Mackinac Island. We used to do it at least once a year. It's an easy run up from Traverse City. My dad kept his 40-foot Silverton in the marina there.

"At the island we always moored in the State Marina downtown right off Marquette Park. They charge an arm and a leg there and the service is lousy, but it's the only game in town, so the state can get away with it.

"Anyway, we get in just about dusk after a miserable run. The lake was fairly calm, but we had rain and fog most of the way up. We only came because the weather was supposed to clear for a good weekend. It never did. The weatherman was wrong as usual. We had the same lousy trip back home on Sunday.

"Once we moored the boat, we went up to town for dinner. We ate in one of the little joints off Main Street. They charge way too much, but the season is short and I guess they figure they can soak the tourists, so they do.

"Then we went to Horne's Bar down near the park. It is my favorite bar on the island. They usually have a decent band and once all the Fudgies leave for the day, the kids working in the hotels come out for the night and hit the bars, so it can be a lot of fun. That's one of the little secrets of the island. All day long the tourists own the town, but once the late ferries are done bringing the day-trippers over from the mainland and the ones staying overnight have finished their evening walks and gone to bed like good little Fudgies, well, then the workers come out. By 10 p.m. the turnover is finished and the bars are rocking.

"Well, we got to partying pretty good. In fact, closing time comes around and my buddies and I are still slamming them down. When they stopped serving us, my friends went back to the boat, but I knew one of the girls bartending so I hung on a bit longer hoping to get lucky. ... In the end, I didn't and left for the boat alone.

"It was a gloomy night. Cold and misty, almost raining. Puddles on the road and the streetlights had that yellow halo effect around them. Visibility was maybe 100 feet. The street was absolutely empty. Not a soul was around.

"Now I am, as we sailors say, 'three sheets to the wind' and a little unsteady, but the road is wide and the boat isn't far, so no problem. No sooner am I stumbling along Main Street toward the marina than I hear the clip-clop of a carriage coming up behind me. This is very odd because in all the years I have been coming to the island I never recall seeing a carriage this late at night. So I turn and look, but no carriage and the clip-clop stops. So I keep walking down the road and the clip-clop starts again and it is closer now. Again I turn and look, but still no carriage. So I start walking. Again I hear the carriage and now it is really close. As I turn and look, it appears out of the mist.

"It is no ordinary Mackinac Island carriage. It's a damn hearse!

"I stumbled backward to the sidewalk to get out of its way and stare at it. Maybe it was the cold and wet, but a shiver ran up my back.

"I remember this part clear as anything, regardless of the booze. A matched team of two completely black horses was pulling it. Each had a high-feathered thing mounted on its head. The two big brass oil headlights were burning a dull yellow. Damn things looked like eyes! The black leather harnesses were all decorated in silver. Otherwise, the hearse was totally black, sides, doors, wheels and everything except for the brass work which gleamed like gold. Hell, maybe it was gold.

"A single driver was on the seat and he wore a long black coat with a black top hat. A high collar pulled up against the cold and wet hid his face. I couldn't see anything but his eyes. He just stared straight ahead and never even glanced at me.

"As it clattered past, I noticed an old-fashioned narrow coffin visible through the windows in the back. The coffin was on a bed

of white satin-like cloth and white drapes hung around the edges of the windows. There was some kind of black filigree scrolling on the windows, too.

"In a minute or so it was gone, just swallowed up by the fog, but I heard the clip-clop for several minutes before it just faded away to silence. My guess is it was heading toward Mission Point. I had never seen anything like it before or since.

"I ran back to the boat and made a good racket climbing aboard, but my buddies were too far gone to even notice me.

"The following morning I said nothing about it. I wasn't sure anyone would believe me. That afternoon we rented saddle horses at the livery up near the Grand Hotel. I made a point of asking the manager if there was a horse-drawn hearse anywhere on the island. Clyde, the guy managing the livery, had been on the island a long time. Someone once told me his family was old island. He was well into his 70s. Clyde looked at me for a stretched minute before he said, 'There hasn't been one of those on the island in a long time, not since the '30s anyway. Why do you ask?' It was like he was expecting something special from me.

"I looked back at him for a while and just said, 'Oh nothing, just curious.' But I am sure he saw something in my eyes that gave him the truth.

"My friends were already outside and as I was getting ready to mount up, he walked over to me and said, 'I heard this morning that one of the cottagers over Mission Point way died last night.'

"I looked back at him and said, 'You know about the hearse, don't you?'

"He waited a second or two, then replied, 'Yeah, I know about it. None of the Fudgies have a clue in hell, even most of the year-rounders don't know about it, but my dad told me about it. Just as an islander is getting ready to up and die, an old horse-drawn hearse comes for the soul. You see the hearse and you know a death is coming. At least that's what my dad told me.'[18]

"So believe me or not, that's what I saw that night."

There is a sheltered location on a small wooded knoll just above Robertson's Folly and down from Huron Road. While it is virtually unknown by modern day visitors, in the days of the French occupation it was a very special spot.

It was a favorite place for the French "coureurs de bois," or "rangers of the woods," also known as "woods runners," to gather between trips. This unique group of men was a direct offshoot of the fur trade. While traders were supposed to be officially licensed, the coureurs de bois ignored the law by trading without government permission. When the trade ended, they did, too, fading quickly into the mists of history. Originally these men, invariably French, went with the Indians to learn the mysterious ways of the deep north woods and the unknown country beyond the small French settlements. They married Indian women and abandoned most of conventional European culture, becoming more Indian than French. Their offspring followed in their fathers' moccasins but were even wilder. They were the kings of the forests, streams and rivers, taking orders from no man but ranging far and wide over the great northern forests. The coureurs de bois earned their living not only by hunting, trapping and fishing but also by paddling the big Montreal canoes, hauling cargoes of rich furs to market at Mackinac or Montreal and trade goods back. Since Mackinac Island was the capital of the Great Lakes fur trade, it was the headquarters of many of the coureurs de bois, too. The quiet little glade in the woods was their private place to rest and cavort.

Some folks speculate that while the coureurs de bois may be gone from this world, they still have a presence on the island. Their spirits are said to go on inhabiting the old shelter where they spent so many pleasant hours, smoking strong tobacco, lounging, swilling good trade brandy, spinning yarns and fighting among themselves. It isn't always the quiet and restful spot you might imagine.

Wander up to this old site deep in the quiet and glade and sit back under a tree at sunset and listen carefully. You may catch a few words of French drifting hard on the soft evening breeze. The spirit of the coureurs de bois still lives.

Fort Holmes' fame comes from a disastrous American attack there during the War of 1812, but its value as an observation point was well known to the Indians for hundreds of years. There is a legend about an Indian wife who drew final consolation of her husband's death from its heights.

It seems Mecostewanda climbed to the hilltop daily to watch for the return of her husband Chi-to-wait, who had left the island as part of a war party. Chi-to-wait was both wise and very brave, but since his ghost never appeared to Mecostewanda, she didn't know if he was dead or alive. Overcome with worry, she sent her four sons off in four different directions to seek word of his fate. They returned empty handed. No one knew what happened to Chi-to-wait.

One sunset, while she was searching from the hilltop, she saw the ghostly image of a strange craft going slowly by the rock she was sitting on. Its sides were stone, the sails feathered wings and the shape that of a canoe. A single brave pulled effortlessly at the oars. He was stripped to the waist and painted for war. An old man stood silently in the bow, pointing out direction with a long stick.

The empty and chill voice of the rower drifted down to her. It was the melancholy chanting of the death song. Recognizing that the voice was her husband's, she knew he was dead. She was a widow and her children, fatherless.[19]

Today's maps of Mackinac Island identify a colorful location just below Fort Holmes on Garrison Road as "Skull Cave." Local legend claims that it was the hiding place for English fur trader Alexander Henry during Pontiac's Rebellion in 1763. Supposedly his friend, Ojibway Chief Wawatam, sent him to hide in the cave on a bed of human bones in order to save him from certain death after the massacre at Fort Mackinac (on the mainland).

When Indian Agent Thomas McKenney visited the cave in 1826 he found it just as Henry described it, filled with bones. How the bones got there is unknown. Even the Indians in McKenney's day didn't know the answer. It was speculated that the bones were those of the original inhabitants of the island who hid there and were subsequently massacred when the Huron invaded in 1650. Henry, however, thought the bones were from prisoners who were sacrificed at war feasts. The answer remains elusive.

There is another legend connected with the cave. It seems "once upon a time," a chief named Kenu or Thunder Bird was faced with a problem so vexing and difficult, he had no choice but to go into the Skull Cave to consult the great god Manitou. The god lived in the caverns of the Great Turtle, as the Indians called Mackinac Island. It was only in the "Place of Sacred Things" that he could hear the Manitou's voice clearly.

In his youth, Kenu was a skilled artisan in clay and produced extraordinarily beautiful peace pipes. Before going to Skull Cave, he obtained a mass of good red clay from a hill on the other side of the island and carried it with him, placing it at his feet as he waited patiently for the Manitou to speak. The gods, especially Manitou, couldn't be rushed. Patience was vital. Kenu's problem was the women in his tribe. They were constantly quarreling and arguing about everything and nothing. Their constant complaining was driving the men crazy. The chief could handle all of the normal tribal problems of leadership, including war, but the women were beyond him.

Kenu had magical powers and could summon the spirits of earth and air, but the women weren't awed by such feats. It was as though they laughed at him. He had to solve his women problem.

He dutifully consulted medicine men and prophets. He brought offerings of sacrifice, made long fasts and imposed nearly unendurable penances upon himself, all in an effort to provide for the welfare of his people. Nothing worked. Finally he went to Skull Cave and prayed that the Manitou would bless the pipes and that they would finally bring peace to his wayward women.

Kenu also had a reputation as a great warrior, brave and wise in all things. But he didn't gain such honor by fighting with women. Regardless of his bravery, entering the cave with its thousands of silently grinning skulls was forbidding. He feared the dark powers hidden in the bone piles of dead warriors.

It was the chief's hope that the great Manitou would bless the pipes that he so painstakingly crafted and give them the real spirit of peace, that whoever smoked from them would accept a feeling of brotherhood and love. When the women smoked the pipes, the problems of the tribe would heal.

With great veneration he bent over a small hollow in the rock wall where the tribe secreted their "sacred things." It was from this hollow that Kenu expected the voice of the Manitou to come. He waited uncomplainingly. The Manitou would speak in its own good time and not before. It could not be rushed.

Suddenly one of the skulls rolled toward him and began speaking. The voice was empty and distant as it flowed from between the chattering jaws. "Beneath thy feet find pliant silver. Out of it make a tube a pipe's length and in its side a small hole, which shall be for a peace note; with a covering of clay, conceal the reed and place it to dry in the sand which thou hast prepared; with thumb and finger, turn the bowl to the shape of thy thought, that thy people may comfort themselves."

Kenu quickly went to work, following exactly the Manitou's directions. He found the silver and made the pipe stems with a single note, covering them with the wet clay. When they dried, the skull blew into each a single note of great sweetness and power, repeating it on each tube in turn until the sound was replicated perfectly. After molding the bowls, Kenu attached them to the stems and placed them between the teeth of several skulls for a trial smoke. This courtesy was repaid by adding to the pipes a magical drawing power no other pipemaker could ever replicate.

The chief prepared to take the enchanted pipes to his people, confident their use would bring peace to them all. But the Manitou wasn't finished with Kenu. By his magical power the skeletons laying about the cave all became living men and, thus reconstituted, left the cave with him. They joined the tribe, becoming his most valiant and brave warriors. Perhaps most important, they also married the quarrelsome women and made them peaceful and docile.[20]

According to Indian legend, Mackinac Island was once the home of a tribe of giant Indians. Eventually the giants passed from the earth, becoming either "wandering spirits" or "wandering demons," according to the whims of the Master of Souls. Wandering spirits took the form of conical rocks, pinnacles or boulders. Wandering demons were transformed into humans but were utterly heartless and unfeeling by nature.

Just north of the island airport and near the west side is a unique geological feature called the "crack." It is a narrow chasm reaching deep into the earth, into the very depths of Mackinac. Even on summer days, when the sky is blue and the sun high overhead, the crack is a frightful place. The shadows are dark and sounds echo weirdly from its uneven surfaces. It is said that the rough and jagged walls prevent the curious from climbing down into the black abyss to explore its mysterious secrets. Reputedly, several folks have slipped and fallen into the crack but none ever returned. Their crushed bodies lay rotting on the bottom of the abyss. Many considered it an open portal to the "Under Land" where the spirits of the dead rule. If the legends are true, it is a place to be avoided.

It is also claimed that island Indians and half-breed hunters and trappers refused to take game from the area and would not eat any taken by others. It was an evil place and they wanted to stay well clear of it.

Legend says the crack is haunted by a giant demon, perhaps one of the wandering giants of eons lost. He tried to climb into the crack to reach the land of the dead but the gods forbade his transgression and his fingers were frozen to the rock where he had handholds, forever trapping him part way down. Some folks claim that if you look carefully and deeply into the chasm, you can just see the giant still hanging to the rock. Five huge fingers, including the knuckles, back of the hand and wrist, are discernable beneath the limestone.[21]

Mackinac Island legends run deep in Indian tradition. Long before the arrival of Europeans, famous fudge emporiums and the Grand Hotel, the island was believed to be a magical place.

By Indian lore, a small band of Ottawa was existing on the island well before Columbus stumbled into the New World. How they came to be there is a remarkable story.

The bulk of the Ottawa were living on Manitoulin Island in the north end of Lake Huron. The Iroquois were their deadly enemy and vigilance was always needed to warn of a sneak attack. During the dead of winter, the Ottawa were celebrating a great victory over the Winnebago of Wisconsin and in the throes of "partying," their vigilance slipped. The hated Iroquois unexpectedly attacked, killing all but two of the Ottawa. The only survivors were a young brave and a maiden who had fled over the winter ice to Mackinac Island. To deceive Iroquois trackers, they reversed their snowshoes. By laying their tracks backward, they eluded their pursuers.

The pair hid from the deadly Iroquois deep in a cave in the wildest part of the island. In time, they "did what came naturally," eventually raising 10 children, all boys. Their existence was a furtive one, always hiding in the shadows and afraid to be seen lest an Iroquois scout see them. One winter, the entire family mysteriously vanished. No explanation was ever given, but the most logical was that a passing Iroquois war party discovered them, killing them all. Eventually, the Iroquois were pushed farther east, opening the island for more peaceful tribes.

When Ottawa and Ojibway later visited the island, they discovered they weren't alone. Strange spirits roamed the lonely island, wafting on the wind and moving silently through the woods. Eventually they came to call them *Paw-gwa-tchaw-nish-bay,* which translates as "Wild roaming supernatural being." Some claim that the spirits still exist, roving the wildest parts of the island. Tourists today, more focused on material things and far out of touch with nature, never even sense them. Prior to the arrival of Europeans, the spirits were part of everyday life for the natives.

The spirits have the ability to be seen or become invisible as the mood strikes them. From time to time they would throw a rock or war club at a brave walking in a lonely place. If a lodge was set in an isolated location, they sometimes threw clubs at it, day or night. The sound of the spirits treading around the lodge was also commonly heard. Is this much different than hearing footsteps upstairs in a haunted house? Or doors open and close? Brave hunters occasionally tried following their tracks in the snow, but were never able to catch them. The spirits owned the woods and humans were a poor adversary.

Occasionally a feeling of dread and foreboding evil would seize a hunter moving alone through the deep woods. It was so strong it made him shake from head to foot. They believed such nameless terror is caused by the closeness of one of the spirits. Would a ghost hunter today not equate this with a "cold spot?" An offering of tobacco or other valuables will be left to appease the spirit.

Should an Indian be lucky enough to talk with one of the spirits, a rare but not unknown event, the spirit will sadly speak of the terrible calamity on the island bemoaning the massacre of the small Ottawa band by the Iroquois. Thereafter, the lucky Indian always became a prophet to his tribe. He did, after all, speak with the spirits.[22]

Indian legend abounds on Mackinac Island. Every natural feature is somehow linked to a legend. For example, scientifically speaking, Arch Rock is a breccia rock formation formed by winds eroding away the softer rocks around it over time. It soars to a height of 146 feet above the water level and spans 50 feet. The structure is visible from many different locations on the island.

In one Ojibway legend the arch is the gateway through which the Great Creator entered to get to his home in Sugar Loaf, another nearby formation.

A different legend maintains that it was created when a beautiful Indian maiden's tears washed away the limestone bluff as she waited in vain for her lover to return.

A third relates the creation to the reprehensible act of an Ottawa chief. What he did was so disgraceful, the Master of Life was greatly offended and in his raging anger sent down a terrible storm in punishment. The very rocks shook with the power of the wind and the lake boiled with crashing waves. The appalling tempest attacked the earth for an entire day. Even the sun, high in the heavens, was affected, stopping when it reached its zenith, unable to continue its course. The Ottawa were greatly distressed by the anger of the gods, and when the sun slowly changed color to blood red they were terrified. Suddenly the sun broke from the sky and plummeted to earth, smashing into the eastern shore of Mackinac Island with horrifying impact. Carefully the Indians went to the place where the sun struck and found some rocks hollowed out to form an arch as if he sun had burned its way through. The next morning the sun rose out of the earth in the east as usual. The anger of the Master of Life had passed. The place where the sun burned through the rocks is now known as Arch Rock.

A large rock, known as Michabou's Rock, lies between the shore and Lake Huron, just below Arch Rock. Geologists guess it was once part of the Arch Rock formation. According to Indian legend, though, it marks the landing place of the Great Manitou of the lakes. From here he climbed the bluff and went through the arch and on to the Sugar Loaf, his wigwam. Over time, his wigwam turned into rock, thus becoming Sugar Loaf. Another legend refers to large swarms of bees that once inhabited the rock and filled every nook and crevasse with sweet honey. A final legend claims that the rock is the transformed body of a giant who once lived in it and he will come to life when Hiawatha returns to Mackinac Island.

From a geological standpoint, Sugar Loaf is another breccia formation soaring 75 feet above the ground and is the largest of Mackinac Island's many limestone stacks. When Lake Algonquin covered all but the center of Mackinac Island centuries ago, only Sugar Loaf protruded from the water. When the water receded, the rock formation remained standing as a tower of rock.[23]

About a mile west of downtown there is a rock formation called "Lover's Leap." This lone rock pinnacle soars about 145 feet above the lake and takes its fame from Ojibway legend.

It seems there was a chief named Wawanosh who had a daughter named Lotah. She was very beautiful and well known for her womanly virtues. When she was 18 years old, a young but humble warrior named Geniwegwon sought her hand in marriage. Her father refused him, although she loved him as no other. The chief wanted a warrior of high rank, more suitable to marry his daughter. He sent the young man away telling him to make a name for himself before daring to seek the hand of his wonderful daughter. Geniwegwon left but wasn't disheartened. If the chief wanted him to win fame and fortune, he would do so.

Within 10 days, he assembled a band of young braves also eager to show their courage and distinguish themselves. Each brave was armed with a bow and arrows, a war club of hardwood, a stone or copper knife and a lance. For food, a deerskin bag of pounded corn flavored with maple sugar and pemmican was carried. They went to the straits where the small band painted and feathered for war. They also performed the ceremonial war dance. For two days and nights they danced to summon the spirits and beg their help. When the preparations finished Geniwegwon returned to Mackinac for a last meeting with his beloved Lotah. He swore he would never come back until his fame as a warrior was made and known far and wide by all. After swearing their faithfulness to each other, the two lovers reluctantly parted.

Once Geniwegwon left on his quest to gain her father's acceptance, Lotah climbed alone to a secluded place high on the bluff and grieved night and day. Two months later the tribe received a message that at the close of a great battle, her lover was struck by an arrow deep in the chest and badly wounded. Whether he would live or die was unknown. She begged the spirits for his recovery and safe return. As she sat on her rocky perch longing desperately for him, a bird with beautiful feathers the color of the rainbow came to her and warbled along with her when she sang the Ojibway love song. She recognized the spirit of her beloved in the bird and from then on prayed to the gods to take her to join him in the Country of Souls. Day after day Lotah sang and fasted while the bird's song accompanied her. One evening her father climbed to the crest of the bluff to convince his daughter to finally return to camp. She was not there, but when he looked down to the foot of the bluff, he saw her lifeless body smashed on the rocks below. She had gone to join her young warrior.

CHAPTER 5

Lighthouse Ghosts

Pipe Island is on the St. Marys River a few miles north of the Detour Passage from Lake Huron to Lake Superior. The shipping channel runs just to the west of the island and a light on the southwest side helps to mark this critical spot.

Pipe Island Light also has the reputation of being haunted. Although little is known of the nature of the spirit, it seems to speculatively center on Norman Hawkins, one of the early keepers. It was said that he was despondent over his only son's death in a hunting accident and, as a result, late one night he committed suicide, although he lingered for days before finally succumbing. A subsequent keeper claims to have seen his ghost standing in a lighthouse doorway clad in dripping oilskins while lightning flashed behind.

Others have reported unexplained poltergeist activity such as slamming doors, unscrewing light bulbs, moving firewood, running water taps, all actions without apparent explanation or cause. Whether there is a ghost or not is unknown, but the signs would seem to say, "Norman's Back."[1]

During a typical upper Great Lakes winter, the northern stretch of Lake Huron freezes over, becoming nothing but an ice-chocked wilderness reminiscent of the Arctic wastes. And herein is the genesis of a ghost story.

Coast Guard crews at both Spectacle Reef Light, 28 miles east of the Mackinac Bridge, and Martin Reef Light, approximately 25 miles west of Detour, were careful to always fully winterize their

128

stations when they closed up for the season. Antifreeze was poured into the drains, windows were shuttered and fully secured against the powerful storms sure to come, heating and generating equipment was serviced and "cold-proofed." If an automated light was to remain lit, all batteries were fully serviced and charged. All foodstuffs were also removed or thrown to the fish. Leaving it behind only invited a vermin feast. Entrance doors were also padlocked to prevent "unauthorized" access.

This simple procedure was common to all the upper Great Lakes lighthouses and worked well for many years until the winter of 1958. That year a small private plane crashed on the ice-covered surface of Lake Huron not far from Spectacle Reef Light. The pilot somehow managed to survive the impact and struggled his way over the frozen ice windrows to reach the lonely sentinel of hope. He also managed to force his way past the locked door into the station and searched desperately for food and a means of getting a fire going for heat. He found neither. The Coast Guard had purposely taken everything away he needed to sustain life. He left a brief note and set off across the desolate and unforgiving ice for land, the closest at Bois Blanc Island just to the west of the mainland. Both were a little more than 10 miles distant. He was never heard from again. Did he freeze to death in the trackless wastes, break through a thin spot and perish in the numbing water or perhaps stumble and break a leg and, unable to continue, just die where he fell? When the ice melted in the spring, his body dropped to the bottom of the lake, forever lost in the depths.

Learning of the terrible tragedy the following spring, the Coast Guard crew at Martin Reef made certain they always left a supply of non-perishable food at the light before leaving for the season. The odds were long that such a tragedy would ever repeat itself, but they felt not to make the effort would be unconscionable.

Meanwhile, Coast Guard crews at Spectacle Reef later claimed to hear steps on the stairs and cupboard doors opening and closing as if someone were searching for something. The activity only happened in the late fall, during the time the men were preparing to close the station for the winter. Is it the wandering spirit of the pilot repeating his desperate search for food, a search doomed to fail?

One of the least known of the Great Lakes lights, Spectacle Reef was a massive engineering project when finished in 1874. The limestone tower walls are 5 feet, 6 inches thick at the base and the structure soars 93 feet from bedrock to top. A second order Fresnel

lens, one of only five on the Great Lakes, provided the vital beam to keep ships clear of the deadly reef, a mere seven feet below the surface, as well as guide them to and from the Straits. The light's importance was unquestioned, with the Lighthouse Board stating that the reef was "probably more dreaded by navigators than any other danger now unmarked throughout the entire chain of lakes." Regardless of its importance, Spectacle was still only rehearsal for the construction of Stannard Rock Light on Lake Superior. The Lighthouse Service needed to develop the skill and techniques necessary before tackling the incredibly difficult project at Stannard Rock. The story of the ghosts at Stannard's is in *Haunted Lakes*. Martin Light became operational in 1927 with the job of guiding shipping on the Detour-Straits track. It replaced a lightship stationed there since 1909, marking a dangerous reef just off the Upper Peninsula coast.[2]

Loneliness was always a problem for lightkeepers and their families, especially at the stations isolated from the many rewards of civilization. Keeping a light was a lonely job under the best of circumstances. The same routine day after day, week after week, month after month, you get the idea. After a time the solitude can affect a person, often pushing them "over the edge." The new Presque Isle light at Alpena was an especially lonely sentinel of the coast and the story of its haunting is partly based on this overwhelming isolation.

Although unverified by fact, the tale is told that the lightkeeper's wife went stark raving mad from the terrible solitude. The lack of human contact and the drab repetition of the station's mind-numbing routine drove the poor woman into the dark pit of insanity. For reasons best known only to him, the lightkeeper felt it necessary to seal his crazy wife in a tunnel beneath the station grounds. There she spent her last miserable days in dreadful shrieking agony until her inevitable but welcome death. Perhaps the keeper hurried her along a bit with a well placed "tap" to the head with his sledgehammer. Reportedly her spirit still haunts the station grounds. When the wind blows from the right quarter and speed, her blood curdling screams are said to echo through the night, the long, low shrieks tearing eerily through the darkness. Or so goes the tale.

Efforts to learn if the story of the crazy wife sealed in a tunnel are true are inconclusive. No mention of the incident is found in official records, although that is not unusual. Every occurrence at isolated stations was not common knowledge or always recorded in government journals. Big brother didn't need to know everything! Besides, what does the lightkeeper write? "I bricked up my loony wife in a tunnel today. Good riddance to the bodacious but bonkers babe!"

A search of the station grounds failed to reveal any major tunnels, although a small one was discovered running from the lightkeeper's house to the base of the tower. In addition, a strange sealed chamber was located directly beneath the rear entrance to the house. The only access was through the floorboards above. Could either chamber have been the mad wife's cell, or is there a yet-undiscovered tunnel?

A slightly different version of the story claims that the keeper had a girlfriend in a nearby village. When he went visiting, he locked his wife away in the brick light tower for safe keeping as well as to prevent her intervention. From the lamp room she could easily watch as her husband traipsed off for a night of pleasant debauchery. His wife, of course, complained bitterly to him about her ill treatment and his trampling of the sacred marriage vows. His response is unknown, but to end her whining he finally killed her outright, explaining her absence by claiming that she had gone home to visit her mother. Whether he hid her body in a tunnel or secret room, or buried her in the nearby forest, isn't known. But the tortured spirit of the wailing wife continues to haunt the tower, a constant reminder to her husband of his unfaithfulness. While the keeper has long since "crossed the bar," as old sailors used to say, when the wind is right, the wife's spirited screams still echo through the grounds.[3]

There is yet another variation of the haunting. Anna Hoge, the daughter of one of the light's latter-day keepers, remembers living at the light as a little girl and hearing the tower cry. The sound was very soft, almost like a cat meowing or purring, but very discernable. When her father heard it, he would always place his hands on the bricks and repeat, "Don't worry. We love you and will care for you." Although the tower always continued to cry, everyone felt better that somehow the tower was reassured.

The old keepers always referred to their lights in the female gender, as a she, and they did their best to take special care of them, to protect them from all harm. Such was not the case when the Coast Guard took over. The men of the old Lighthouse Service kept the lights because they wanted to. It was a job most found great satisfaction in doing well. Coast Guardsmen kept the lights because it was a job they were ordered to do. They didn't join the Coast Guard to be a lightkeeper. The difference in attitude was major, as was the resulting performance.

To properly maintain the light tower, it was necessary to whitewash it annually, a difficult and time-consuming job. One year, to save both time and money, the Coast Guard painted the Presque Isle tower with enamel-based paint. The old-timers railed against the painting, but to no avail. In theory the paint would last many years and eliminate the need for an annual whitewashing. In practice it was a disaster. The enamel didn't allow the bricks to breathe and rapid deterioration set in. The outer course of bricks began pulling out and caused great cracks in the tower facade. The tower that had withstood gale and storm for a century threatened total destruction!

Strong community action convinced the Coast Guard to rectify their grievous error by rebricking the tower. It was an expensive solution to a self-inflicted injury, but at least it saved the gracious lady for future generations.

During the rebricking work a very remarkable thing happened. One of the workers replacing the bricks near the very top of the tower discovered a small gold wedding band wedged into a joint between bricks. Was it lost by one of the men during the original construction or, perhaps more tantalizing, could it have been a women's plain ring stuck into the bricks by the keeper's wife when faced finally with overwhelming evidence of her husband's continuing infidelity? Could it have been, in some strange way, connected with the crying of the tower? The workman kept his unique discovery but did tell Anna Hoge about the ring. To replace the tower's lost keepsake, she had the man place a small locket into the new brick course. The old tower lost one treasure, but gained another.[4]

The Presque Isle lightkeeper isn't the only one to have "done in" his wife. In the mid-1880s, the keeper at Sequin Island Light in Maine chopped up his better half with an axe in a fit of red rage. Legend says that she played the same tune on the piano again and again for hours on end. Finally, the long-suffering keeper snapped and hacked both her and the piano to little, tiny pieces. He later committed suicide, perhaps in remorse for his terrible deed or maybe he missed the old familiar tune. Today, when the air is very still, some passing ships claim they can still hear the wife's monotonous melody eerily wafting over the sea. In the early 1900s the keeper at Block Island, Rhode Island, became so enraged at his spouse, supposedly for her constant nagging and complaining, that he threw her head over heels down the steep spiral tower stairs to her death. Her ghost is also said to haunt the light. Perhaps understandably, the ghost never seems to bother women, but is said to take joy in annoying men.[5]

Old Presque Isle Light, completed in 1840, provided critical navigational aid for vessels seeking shelter in the small harbor at the south end of Presque Isle. It was not only a popular anchorage to wait out gales, but also a fueling point for early wood-burning steamers. The old wood burners could only run for a day and a half or so before needing to reload with fresh cordwood. The white stone light tower stands 30 feet tall, a clear and welcome sight for vessels for more than a century and a half. A small stone keeper's house is just a few feet from the tower base. The light was discontinued in 1871 when the new Presque Isle Light, a mile to the north, was completed.

In the early 1900s, the property was sold to the Stebbins family in whose ownership it remains. The family restored the light, furnished it with period antiques and presently operates it as a museum. In 1977, George and Lorraine Parris, a retired couple, took over as caretakers.[6]

Nothing much happened at the old light until 1979, when the beacon inexplicably began to shine again. This was a serious problem. Once a light is decommissioned, it is removed from the official light list. The sudden reappearance of a light could confuse mariners, leading to disastrous consequences.

Lorraine Parris, the museum manager, remembered it suddenly coming on and revolving as in the old days a century before. It was immediately turned off. There was no rational explanation for the unusual event. To make certain it stayed off, the Coast Guard came out and assisted her husband in disconnecting it, even to the extent of removing the rotating motor and gears. For good measure, all electric power to the tower was also cut off. For museum purposes, the old Fresnel lens was left in place.

For 13 years the tower stayed dark, as it should be. But one day in the spring of 1992, as Lorraine Parris was driving along the lake road toward the light, she noticed a glow in the tower. Afraid of ridicule, she didn't mention the light incident to anyone. Finally, she told her son-in-law. He and her daughter said it must have been nothing more than a reflection of car headlights. After all, what else could it be?

Thinking that it just might be something more, Parris took two friends to the point where she first saw the strange light. One of the friends, Anna Hoge, had grown up around lighthouses. Her father had been a lightkeeper at Presque Isle and at Passage Island on Lake Superior and she was well familiar with every facet of lighthouse operation. They saw the light again! The three friends thought the curious glow just might be caused by a reflection from the floodlights that illuminate the tower at night. To test the theory they were turned off. The unexplained incandescence remained. Moving about the area, they determined that the mysterious glow is best seen from the marina pier. The following night they repeated the test, with the same result. One member of the group closely observed the tower with powerful binoculars. She thought she saw a shadowy figure faintly visible in the lantern room. Parris also believed she saw it. The tower was locked and entry was impossible. Whatever it was, it wasn't human. When seen on other occasions, Parris thought the strange figure even seemed to dance.

Several other methods to extinguish the light were tried. The lens was covered with a thick army blanket. It still showed. The next night thick black plastic was taped over the lamp room windows. It continued to show. During the summer of 1995, a Boy Scout group covered the lens with a heavy tarp without effect.

To preclude any possible chicanery, the old light bulb in the tower was removed. The Coast Guard later even changed the direction of the lens to defeat any unusual reflection. Still the glow appeared. Lake freighters steaming far offshore also observed the phenomenon. Other local people besides Parris and her friends have seen the light and although some may not accept it as real, they also can't explain it. In at least one instance, people were in the

134

tower when watchers on the pier saw the glow. Those in the tower saw nothing, however. Others claimed having had disturbing experiences there, feelings of foreboding and dread. Climbing the stairs at night with only a flashlight has unnerved some people, giving them a feeling that the stone walls were closing in on them, the resulting anxiety forcing them to flee. Some visitors say they also heard footsteps echoing on the old stone steps.

At one point a church group held a candlelight meeting on the grounds with the intention of praying the ghosts out of the light. The following night the light still glowed, leaving the pastor to conclude that at least the haunt wasn't a demon.

Once a small girl climbed to the top of the old tower and was chuckling when she came down. When someone asked why, she related that she had been talking to "the man in the tower." After she saw a picture of George in the keeper's cottage, she identified him as the man in the tower. A local resident suggests that the daughter of one of the old keepers likely haunts the tower. Does this mean George has company?

During an interview, Lorraine Parris related another incident. "Little things happened that you don't know what to make of. On September 5, 1992, a bad storm struck. The light was on then. I was sitting (here) doing my bookwork and everything and it was an awfully bad lightning storm. I went to get out my back door to move my car up to the light and I couldn't get out. These two white chairs (outside) were braced up against the door, just like there were two people sitting talking. I couldn't open the door. It would not open! Well, I thought, I guess I am not supposed to go outside so I came back, sat down and started to do my work. All of a sudden, a bolt of lightning hit just outside. It blew my nightlight and sensor right out of the wall! If I had been outside I would have been hit."

Parris, however, does have an explanation for some of the strange events. For 14 years she and her husband, George, ran the light and museum. Their lives were deeply intertwined with it. George died of a heart attack at the lighthouse just a few months before she first saw the light in 1992. It is her conclusion that it's just her husband. He had just come back to help. A master electrician, what could be simpler for him than to "power up" the old light? "It was always so peaceful living here. The water would just lullaby you right to sleep," she related to a reporter. "And George is here. He's still protecting the property." Others say it's the spirit of the first keeper, old Patrick Garrity, still trying to do his duty.[7]

During the 1930s and '40s, the ghost of an old keeper known only as Morgan reputedly haunted the light at Thunder Bay Island off Alpena, Michigan. His uneasy spirit is said to still walk the desolate shore of the island. Although no particular reason for his wanderings is known, his presence unnerved Coast Guardsmen during their own lonely night patrols, especially on moonless nights when the wind howled with a wild abandon and endless waves crashed on the rocky shore. Young surfmen often claimed that the ghost followed them just out of their sight. Although they couldn't see him, they knew he was there, ... watching ... and waiting.[8]

Thunder Bay Island light is one of the oldest on the lake, being established in 1832. The original stone tower stood 40 feet tall. In 1857 it was raised 10 feet, to reach the present height of 50 feet. The keeper's quarters was added in 1868.

In May 1993, I was making some copies of Life-Saving Service photographs in the old Sturgeon Point Lighthouse Museum on the shores of Lake Huron. One of the older lights on the lakes, the stone structure was built in 1870. The Life-Saving Service station was established adjacent to it in 1876, however, today the buildings are long gone.

The day I visited was bright and sunny, the type to push all thoughts of things that go bump in the night to the deepest recesses of the mind. The museum was not yet open for the season and was still shuttered against the icy blasts of winter. Inside it was damp, chilly and dark. The only illumination came from a few low-wattage bulbs. The furniture and general decor were from the 1870 period, adding to the effort of stepping back in time.

Immediately on entering the building the hair on the back of my neck began to tingle. Intuitively I felt uncomfortable, that I wasn't alone. After setting up my copy camera gear in the restored living room on the first floor, I climbed the stairs to the second floor and entered a room fitted out as a display area for lighthouse memorabilia and relics. Long glass cases filled with small artifacts lined one wall. A single switch near the door controlled the electric lights in the case. Turning it on, I quickly examined the contents. Finding nothing of immediate interest, I turned the light off. I removed several Life-Saving Service photos from the adjacent wall and carried them downstairs to my camera set up in the living room. When I returned with the photos several minutes later, the display case light was back on. After replacing the photos on the wall and selecting two more, I again turned the light off and went back down to my camera. All the while I felt a vague apprehension. The hair on my neck continued to tingle and a penetrating shot of cold shot up my neck.

Again I returned to the display room and again the case light was on! Enough was enough. Replacing the photos, I turned the case light off a third time and retreated downstairs. I hastily picked up my camera gear and left the building. Outside, the blue skies and warm temperatures instantly relieved my apprehension. Somewhat embarrassed by my experience, I said nothing about it.

All the while I was in the lighthouse I saw nothing unusual, only felt it. Knowing nothing of the light in terms of ghost stories or the like, I had no reason to suspect anything unnatural. But I did experience something. It wasn't just a reaction to an old building.

A year later when I spoke to one of the museum personnel regarding whether there was any reason for my strange feelings, she stated that she wasn't aware of any ghost stories connected to the light. Coincidently, though, she related that on occasion she did have a difficult time turning the lights out. After closing down at the end of the day, she sometimes opened the next morning to find lights burning that she was certain she had turned off. She was forced to put it down to her error. But I wonder. Could it be that the playful spirit of the first keeper, Percy Silverthorn, is still keeping his light? Something was definitely going on in there.[9]

The spirits in some lighthouses are more active than others. At Old Presque Isle, for example, it seems that they are lively every month or so. Other lights are quieter, with just a hint of spectral motion.

I visited Forty Mile Point Lighthouse in October 2002 en route to the Great Lakes Lighthouse Festival in Alpena, Michigan. As part of the overall celebration, local lighthouses, including Forty Mile Point, open to the public for exploration. Hundreds of people take advantage of the opportunity to see some great lighthouses.

Forty Mile Point Light proved especially interesting. It's a brick duplex much like the Big Bay Light on Lake Superior. While waiting to climb the tower, I playfully asked one of the guides, "How's the ghost doing?" I had never found a ghost story associated with the lighthouse, but sincerely believing "all lighthouses are haunted," I asked the question. If you don't ask the question, you don't get the answer.

Her response surprised me. As I remember her words, it went something like, "Well I've never seen one, but one of our volunteers did." The story goes that the volunteer was working in the basement. He was alone in the lighthouse, at least he was the only living person around. When he finished the job at hand, he carefully locked up all the doors, double-checking them all and went upstairs to the kitchen and out the back stairs, heading for his car. Glancing back toward the lighthouse, he was startled to see a shadowy figure looking back at him from the kitchen window.

Being braver than most, the man turned around and went back inside to investigate. He was certain that he was the only one in the building, but he definitely saw someone or something. Despite searching high and low, the building was empty. Whatever he saw simply wasn't there anymore.

The volunteer also related several years before that a body was found buried in the woods behind the lighthouse. Although only a skeleton, the skull was pierced by a bullet hole. The remains were never identified or explained. Was the body connected to the figure in the kitchen, or just a bizarre coincidence? Was it an unreported hunting accident, suicide or murder?

The Forty Mile Point Lighthouse Historical Society has been working hard to restore the old light. Has its energetic activity somehow released the spirit? Some paranormal investigators claim that ghosts become active when their "homes" are disturbed by such enterprise.[10]

The tower of Saginaw River Light is said to be haunted, but by whom or what isn't known. Suspicion falls on an old lightkeeper who died at the station. The story is told that before succumbing, he admonished his family to continue in his place and to faithfully keep the light burning. They were to maintain a never-ending vigil over "his" light. In any case, the loud echoes of steps on the old circular iron stairway leading up the 77-foot tower are said to still be heard.

In one instance in the 1960s, two Coast Guardsmen were standing a late watch in the building. As was typical, one stayed awake while the other napped on a nearby cot. In the early hours of the morning, the sleeping man was shaken awake by the watch stander. "Something is in the tower, something is in the tower," was all the frightened sailor could yell. Together, both men went to the tower door. They could clearly hear the slow thumping of heavy boots climbing the stairs. Blankly they stared at the heavy steel door and back at each other. What was happening was beyond their comprehension. An oversize padlock still secured the hasp. It was locked tight. Obviously no one had entered the tower. But what was making the sound? They never found out. As suddenly as it started, it stopped. Was it the old keeper, or his family still carrying out his last desperate instructions?

The *Coast Pilot* describes the reef at Lake Huron's Pointe aux Barques as "dangerous … with rocks covered by less than 6 feet near its outer edge, extends two miles E from Pointe aux Barques Light. A 5-foot spot is 1.2 miles NE of the light and boulders covered 13 to 15 feet extend up to 2.5 miles N and NE. …" Under any circumstance, it is a dangerous place for a sailor to be.

To warn mariners away from the reef's deadly stone talons, in 1847 Congress provided $5,000 to construct a lighthouse. The beacon became operational the following year, a remarkably short period of time. In the 1850s, the light had to be rebuilt, due to the era's poor building standards for lighthouses. An assistant keeper's quarters was added in 1908. The present tower stands 80 feet high.

As a result of the large number of vessels wrecked in the area, regardless of the light's effort to warn them clear, in 1876, a first class lifesaving station was built several hundred yards to the south. Time and time again, these brave surfmen ventured forth into the teeth of gale and storm to rescue shipwrecked sailors and passengers.

In 1958, the Coast Guard turned the land and facility over to Huron County, which presently operates it as a park, campground and museum. The old stick-style lifesaving station building was moved several miles to the west to the Huron City Museum complex.

Pointe aux Barques is fraught with maritime tragedy. Many sailors drowned just offshore in numerous shipwrecks. The latest major disaster was the 567-foot steel steamer *Daniel J. Morrell* lost on November 29, 1966. Dennis Hale, the sole survivor from her 34-man crew, actually washed ashore at the point on a life raft.

An especially terrible loss for local families occurred in April 1879 when seven of eight members of the lifesaving station crew perished when their surfboat overturned in heavy seas while they were going to the aid of a schooner in distress. The only survivor was the keeper, Jerome Kiah.

From a sailor's perspective, Pointe aux Barques is certainly a place of both pulse-quickening danger and deep sadness. If, as the old sailors believed, the spirits of drowned mariners haunted the places where good vessels and crews died in screaming agony, then

this dreadful point is home to many a restless soul. But it is also home to at least one very gentle and concerned guardian ghost.

Because the old lighthouse grounds are now a county park, a resident manager is employed during the summer to handle the multitude of tasks necessary to make it a successful enterprise. The manager lives in the old assistant keeper's quarters, a hundred yards or so distant from the lighthouse proper. The building is far more spacious and comfortable than the old 1857 keeper's house, which is now used as a small museum.

A dozen or so years ago, the manager's adult daughter was staying with her parents in the old assistant's house when she awoke suddenly in the middle of the night to a strange and unidentifiable noise. She was staying in a second-story bedroom. Knowing that something was there, but not what, she slowly opened her door and nervously peered out into the dark but empty hallway. Seeing nothing, she crept carefully to the head of the stairs and looked down.

What she saw should have scared the wits out of her, but it didn't. Instead she was overcome by a feeling of intense calm, of pervasive relaxation. Instinctively she knew that everything was all right. Standing at the base of the stairs, shimmering slightly in the pale moonlight streaming through the windows, was the distinct, almost solid apparition of a woman from a time long past.

The woman appeared average in height, perhaps a bit on the thin side and wore a long old-fashioned dress with an apron tied about her waist. Her hair was done up in a tight bun. The face was neither old nor young but instead had an ethereal and ageless quality. Her left hand rested easily on the banister, as if in preparation for climbing the steps. The woman had shape and substance, none of the half-formed appearance commonly accepted as spirit manifestations. The strange visitor spoke not a word nor made a motion, but the daughter clearly received the overwhelming impression that the woman was the old lightkeeper's wife and came over from the original quarters to see what was going on in the new house, to determine if the new residents posed any threat to the old light. For the longest time, it seemed minutes but probably was mere seconds, human and spirit stood silently staring at each other, their eyes locked in eerie understanding. Reassured by the bizarre visitor, the daughter returned to her bed for a deep and restful sleep.

Before her encounter with the ghost, the daughter had always been uneasy when she visited the light, sensing a feeling of foreboding – that something didn't want her there. But after encountering the ghostly woman, she found the light to be relaxing and peaceful, and looked forward to her visits. The wandering spirits of sailors drowned in the wrecks may haunt the offshore waters, but the old lightkeeper's wife owns the land and there she would welcome friends.[11]

The following story came from an old Coastie who ended up at a Lake Huron lighthouse in the 1940s, while some of the civilian lightkeepers were still serving. He asked that the light not be identified, feeling it opened him to ridicule. I honor his request.

"The old guy I replaced was at the light for a long time, 30 years or so. Among the men in the old Coast Guard, he was a real legend, kind of an old man of the sea kind of thing. Anyway, when I arrived at the lighthouse he was still there. Normally, the keeper, especially one retiring, would be long gone, happy to finally be away from the damn place. But he was still there. He gave me the grand tour, showing me every little nook and cranny the old place had. It pretty much took the whole day.

"In late afternoon, we finally sat down for a cup of coffee. 'Bud,' he says, for some reason he called everybody bud, 'Bud,' he says, 'I've seen many strange and wondrous things. You stay here long enough and you will, too. But you listen to me now, real close, 'cause this is important. Sometimes at night you will see something down on the beach. Just ignore it. Whatever you do, don't go near it, just stay away and it will stay away from you. If you bother it, you will regret it. I've lived with it for these 30 years and you can too, nice and easy, but should you do anything to it, I can't be responsible." With that, he put down his coffee cup, picked up his old cane and hobbled out the door. My questions concerning what the hell he was talking about went unanswered.

"Everything went along fine for several months, then one dark November night, I was in the tower enjoying a good pipe and looked out toward the beach. I saw a dark shadow shifting over the sand. It moved down the beach slowly, as if searching for something in the wave wash. When it crossed the pale of the moon, I could see it a little better. The form appeared human, but instead of walking normally, it moved somewhat hesitatingly, as if dragging a leg. I watched for a while, and then it just disappeared. It was there, and then it was gone!

"I didn't see it again until the spring of the following year. It followed the same routine as before, moving along the beach as if searching for something and lasting for 10 to 15 minutes before just fading away. One day I asked the assistant keeper if he had ever seen anything out of the ordinary during the night watch. He said he didn't; everything was always the same.

"I saw it again in mid-summer. It was the same as before, just walking along then vanishing. I am not a brave man, but I had to find out what was going on. I resolved that the next time I would go down to the beach and have a closer look.

"In late fall, just before we would close for the season, it came again. I was ready for it and charged off to the beach with a flashlight. There was a break in the dunes directly in front of the lighthouse and that's where I reached the beach. I was only about 50 feet away when it loomed up in front of me. It was tall and dressed in rough clothes. The head was bare with a scraggly growth of black hair hanging down. The figure was still looking down to the sand and had not seen me.

"I switched on the flashlight and put the beam right on it and with a loud voice said, 'Who are you? What are you looking for?' The figure stopped dead in its tracks and gazed up at me. The eyes glowed bright red. I'll never forget the eyes, the dreadful, burning eyes.

"The damn thing ran right for me! I took a couple of steps back and it kept coming. Then I turned and ran, not looking back until I got to the cut of the dunes. It was still coming right behind me! I ran straight into the lighthouse and slammed and bolted the door. For some reason I thought I was safe. The door started to shake, lightly at first then harder and more violently. The heavy door began to come apart in front of my eyes, to slowly burst, if you can understand what I mean.

"I ran through the dining room and past my office to the door to the tower. I heard a loud crash and surmised that it was the kitchen door shattering. All I could think of was to run up the tower with the hope that I could figure how to lock one of the scuttle doors behind me. I ran up the stairs as fast as I could, the creature pounding along behind me. I shot through the first scuttle and slammed it tight, then stood on it. When it reached it, the door just raised up into the air with me on top. I weigh almost 200 pounds, but it was as if I wasn't even there. I jumped off and ran up the last few steps to the lamproom and out to the galley. As I burst out on the walkway, I could feel its breath. I ran to the left, hoping to get around the galley and back inside and down the stairs before it got me. The door at the base of the tower was steel and could be bolted from the outside. Maybe it could contain it.

"Then a miracle happened. The first light of dawn broke over the horizon. Being that high up, with the ground still in darkness, the new light was in sharp contrast with the shadows of the night. The light evidently chased the figure off. I was suddenly conscious of being alone. It was gone!

"I never bothered the mysterious figure again and it never bothered me. I have no idea what it is, or was searching for, but I decided to take the old keeper's advice just to leave it alone."[12]

Lighthouse ghosts are not only the spirits of gray-bearded old keepers. Sometimes they can be the shades of others who experienced both joy and sorrow at the lights. The ghostly girl at Tawas Light, Michigan, on the Lake Huron shore, is a fine example of the latter variety of specter.

The first lighthouse at Tawas Point, a rubble tower similar to the one at Old Presque Isle, 70 miles to the north, was operational in 1853. By the early 1870s, the point had shifted enough that a new light was needed and the present one was constructed as a result. The brick tower stands 67 feet high, giving the fourth order Fresnel lens a focal plane 70 feet above the lake. A two-story red keeper's house is attached. It is all very picturesque.

Pinning down the reason for the ghost is always the purest conjecture. In this instance, it seems that a young girl, thought to be the daughter of a lightkeeper, died in one of the upstairs bedrooms around the turn of the century. Apparently the death was caused by pneumonia. Old-timers say her spirit has haunted the light ever since. She isn't confined to the building, but has also been seen on the grounds around the lighthouse.

One of the more modern stories involves the wife of a Coast Guard officer-in-charge of the station. Up until fairly recently the lighthouse was an active part of Coast Guard Station Tawas Point. Before the new officer-in-charge and his wife moved into their quarters at the station, they were staying in a camper parked near the lighthouse. It was a pleasant spring morning and since the station was closed to the public, the grounds were deserted. The wife was sitting at a picnic table enjoying her morning coffee when, to her surprise, she noticed a young girl in a pink sleeping gown sitting on the stone steps to the rear of the lighthouse. The little girl was crying. The woman thought this was very odd and walked over to ask the girl where she was from and why she was crying The girl looked up at her for a long moment, her red eyes streaming tears, and then dashed through the back door and into the lighthouse. Since the door was locked with a large padlock this was clearly impossible! Startled, the woman ran to the camper and got her husband. Between them, they couldn't figure out what had happened. All the doors were locked, as were the windows. When the husband searched the building, no evidence of the little girl was found.

There have been other encounters with the mysterious little girl. She has been sighted looking forlornly out of her top floor bedroom. Reportedly this was the room she was in when she died. She has also been seen peering out of the upstairs windows at the rear of the house. Is she looking for playmates that will never come? Why is she trapped in the lighthouse at all? Why didn't she "pass over?"

It is reported that in 1998 a group of Coast Guardsmen had another brush with the little ghost. The officer-in-charge of the station, engineering officer and two Coast Guard engineers from Coast Guard Group Detroit were working in the lighthouse basement when they heard a little girl's voice outside. It sounded as if she were playing, laughing and carrying on the way children do. Finding this odd, since they knew there were no children in the area, the men went outside to see what was going on. They discovered no one anywhere near the light. As far as they could see, they were completely alone. Thinking that they must have been mistaken in what they thought they heard, they returned to the basement to finish their work. As soon as the men reached the cellar, they heard the little girl again. One of the Coast Guardsmen was so rattled by the unearthly experience that he refused to ever return to the lighthouse. The man was also involved in scouting and when he brought his troop to the lighthouse for a tour, he refused to enter the building but stood outside in the bright sunshine instead while another Coast Guardsman led the tour.

Perhaps there are more wandering ghosts at Tawas than just the little girl in pink. Just to the northwest of the light is the old Tawas Coast Guard Station. A new, "state of the art" Coast Guard station was built across the road, so the old one was abandoned. The original station was built by the U.S. Life-Saving Service in 1876, making it one of the oldest on the Great Lakes. There are numerous stories of bizarre events happening in the old station house. One evening after the men moved to the new station, the Search and Rescue (SAR) alarm in the old station suddenly blared to life as if to summon the crew to a rescue. Considering that there was no electrical power in the building, the alarm blaring was most remarkable. It continued to sound until station men came to see what was happening, then mysteriously stopped. This wasn't the only odd thing happening in the old building. On previous occasions Coast Guardsmen working on the ground floor of the building clearly heard people moving about and talking on the second floor. In the old Life-Saving Service days, this was where the men had their bunks and personal lockers. When the Coast Guardsmen climbed to the second floor and checked, the room was empty – of the living anyway. After hearing the steps and voices numerous times, they just stopped bothering to look anymore. It was just part of life at the old lifesaving station.

Hearing the sounds of the old surfmen (for want of a better description) on the second floor of old lifesaving stations isn't all that unusual. Just as all lighthouses seem to be haunted, so, too, do many of the old lifesaving stations. Similar tales have come from the Hammonds Bay station on Lake Huron, both South and North Manitou Islands on Lake Michigan and Marquette station on Lake Superior, among others. In addition, the surfboat from Pointe aux Barques Station on Lake Huron has also supposedly been seen again. The old surfmen are not going quietly into the night and neither is the old station. In 2005, a developer purchased the disused Coast Guard station property and intended to tear down the old Life-Saving Service building. The room was needed for a set of brand new condos. Luckily, a historian convinced the developer of the importance of the old station and the value of incorporating it into the project, thus saving part of Great Lakes history. How the ghosts respond is still open.[13]

One of the more engaging lighthouse ghost stories involves Georgian Bay's Cove Island Light and Captain Amos Tripp of the schooner *Regina*. It seems that one storm-lashed November night, no one quite remembers the year, the steady beacon on Cove Island winked out. Since October 1858, the massive stone tower at the northeast tip of Gig Point at the entrance to Georgian Bay had faithfully kept the light for all to see. Without its steady beam to guide the ships past the treacherous rocks and shoals, disaster was certain to strike. When all looked the blackest, the light suddenly came back on, the steady and powerful glow reassuring mariners struggling on the stormy lake.

When later asked why the light went dark, the lightkeeper first explained that although the lamp had indeed gone out, it was only through his skill that he was able to relight it. Many years later he reluctantly revealed the shocking truth: he was not at his station that tempestuous night. He was in fact, not on the island at all. The light failed due to his inexcusable neglect. His explanation for why the light came back on was even more unusual. It was relit by the ghost of Captain Tripp!

Tripp's story goes back many years before, to October 22, 1881. He was the master of the small 75-foot, 118-ton schooner *Regina* bound from Goderich with a cargo of salt. The schooner, built in 1866, was overtaken by a fierce gale and badly beat about. The old hull soon started to spit her oakum caulking and great quantities of water began flooding into her hold. *Regina* was heading for the bottom, the only question was how quickly. Captain Tripp thought he could nurse her to safety on a sandbar off Cove Island. His crew didn't give a plugged nickel for her chances and voted with their feet, deserting her in the yawl, leaving Tripp standing alone on his quarterdeck. The crew's assessment of the *Regina*'s seaworthiness was correct and the schooner sank just short of the sandbar. Tripp paid for his overconfidence with his life, drowning when the schooner dove for the bottom. The old captain's body eventually washed ashore on the island 13 days later and was buried without ceremony behind the dunes. Since no coffin was available, he was simply wrapped in a canvas sail. Perhaps for an old sailor like Tripp this was most appropriate anyway. Weeks later, Captain Tripp was dug up and taken home to an "official" cemetery at Collingwood farther down Georgian Bay. Apparently the captain didn't want to go. They may have planted his mortal remains in that cold and formal burying ground, but he lived, died and was buried as a sailor. His spirit stayed at Cove Island.

Regardless of the facts surrounding the event, the unfaithful Cove Island lightkeeper always believed that Tripp's presence was with him on the island. He constantly felt the presence of the old captain's energy. And it was his noble spirit that relit the light and kept it burning throughout the storm. Another variation of the tale holds that when the cold north wind blows hard, the ghost of old Captain Tripp returns to the light to play a hand of cards with the keeper, safe and snug in the little stone cottage. None of the keepers ever objected to sharing their old home with the venerable captain. It was nice to have such faithful company. The light was manned until 1991, so from then on Captain Tripp had the island to himself.

It appears old Captain Tripp is not just a "historic" ghost, one only reported a long time ago. In the last couple of years, some folks visiting the island claimed an eerie feeling of being watched, that they were not alone. One person even said that he saw a shadowy figure moving just out of clear vision. Evidently the captain is still on duty.[14]

"There it is! It must be the light," said the wheelsman. The captain agreed that it was indeed the light and ordered the *Mary Ward*'s bow swung to starboard. It was November 24, 1872, and the 120-foot steamer was bound east from Owen Sound for Collingwood, normally an easy 45-mile run. But visibility was very poor and both men were straining hard to see the beam of Nottawasaga Light in the black night. When they saw a faint glimmer through the dark just where they thought the light should be, they assumed it was the light. It wasn't. The glow was from an old oil lantern on the porch of a boarding house at Craigleith (also identified as a tavern) five miles short of Collingwood. With a shutter and crunch, the steamer ran hard up on a limestone reef three miles or so offshore.

Since the weather was still calm and there was no reason for immediate panic, the captain sent several men in a ship's lifeboat to Collingwood to get a tug. They were eventually successful in arranging for the services of the 86-ton tug *Mary Ann*.

November, though, is never quiet for long on the Great Lakes and during the delay, the water turned ugly and the captain, with seven others, launched another boat and headed for the now-visible lighthouse for help. The waves were so roiled that the small boat just made it to the beach without foundering.

The tug *Mary Ann* reached the area of the stranded steamer the day after she went on the reef, but the combination of storm and shoal water prevented her from getting close enough to help. She could neither remove the passengers and crew nor even get a hawser to her. Helpless to assist, she steamed back to the safety of Collingwood.

The power of the rising storm and the sight of the tug abandoning them were too much for the folks left aboard the *Mary Ward*. Without the captain to keep order, they panicked. Eight of the men launched another boat and, disdaining other passengers, headed for the nearby beach. They never made it. Capsizing in the crashing waves, the deserters "fed the fishes" the hard way. The 24 souls remaining aboard the *Mary Ward* were the lucky ones, surviving the battering of the gale until the following day when the weather calmed and they were rescued by fishing tugs from Collingwood and the lighthouse keeper in his boat. Although much of her cargo and fittings were later salvaged, the vessel itself was a total loss. The shoal is now known as *Mary Ward* Ledges.

The fisherman, lighthouse keeper and his assistant each received $15 as a reward for their rescue work. The lightkeeper was an old hand at taking people off shipwrecks. In 31 years at Nottawasaga Light, he reputedly helped bring 52 ashore from different wrecks.

But the ghosts rose from the wreck of the *Mary Ward* and, for years afterward, it was claimed that the boarding house whose light caused the loss of the vessel was haunted by the spirits of the men drowned in the wreck. It was their revenge for the lantern that led them to their deaths. By rights, though, the ghosts should have haunted the captain. It was his error that put the steamer on the rocks and his failure to stay with his ship that allowed the panicked men to make their ill-fated attempt to land. The haunting only stopped when the old structure was finally demolished.[15]

CHAPTER 6

Sea Monsters

Contemporary sightings of lake monsters are still being reported. A St. Ignace, Michigan, husband and wife were standing on the Lake Huron shore on Easter Sunday 1989. It was mid-morning and the weather was warm and pleasant. There was every indication of a hoped-for early spring. The lake was calm with hardly a ripple to break the surface. While the wife was looking elsewhere, the husband noticed a "… large wake in the water heading northeast," toward Rabbit's Back Point. He quickly pointed out the strange phenomenon to his wife. There was no boat or obvious explanation for the wake. The pair swiftly returned home, about a half-mile distant, and grabbed a pair of powerful binoculars. Looking through the glasses they saw that a boat or Jet Ski was not causing the wake. Instead, it came from an object projecting about two feet out of the water, almost like a submarine's periscope. But why would a submarine be running between Mackinac Island and St. Ignace? After a while the strange wake disappeared behind Mackinac Island. The couple, long-time residents of the area, had never seen anything like it before or since.

This was not the first report of a "sea serpent" in the area. In August 1975, there was an account of a "40-foot snakelike creature" sighted in the Straits, swimming north from Cheboygan, Michigan.[1]

The following year other "sea monsters" were reported around Cheboygan, about 15 miles south of the Straits. In June 1976 frantic calls to the local sheriff claimed a "sea monster" was cavorting along the shore. One eyewitness even reported seeing several snakes about 40 feet long swimming in Lake Huron about 600 feet offshore, but when a deputy arrived on scene the creatures were gone. The following day the sheriff went to the beach to personally investigate and was shocked to see a creature "20, maybe 30 feet long swimming just below the surface." He further stated, "I was amazed. I didn't know what it was, but it sure wasn't a publicity stunt. Anyway, I'm watching this thing through field glasses and I see no wiggling so I judged it traveling maybe three miles an hour. Something is protruding about an inch out of the water, but if there was any movement, any disturbance from shore, it would duck under." The sheriff sent a deputy out in a canoe for a closer look, but he couldn't get close enough before it dropped out of sight.

Some of the possible explanations tested the bounds of credibility as much as the idea of a sea serpent. One local expert claimed that it was nothing but migrating carp. Another specialist from the Michigan Department of Natural Resources theorized that it could be a salt-water eel that migrated up the St. Lawrence Seaway. Certainly it was a good explanation but ignored the fact that eels aren't 20 to 30 feet long![2]

Sea monsters are an old American tradition. The first major sightings were in the summers of 1817 and 1818 in the waters off Gloucester, Massachusetts. Reported as a large, multi-humped creature, at one time more than 200 people claimed to have seen it simultaneously. Some folks estimated it at 40 to 70 long and said it moved very fast. After a time sightings ceased but it supposedly reappeared in 1877 for a brief encore. Similar creatures were seen around northeastern waters from Long Island Sound to Portland, Maine.

While we never had any sea monsters as spectacular as the Gloucester creature, Great Lakes sea monsters aren't unique in American folklore, or just a relic of the past. Folks continue to report sighting strange beasts in modern times.

For example, a large school of mysterious creatures was spotted in 1975 near Kincardine, Ontario, at the southern end of Lake Huron. Witnesses were unable to determine their identity but knew they were definitely something they never saw before. In addition, two long, loglike creatures were spotted swimming in the water off Goderich, just to the south, in 1989.[3]

Some sea serpents may have been more "real" than others. An October 24, 1890, story in the *Detroit Free Press* described a monster snake that occasionally appeared along the waterfront near the F.E. Bradley sawmill. The monster normally was sighted at night and scared the wits out of several mill workers. One witness said the dead glow in its eyes shook the men to their souls. Others claimed that it was 12 feet long with a head shaped like an ox. A more rational explanation was that the creature may have been a large anaconda that had escaped during a fire at a local museum. If it was the missing anaconda, winter certainly spelled the end of it, or maybe it found a nice warm attic somewhere.[4]

On a warm summer day in the early 1960s, an entire family watched another huge creature, alternatively showing humps and then stretching out straight, swimming up the St. Marys River past Sugar Island. They never saw a head or tail, but it just kept moving along until finally disappearing in the distance. I wonder if it locked through? If so, did it use the American or Canadian locks?

A group of Detroit men came face to face with a monster off Sarnia in the summer of 1897. They were fishing about three miles offshore in 145 feet of water when their boat began moving at a very rapid speed, as if being towed by the anchor line. Suddenly a "black mass, a swiftly moving ribbon-shaped monster, dashed to the surface. One of the party began firing at it with his revolver (and) four rods away the water was lashed into bloody foam. The monster was at least 88 feet long, was flexible as a snake (with) a double row of fins ... it had long whiskers." As quick as it came it left, leaving the group to wonder what they had witnessed.[5]

In early October 1938, six otherwise sober Sarnia fishermen claimed to have been forced to run their boat ashore by a huge sea serpent. Estimated at 30 feet long, it undulated in and out of the water as it swam and its menacing tail swished back and forth. The year before, a similar serpent was reported near Southampton, Ontario, 100 miles to the north.[6]

Georgian Bay commercial fishermen occasionally reported encounters with sea monsters, too. Locations varied and include Manitoulin Island, northwest of Parry Sound at the Limestone Islands and Gull Island. None of the beasts were ever caught, killed or photographed.

A seal-like monster estimated at 8 feet in length was supposedly sighted off Wasaga Beach at the foot of Nottawasaga Bay in 1938. Unlike the serpentlike creatures sighted elsewhere, Georgian Bay monsters tended to be on the small side. One was said to be approximately 4 feet long with four feet and fins. Another was a larger version of the famous Lake Superior merman with fins and a tail.[7]

Another fascinating sighting came from folks aboard the big excursion steamer *City of Detroit III,* according to a report in the *Owen Sound Sun Times,* dated July 23, 1948.

"While men yelled and one woman fainted aboard the *City of Detroit III*, a Detroit and Cleveland Navigation Co., liner, a sea serpent slithered through Georgian Bay.

"That was the report of an eyewitness, Miss Bess Munroe of Michigan, the ship's social hostess.

"Miss Munroe's report of a 60-foot green-and-purple-scaled monster with a huge horned head was confirmed by more than a dozen passengers and several of the ship's crew.

"The 'thing' was sighted by the travelers as the ship was entering the bay near Flowerpot Island. It came within 500 feet of the ship and remained in sight for approximately 15 minutes. It then disappeared in the fog and rain.

"'I've sailed the Great Lakes for many years,' said the captain, 'and have yet to see any monster. However, some of the informants in this case have always been persons of sound judgment and character.'

"When the news of the sighting reached Tobermory, one local old-timer was heard to comment, 'I am sure this "spirit" came from a bottle!'"[8]

This story was compiled from several sources. How accurate it is, of course, is open to speculation. When you try to combine oral tradition recorded by a wandering priest, barely discernable French records interspersed with conjecture and other like-sounding tales, veracity is very questionable. All that said, there is an interesting aspect to the tale.

Middle Island is just north of Alpena, Michigan, and several miles offshore. Even today it has little to recommend it beyond an old lighthouse. Lake Huron was never a priority for the early French voyageurs and explorers. The fur was all north and west, not south. When their canoes emerged from the mouth of the French River in eastern Georgian Bay, it was west to fur and fortune, not south into the vast nothing of Lake Huron.

There was one exception, a voyageur named Marcel LaFontaine. For reasons he kept to himself and a version he spun to his crew, he decided to go south. Common knowledge said that there wasn't anything of value there, but he had heard about a mysterious silver mine nearly two week's paddle to the southwest.

His information was at best sketchy, coming from an old coureur de bois he met in a Montreal tavern who had too much brandy. Marcel heard the wonderful stories of the riches the Spanish pulled out of the wilderness far to the south. Why not here, too? Yes, why couldn't gold and silver be in the north woods? His compatriots were satisfied with the beaver, but Marcel hungered after more. Over time and much brandy, he managed to convince five other men to go together with him. They all shared dreams of wealth beyond the dirty beaver.

The Jesuit priest accompanying them could be a problem.

The stupid fool thought they were still going to Grand Portage on Lake Superior! All he did was pray and complain. Never picked up a paddle, helped to make camp or even gather firewood. Every time they stopped he was doing a Mass to some saint or another. He was dead weight, pure and simple. Marcel didn't know what the church was coming to, sending such fools into the forests. When they found the mine, the priest would have to be satisfied with his share or he would disappear on the return trip. God surely wouldn't punish them for ridding the world of a fool like this good-for-nothing priest.

Rather than risk going across the open waters of Georgian Bay and Lake Huron in their canoe, Marcel and company had to paddle up the coast and through a maze of small islands (now called the North Channel) past the broad entrance to the St. Marys River and on toward the post at Michilimackinac. Short of the island, he turned south, skirting Bois Blanc Island before reaching the mainland shore. They were far off the approved voyageur route now and it was best that they were not seen by anyone lest questions be asked. The French regulated the fur trade tightly and Marcel's license only allowed him to go to Grand Portage.

Ten days after leaving the French River, they came to a beach near an area of reddish clay banks running nearly up to the water. They suddenly thought they heard noise from the bush, as loud as the crashing of a tick-crazed moose. The priest plucked at his rosary nervously.

There was a large rock on the shore, nearly as tall as a man and flat on top. It appeared to be covered in old blood. A sacrificial site? For a brief instant, they thought they saw something writhing across the stone. Suddenly there was a woman's scream and something large, very large indeed, splashed into the water. Was it coming toward them?

The priest, who had watched without comment, collapsed into a faint. The Frenchmen paddled harder, trying to put as much distance as possible between them and whatever was now in the water with them. But the water remained calm behind them and soon they settled into a less harried pace. None spoke of what they'd heard and seen.

A day later Marcel and his men arrived at the island. It was just as the old coureur de bois said, three days' paddle from Michilimackinac and the first one encountered. The old man had muttered something about snakes, so Marcel reminded his men to be careful.

They landed at the small cove on the west side of the island. With the mainland just a couple of miles to the west and the bulk of the island blocking east winds and seas, it was a protected spot. The shore was all rocky, but the interior was deeply forested with some elevation. It looked like a pleasing place.

By now the Jesuit priest had figured out they weren't going to Grand Portage and questioned Marcel about why they were at this unknown place. Marcel told him he was doing God's work and to keep quiet. In time it would all be clear.

As they were making camp, a young Indian woman walked out of the forest. She was dressed in deerskin, highly decorated with bright shells and shiny white metal. Her black hair hung in two long braids, one on each side of her face. But it was her eyes the men focused on. Instead of round, they were more elliptical, with the dark pupils reflecting the unusual shape.

Smiling, she welcomed them to "Serpent Island" in a language that Marcel somehow understood, though he could not place it.

She said her name was Coatilique and she lived alone on the island with her children. There was no one else, just she and her children. When Marcel asked why, she replied that it was what her people wanted. Every moon they came by with food, and she was happy to remain apart.

Marcel explained that they were seeking the white and shiny metal like that adorning her dress. She replied that it could be found on the island. In the morning she would show them where. Abruptly she turned and left, melting into the dark forest.

That night the Frenchmen enjoyed their pipes and brandy as they lounged around the campfire, dreaming of riches sure to come. With silver they could retire to a life of ease, with wives to keep them warm at night and brandy to forget the cares of the world. Only the priest was in a foul mood. He complained about not going to Grand Portage as promised and this foolish treasure hunt was certain to fail. God would punish them for not doing their duty.

The next morning broke clear and beautiful. A little after breakfast, the woman again came out of the forest and greeted the Frenchmen. Marcel inquired after her children, and she replied that they were all well.

Quickly turning, she headed for the forest. Marcel and his men hurried to keep up, the priest complaining about not finishing his morning Mass. For half an hour, Coatilique led the men through the thick forest, along an old and little-used trail eventually reaching a fork. Turning to the men, she warned that they must never go down the left path but must always keep to the right. After repeating the warning, she again strode quickly down the trail.

Marcel noticed her walk as almost like a sailor's, rolling a bit left and right. After a few more minutes, she stopped in front of a low rock cliff. A small cave was visible at the base. Looking squarely at the men, she said that the white metal was in the cave.

Making a hasty torch from a pine knot and stick, and striking it into a fire with flint and stone, Marcel slithered through the small entrance. Inside, the sides glistened with silver! Hunks of it hung from the rock walls. The other men followed, even the priest. All were astounded with the amount of silver and the relative ease of mining it. It was there for the taking. Perhaps realizing that the Church's share would be immense, even the priest relented from his constant complaining. Privately he began to scheme ways he could claim credit for the discovery.

For the next week the men worked to extract the silver. Marcel had managed to smuggle picks and shovels inside his trade bundles instead of the normal blankets, knives and brandy. All sweated, dug and carried equally, except the priest who as usual did nothing worthwhile. Several times a day Coatilique came by to check the progress.

On the third night she came to the camp at stood quietly at the edge of the forest. Only Marcel noticed her and walked over to ask if she wanted anything. She said nothing, but took him by the hand, leading him to a small glade covered with soft grass. They made quiet love. Her soft body seemed to wrap around him, drawing him within her. When he awoke in the morning she was gone. Was it all a dream?

One day the priest, who still was no help, grew bored and decided to go down the left fork, the one forbidden by Coatilique. After several hundred yards he came to an open area. Waking to the center, he found a pit about 10 feet across and 10 feet deep. At the bottom was a writhing, twisting mass of the largest snakes he had ever seen. They were huge, maybe 10 feet or more in length and hissed evilly at him. Several rose high on their tails and swayed rhythmically. He imagined their beady little eyes staring into his very soul. Their heads were strange, too. Rather than the square and angular shape characteristic of snakes, these were more round as were the eyes. There was even the suggestion of nose and ears.

Repelled by the discovery, he fled to the mine and told the other men of his horrible discovery. He told them that the serpents were evil and had to be destroyed. Was it not a horrid serpent that tempted Adam and Eve in the garden? Snakes of any kind were the spawn of the devil and it was the duty of every Christian to kill them. Marcel was gone to the camp. The priest's powerful personality overwhelmed the men's good sense.

The men agreed to kill the nest of deadly vipers. Taking a small keg of gunpowder to the pit, they fused it and pushed the makeshift bomb into the den. The resulting explosion echoed through the forest, followed by the most unholy scream any of the men ever heard. It was more wail than anything else and lasted for several minutes before dying off to a whimper and finally ominous silence. All of the sounds of forest ceased. No birds chirped or squirrels scampered. Even the wind stopped blowing. The silence was deafening.

When Marcel returned, he was angry that they had acted without him. He was leader and it was his responsibility. Killing a den of snakes that didn't threaten them was foolish. All it did was waste good gunpowder needed for mining and muskets.

Marcel sensed that it was time to leave the island. That night they loaded the canoe for the trip back to Montreal. To make room for the silver, Marcel ordered all the picks and shovels be left behind, carefully hidden in the mine. A large pile of silver was left, too. They had mined far more than they could carry. Perhaps they would return for silver later. He also swore each man to secrecy, using the priest's Bible. The priest, of course, refused to be sworn, claiming that as a man of God he was already sworn. In reality, he was plotting how to use the mine to buy his own rise up the Jesuit hierarchy. Was a bishop's miter out of the question? Marcel, too, plotted, thinking of ways the priest would not survive the return journey.

That night the coureurs de bois enjoyed a last smoke and brandy, jovial over the success of their strange foray. The priest stayed away, choosing his own company over theirs, sleeping a hundred yards distant. By the dying embers of the fire, the men fell into their dreams.

When Marcel awoke in the morning he found that the camp was a scene of bedlam. His companions lay sprawled in grotesque shapes, their faces twisted in horrible agony. Each neck was punctured by two huge fang marks, fully two inches apart. If this was the work of a snake, it was huge!

As Marcel went frantically from man to man looking for some sign of life, he heard the voice of Coatilique.

"Murderers all! You killed my children!"

Marcel whipped around and there was the woman, her eyes blazing as she said, "I told you to stay away from that trail. I gave you all the white metal you wanted and you repaid me by murdering my children."

The priest, unharmed by the death in the night, since he slept apart, ran up to the woman, pronouncing, "Evil creature! They were serpents, spawn of the devil and the forever enemy of man. Killing them was God's work I say, God's work," and he held his small gold crucifix toward the woman as mystical protection.

She recoiled and a strange shimmering of colors encompassed her. Within a smattering of moments her legs morphed into a tail and head into that of a timber rattler. It seemed only a heartbeat before she was a serpent, and she struck the priest with lightning speed, grasping him in her powerful tail as her eyes stared deep into his misbegotten soul. He could neither move nor speak, not to beg forgiveness or curse the evil ready to destroy him. Slowly her long sharp fangs emerged from her mouth. Once fully extended, she struck with lightning speed, sinking them deep into his neck. The priest screamed the shriek of the damned then went limp. When she released his body, it slipped silently to the ground.

The snake monster turned slowly to Marcel, who was too mesmerized to move. After a long moment the snake morphed back into the woman. Coatilique carefully wiped a drop of blood from her lips with the back of her hand and looked hard at Marcel with her piecing eyes.

"You were kind to me," she said. "You gave me the gift of life yet to be. It was the sorcerer who was evil. You may go in peace and take whatever you can carry, but never tell anyone of this place or return. Leave the bones of your comrades to bleach in the sun … an offering to wild beasts. It is all they deserve."

She turned and melted back into the forest.

Marcel left most of the silver on the beach. He could barely launch the canoe and paddle it alone. All he had for his adventure was a small pile of silver in a deerskin pouch, but that small pile was still a fortune.

He would have to spin a tail of an Indian attack and perhaps capsizing in the river to explain the loss of his men and the priest, but such things did happen and it would be believed. After several weeks, he reached the French River. In a moment of inattention disaster struck. The canoe hit a rock and went over, spilling the heavy silver to the bottom of the river where it was lost forever. When Marcel finally arrived in Montreal, his tale of disaster and treachery was accepted. After all it was almost true.

Marcel returned to the life of a coureur de bois. It was the only life he knew. Returning to Serpent Island was not possible, not with a protector like the snake goddess there. When he grew too old to make the long portages and swing the paddle, he told great tales in the taverns of Montreal. He had no fear of letting the secret out. Who would believe him anyway?

CHAPTER 7

Shipboard Spirits

There are many strange stories of shipwreck and survival on the Great Lakes. Perhaps none is more bizarre than that of Dennis Hale of the bulker *Daniel J. Morrell*.

"I told you not to eat the ice off the peacoat. If you do, it will lower your body temperature and you will die!" Hale looked up at the strange figure of a man floating in air above him and silently obeyed. Then Hale collapsed back on the raft.

The last major shipwreck before the *Edmund Fitzgerald* in November 1975 was the 580-foot steamer *Daniel J. Morrell*, on Lake Huron on November 28, 1966. The Bay City Shipbuilding Company built the *Morrell* in West Bay City, Michigan, in 1906. She was very typical of the many bulk carriers in service on the lakes at that time. During the time of her construction it was a common joke that they "built 'em by the mile and cut 'em off at whatever length they needed."

The big steamer left Mullin's Fuel Dock in Windsor, Ontario, on the Detroit River at 7:30 a.m., November 28, 1966. When she passed under the Blue Water Bridge between Port Huron, Michigan and Sarnia, Ontario, Lake Huron was being whipped by a rising storm. As the *Morrell* churned her way north, it was hard going and many larger boats had gone to shelter, but the *Morrell* kept plugging her way north, shouldering aside the big waves as she had for more than five decades.

Watchman Dennis Hale, a young sailor from Ashtabula, Ohio, crawled into his bunk in the forward end and read a book for a while. He could hear the waves pounding hard into the steel hull, but it was a sound he had heard many times before. About 10 p.m., he turned off his reading light, rolled over and dropped off to sleep. He had no premonition of events to come.

Hale was suddenly wakened by a loud bang! He tried to turn his light on, but there was no power. Searching in the dark he found his life jacket, pulled it on and ran topside.

On the spar deck he and other crewmen tried to make sense out of what they were seeing. Looking to the stern, he saw the *Morrell* had hogged, with the middle of the ship up and the bow and stern down. All lights were off on the bow, making it terribly dark. The stern, by contrast, was still blazing with light. Realizing that he was standing only in his shorts, Hale took a chance and ran back to his cabin. Fumbling again in the dark, he was able to find his heavy wool pea jacket, but his trousers eluded him. Returning to the deck, he joined a group of men standing around the life raft stored between the No. 2 and No. 3 hatches. The wind blew hard and cold, chilling them all to the bone.

Looking back toward the stern, they watched the great ship slowly break in two, the steel deck tearing apart with a terrific screeching sound. Great showers of sparks and clouds of steam from broken electric lines and steam pipes added to the surrealistic effect. Finally the stern, still under power and with lights blazing, tore free of the dead forward end. The men looked on in amazement and horror as the stern steamed past, plowing its way out into the wild storm.

The next thing Hale remembered, he was struggling in the water. He and three other men finally ended up on the small raft, which was nothing more than two steel pontoons with a rough wood grating on top. It would keep them above the water, but provided no shelter from wind or wave. It was nothing more than a platform for dying.

All the survivors on the raft were in shock. None was thinking too clearly. They broke open the box of flares and fired several off, hoping to attract another vessel. No one saw them. They were utterly alone in the black storm-blown night.

The waves grew in violence and began to break over the raft. To conserve heat and try to stay out of the cutting wind as much as possible, all of the men lay down on the wood grating. By chance, Hale was in the middle, protected by other men's bodies. None of the men were properly dressed for the cold and wet. Hale was only in his shorts and pea jacket. One man wore only his pajamas, another blue jeans and a sweatshirt. The last man was fully clothed with a short jacket. All wore life jackets.

They were constantly drenched by the cresting waves and viciously attacked by the icy wind and cutting spray. Rescue had to come quickly or not at all. As the long night wore on, Hale alternately prayed and cursed. The men talked among themselves, but as the cold continued to sap their energy, conversation grew less and less.

By dawn the storm had lessened, but two of the men were already dead. Later in the afternoon, the third man died. Hale and his three dead shipmates continued to ride the small raft. He kept weakening, the terrible cold inexorably draining away his strength.

All through the next night Hale lay on the raft as it rode the falling seas westward, eventually washing up on some rocks several hundred feet off the Michigan shore, east of Pointe aux Barques. He had drifted roughly 19 miles from the position the steamer sank. Although he could see the lights of a nearby farmhouse, he was nearly powerless to act. Hale was too weak to walk or even crawl to it, but maybe he could attract attention somehow. Eagerly, with frozen and fumbling hands, he fitted a flare into the gun, pointed it skyward and pulled the trigger. The gun had broken into two pieces after the first time the men used it, so Hale had to hold the parts together to get it to work. The lonely flare arced high into the black sky and exploded into a brilliant show of colored light. There was no reaction from the farmhouse. No one saw it. Working as quickly as he could, he fired another one. No one saw it, either. He yelled and screamed, but no one heard him. Too stiff to move, he could only lay helplessly on the raft and watch the house. Eventually the lights inside winked out. The farmer and his family had gone to bed. The night was terribly cold. The water wasn't washing over the raft anymore, but the awful piercing cold struck deep into his bones. That night he slept in fitful snatches.

The next morning, November 30, the farmhouse lights blinked on. He yelled again. There was no response. So near but yet so far. If only someone would look out on the lake. They had to see him. They never did!

It wasn't until 12:15 p.m. on the 30th that the Coast Guard was notified that the *Morrell* was overdue. The steamer broke so quickly, there wasn't time for a distress call, thus delaying the Coast Guard search-and-rescue effort. The first break of the hull also severed the power lines from the engine room generator to the pilothouse, killing the radios. There was no battery-powered backup. During the subsequent official investigation, the Coast Guard estimated that the vessel sank in a mere eight minutes.

During the afternoon, overcome with thirst, Hale started to pick at the ice on his peacoat and put it in his mouth. Then the mysterious specter appeared. In Hale's words, "Hovering above the raft was a man dressed in white. His skin was almost translucent, with a bluish tinge. He had moderately long wavy, white hair and a neatly trimmed mustache. His eyebrows were bushy and his eyes deep-set. I remember his eyes seemed to burn with an incredible intensity." The figure Hale always referred to as Doc, told him, "Stop eating the ice off your peacoat," then disappeared into nothing.

After his conversation with the strange visitor, Hale felt himself floating above the raft, and then spinning wildly into a bizarre white cloud. He arrived at a large green field when he met his mother and was questioned by a man in white. When he asked about his friends on the *Morrell*, he was sent over a hill where he found the bow of the vessel and his shipmates. As the men watched, the stern arrived and mated with the bow, becoming one ship again. He and his forward end fellows went back to visit their friends on the stern. When the two groups got together, they greeted each other in joyous reunion. Then everyone grew quiet. The men looked at Hale with big sad eyes. One turned to him and said, "It's not your time yet. You have to go back."

Hale was then immersed again in the strange spinning cloud and returned to the raft. Still thirsty, he began to again eat the ice off his peacoat. The mysterious specter again appeared and shook his bony white finger at Hale, telling him, "I told you not to eat the ice off the peacoat. If you do, you will lower your body temperature and die." Hale stopped eating the ice and fell back on the raft. Drifting in and out of consciousness, he waited for either rescue or death. Suddenly a Coast Guard helicopter was hovering overhead, then landed next to him. After hustling him aboard, the flight crew rushed him to the Harbor Beach, Michigan, hospital. It was touch and go for Hale for a while. His core body temperature was down to 94 degrees. "Doc" was right. Eating ice would indeed have killed him. A priest also gave him the last rites. He was that close to death.

Hale kept the "Doc" part of his story to himself, afraid of being ridiculed. He didn't speak about his experiences for 20 years.

When the *Morrell* sank, 28 of 29 men aboard lost their lives. The steamer was the first major vessel to founder in Lake Huron in 42 years. Ironically, she sank nearly in the same position as the steamer *Clifton*, lost in 1924.[1]

Aviation writer Ernest K. Gann coined the phrase "fate is the hunter," and in the case of Dennis Hale, it surely was. That night Hale was not in fate's sights. Consider:

Of all the ships on the lakes that night, why was it the *Morrell* that snapped in two?

Why did Hale make it back from his quarters with his peacoat without which he surely would have died? Why did he think to go get it at all?

Why did Hale make it onto the life raft when others nearby did not?

Why did he end up in the middle of the raft and comparatively protected from the wind?

Why did he not perish from the cold when his companions did?

Why did the strange specter visit Hale, and not once but twice? Without his intervention, he surely would have died from eating the ice. Who was "Doc?" Was he a reincarnation of the Ancient Mariner of saltwater lore or the spirit of one of the old Pointe aux Barques lifesaving crew?

Why was Hale the only survivor of 29 men?

Perhaps the only answer is that there must be a muster book up yonder and if your name is not in it, you will not be called. Fate is indeed the hunter.

"I alone survived the wreck of the brig *H.G. Stamback*. The loss was attributed in the papers to the tremendous storm, of course, not what I am going to tell you, but take it from someone who was there. This is the true story of the wreck.

"Before I relate this narrative, I must point out that I am a well educated man, private schools in New England and enough time in one of the old colleges to allow me to successfully read for the law. I was by any standard a gentlemen. My path in life was set: Practice law in my father's firm, a good marriage, a seat or two on a good corporate board, in the end a very comfortable and pleasant life. For inexplicable reasons, though, my health began to fail and my physician suggested a trip to the lakes to regain it. His advise worked, perhaps too well. I got on so well here, I decided to stay. Eventually I meet up with Captain John and took a couple of trips with him on his brig. We got on well enough together that after a while he made me his mate, the position I held when the vessel was lost.

"It was the fall of 1857, and we were at Buffalo. Shipping was down and it looked like the end of the season when the captain was chartered for a trip to Chicago by a woman anxious to get there before winter and not desiring to make the tedious overland journey. As a bonus, the captain also arranged for a partial cargo of barreled whiskey. That's a commodity always in demand and, as it was on his account, should fetch a good profit!

"The woman arrived at the dock well after dark in a closed carriage. A considerable amount of baggage accompanied her, including several large trunks and an unusual box about 5 feet long, 2 feet deep and 2 feet wide. Since she wanted this in her cabin, a couple of the boys wrestled it in for her. The woman was very finely dressed and a great beauty in a dark and mysterious fashion. I'd guess her about 30 or so, with a very pale, almost white complexion. Her eyes were very dark, nearly black, and most engaging, nearly hypnotic. From her overall appearance, however, I guessed her to have been recently ill. The lake trip would be far easier than overland for a woman as delicate as she. The captain immediately escorted her to her cabin. I noticed that she leaned heavily on his arm as he led her below. He never mentioned to me how he had arranged the charter. Within the hour we were under the tow of one of the numerous little harbor tugs that brought us to the harbor mouth and soon after under easy sail bound west. We were sailing with a short crew, our regular men having left for their homes or other employment. Other than the captain and myself, there was the cook, an old fellow named Hobbs, I think, a ship's boy and five men forward. As was my job, I obtained the forecastle men from our usual saloon, the bartender being very adept at providing our needs. The captain hired on the cook, who had sailed with him before. I found the boy hanging around the saloon, too, and hired him thinking that he could be of use helping the passenger. Because of the lateness of the season, a bonus was promised on arrival in Chicago.

"The first night out everything went well, a good northeast breeze kept us bowling along and I saw nothing of the woman. The breeze was slanting northeast the next day resulting in a sharp chop, so it didn't surprise me not to see her all day. The captain and I assumed that she was suffering from the seasickness and decided to stay in her cabin. The cook said he rapped at the door offering some tea and biscuits, but received no answer. Later in the day I realized I had not seen the boy about the ship. On my inquiry, neither had the captain, cook or crew. He had just disappeared. Searching the ship failed to find him, so we had to assume he had somehow fallen overboard during the night.

"Just after dark she came on deck, looking as beautiful as I remembered from my brief glimpse the previous night. Although still somewhat pale, she did appear stronger. She confessed it was as we had surmised, that a touch of the 'mal de mer' kept her confined. At this point the cook came up and inquired if she would like a little late supper, he could put something together for her. She replied that her stomach still was too delicate for food, and then walked to the lee rail and just stood there gazing out at the black lake. Her accent was unusual. I had traveled in Europe with my father as a youngster but still could not place it. After a while, I went over to her and tried to make a little polite conversation, but she rebuffed me, saying she would rather be alone. Wounded, I retreated to my post at the weather rail for while, then down to my cabin after leaving orders with the wheelsman to call me if the weather changed or anything looked dangerous.

"About an hour later the violent motion of the ship awakened me. She had nearly broached! Rushing to the deck just seconds ahead of the captain, I saw the wheelsman standing unsteady at the wheel. Cursing him loudly for his inattention I grabbed the wheel and horsed the ship back around. Had the weather been foul, his error could have been disastrous. The man appeared almost drunk, staggering on his feet and eventually collapsing in a heap on the deck. Two of the boys from forward, also awakened by the motion, carried him to his bunk. Another assumed his trick at the wheel. The woman was nowhere around, evidently having gone to her cabin before the excitement.

"Dawn the next day found us off Erie. A hard day's sail with the northeasterly breeze brought the ship to Colchester Reef by nightfall. It was a good run for the old girl. The woman continued to stay in her cabin. That night the captain stayed on deck given the dangerous area we were in as he worked her up toward the Detroit River. The old man told me the next morning that the woman came up around midnight, said a brief hello to him and then walked forward. The seas were calm enough, so he thought a stroll would be safe. Once she passed the foremast she was too deep in the gloom to be seen. About 10 minutes later she walked back to the stern, passing him without comment and went directly down to her cabin.

"As dawn broke the following morning, the captain saw a man collapsed on the foredeck. Rushing forward, the old man immediately saw how pale his skin was and the lethargic look in his eyes. He was taken to his bunk and given a dose of salts from the captain's medicine box. We both put it down to a case of the DTs, considering the quality of the crew. The rest of the day was spent going up the Detroit River, a job much speeded by a powerful tug. Around nightfall, we dropped the tow, put up our rags and continued out onto Lake Huron. Again the wind was favorable and easy. The woman came up a couple hours afterward and gave no explanation for her absence during the day. She looked much better than the previous night. There was more color on her cheeks and her lips were pleasantly red. The lake air must agree with her. She gave me a casual and cold good evening and took her lonely place at the rail.

"The next morning the cook was too ill to make breakfast. When the captain looked him over, it was plain he was not shamming. His skin was ghastly white and eyes dull, as if he was in a trance. These were the same symptoms as the two sick crewmen. Captain John told him to lie back in his bunk and take it easy, although I am not certain the man heard a word he said. The rest of the day was uneventful. The winds continued fair and by nightfall we were abeam Thunder Bay Island. At dusk the captain went below for what he said was a short nap and never came back topside. When he didn't respond to stomping the deck over his cabin, our signal to him that his time was up, I went down to check on him. He seemed to have taken sick with whatever malady struck the cook and sailor down. He was dreadfully white and eyes absent all spark. My shaking could not fully waken him. I went back on deck and sent one of the men down to sit with him and to look in on the cook, too.

"Perhaps an hour later, the woman came up for her nightly air. If she was beautiful before, tonight she was positively ravishing. Her skin was flushed pink and full lips literally glowed red. Her eyes were more sparkling then previously, too. By the pale light of the full moon, she was exquisite. She gave me her cursory good evening and retreated to the lee rail. What a shame her personality didn't match her beauty.

"I stayed on deck until 3 a.m., and then retreated to my bunk, instructing the watch to call me at dawn. It was a quiet night. When day broke, we were abeam Bois Blanc Island. Sometime during the night, the cook had died. The crewman, who had been alternating between the captain and the cook, had fallen asleep. When he awoke a little past daybreak and belatedly checked the cook, he found him lifeless. He immediately summoned me to the cook's little sleeping corner in the galley. There was no doubt that he was stone cold dead. Whatever was striking down the crew was indeed fatal. Most odd was the evident loss of blood. The skin was almost white. Curious, I stuck my knife blade into his arm and there was no bleeding, only the barest hint of redness. This was very strange. I had never heard of any illness that would so destroy the blood. If this were salt water, we would have immediately buried him at sea. On the lakes, such things are not done. We wrapped him tightly in his blanket and carried him to the hold. We would be at Chicago in a couple of days and he would keep until then.

"The winds turned westerly and it took most of the day to get to the Straits. By the time we came abeam of Old Mission Light, it was well after nightfall. Several hours later the woman came up on deck, as was by now her habit. By the light of the pale moon, she was as lovely as ever. Short-handed as we were with the strange sickness, I told the man at the wheel to get some sleep. I would take his place for a few hours. The woman climbed down the stairs to the deck and started to walk forward. The moon was sliding in and out of the clouds. When it was out I could see the bow. When the clouds obscured it, I had trouble seeing as far as the mainmast. I noticed though, that she appeared to glide rather than walk. Captured by her face, I had never noticed this before. But with her long, flowing white gown I was certain that this was just an illusion. I watched her carefully as she moved toward the bow, and then she disappeared from view in the gloom. Ten or so minutes later, she recrossed the deck and descended the stairs to her cabin. Again, she seemed to glide rather than walk, her motion was so graceful.

"The next morning another man was found unconscious on the foredeck. Like the others, his skin was pale and he could not be roused. He, too, was carried to his bunk. The two remaining crewman and I would have a tough time bringing her to Chicago, but we resolved to continue. If the weather held, and the confounded sickness would stay away, we could do it.

"Then the storm struck! I had seen no warning of it, or any of the traditional weather signs of its approach. In an instant it was on us!

"The first blast blew out the foretopsail. Since we were too short-handed to bring it in, that was fine with me. The second burst nearly knocked us over before the mainsail let go, followed by the foresail. Only the forestaysail remained and that was only for a few minutes before it, too, went flying off into the dark. We were now under bare poles. The wind increased by the minute, each gust more powerful than the last. I put both of the remaining healthy hands on the wheel, trying to keep her steady in the overwhelming wind.

"When everything seemed to be under control, at least for the moment, I went below to see how the captain and woman passenger were faring. I knocked hard on her door but got no response. Even considering the storm, she should have heard me. I opened the door, an act I, as a gentlemen, never would have done except for this emergency. She wasn't there. The box the crew had manhandled into the cabin was lying open on the floor. It was empty except for a thin layer of dirt. This was most strange, but considering the terrible danger we were in, of no immediate concern. Out of the corner of my eye, I saw a leg projecting from behind the box. It was the boy and he was very dead. Like the others, he was nearly white. He had not fallen overboard after all. But what was he doing in the woman's room? Next I went to the captain's cabin. When I opened the door, there she was, on her knees bent over him, her slender back toward me. She must have heard the door, but with all the screaming of the wind and creaking of the ship, I'll never know how. She quickly looked up at me. I'll never forget the terrible scene before me. Blood was dripping from her lips and her wild, glowing eyes burned with an unholy intensity. Two short white fangs extended down from her mouth. I turned and started to flee from that horrible sight.

"At that very moment the ship lurched violently, knocking the woman to the deck and throwing me hard against a bulwark. Being a sailor I was more used to such extreme motion, I quickly recovered and ran up the companionway to the quarter deck.

"The two men I had left at the wheel were gone and the wheel itself smashed. Apparently a massive wave had crashed aboard and swept them away. We were rolling wildly, caught in the very jaws of the storm. Thunder rolled overhead and sharp flashes of lightning lit the night sky. Our poles were still up but the strain on them was immense. They could not long last. The ship was doomed as were all of us in her.

"Then the woman struck me from behind with tremendous force, sending me tumbling down the deck and crashing into the mainmast fife rail. Looking up I saw her in all her evil. What kind of creature she was, what beast in human form, I do not know. In the cutting wind she was the pure embodiment of the devil. Her white gown, torn and streaked black with the captain's blood, blew stiffly out behind her, as did her long black hair. Her eyes flashed red with a blood lust unsatisfied. All this said, there was an evil beauty to her undeniable in its power. As she advanced to me over the heaving deck, I was frozen to the rail and could not run, her

glaring eyes riveting me to my place. I was caught just as surely as any animal in a leg trap. In that instance I finally realized that she was the cause of the strange sickness and death among the crew. Perhaps the storm was the consequence of the heavens lashing out against her evil!

"When she reached me, her powerful hands grabbed my shoulders and pulled me easily to my feet. Her strength was incredible! She gave a short growl, baring her sharp fangs, and lifted her head back, preparing to plunge them deep into my neck. Again, I could not move, held as motionless as a statue, as much by fear as by her hold.

"The ship suddenly pitched wildly, breaking her grip and forcing her to step backwards. I held fast to the fife rail. A tremendous clap of thunder boomed overhead and a bolt of lightning shot to the main topmast, shattering it into several pieces. One of them, 5 or 6 feet long, fell directly to the deck, impaling the woman through her chest just as Ahab struck the whale.

"I watched dumbly as her blood gushed black on the deck, only to be washed immediately away by the rain and wave wash. Mesmerized by the sight, I must have held to the rail for several minutes, watching as her lifeless body drifted to and fro across the deck.

"Then the ship went over, rolling bottom up, and I was thrown into the lake. Fighting my way back to the surface, I grabbed a floating hatch grate and hung on to it. The storm ended very soon after. After six or so hours, I came ashore at one of the Manitous.

"I found a farmhouse where I was given food and sheltered for several days, then hitched a ride on a fish boat to the mainland. I never told the full story of what really happened, only that a violent squall had sunk the ship and I was the only survivor. Who would believe the true story anyway? Considering the time of the year, no one questioned me closely. Old captain John owned the ship and carried no insurance, so there were no underwriters to satisfy with an endless stream of details. He was a bachelor, too, and had no family I knew of. The crew was a scratch one, mostly just drifters. In short, no one had any personal interest in what happened to the ship. The woman, or whatever she was, was dead, killed by the topmast, so she was of no consequence. Later I heard that the hull drifted on a reef off North Manitou Island, but soon slipped off into deep water. When I arrived at Buffalo, I gathered my meager gear from my room at the boarding house and went back east. After all, I had recovered my health and, considering the circumstances, had no reason to remain. I spent the last 30-odd years at the law and my end is coming near. Regardless of what anyone may think, I wanted the full story of the loss of the *Stamback* to be a matter of record, official or not. By this date, more than 40 years later, whatever anyone thinks of my senses or me is immaterial."[2]

CHAPTER 8

Beyond Understanding

Sometimes captains had the ability to look into the future, to "feel" what was going to happen, but caught in the need to keep a schedule they had to sail anyway and trust they were wrong.

When the propeller *Galena* finished loading her cargo of lumber at Alpena, her captain thought about holding in port for a while. It fact he had a very strong feeling he should delay in Alpena. He felt it in his bones! A strong southwest gale was blowing and at best would make his run to Chicago miserable. At worst, it could sink him and that's what concerned the captain. While the lumber cargo was important, there were also 20 people aboard, five of them passengers. Captains are paid to make decisions and he made his.

Before leaving Alpena at 11 p.m. he told the mate that his biggest concern was getting around North Point and the offshore reefs. Once the *Galena* cleared them, the waves would be on her stern and the going would be comparatively easy. When the captain figured he had gone far enough plus a little more for safety's sake, he ordered the wheelsman to turn to port and steady up on a course for Mackinac Island. The gale was a real "gagger" and visibility nil. The night was black as sin and everything was being done by compass and time. Keep a given course for a given time and the ship should be at a given location. It was almost, but not quite, foolproof. This was one of those times when it didn't work and the captain should have listened to his internal premonition of trouble. Within minutes of the turn she drove hard up on the outer reef at North Point, about a mile and a half offshore. Apparently the southeasterly wind pushed her farther west than the captain realized.

The captain tried to back off, but the *Galena* was on too far. She wasn't going anywhere, which was probably a good thing. A quick check showed a hole in her bow big enough to sink her had she managed to back off into deep water. Meanwhile, the southeast seas smashed into the stranded beast with powerful blows, sending water high over her decks. To ease the working of the hull, the captain scuttled her so she rested solidly on the rocky bottom instead of rocking back and forth with the wave action. Soon the boiler flooded out and the ship was without heat. The upper deck also showed signs of coming loose, the victim of the battering waves.

The steamer *Wenona* passed the *Galena* the following morning, but it was too rough for her to stop and investigate. When she reached Alpena, the *Wenona* captain reported that the *Galena* was on the reef and she appeared to be breaking up. In mid-afternoon the bark *Erastus Corning* sighted the beleaguered *Galena*. Her captain was more of a seaman, coming up to anchor two miles away and sending his yawl to investigate. It took an hour of hard rowing, but when they reached the battered propeller the sailors discovered everyone was alive and well, although certainly very cold. The bark's men offered to take some of the survivors back to the *Corning*, but the offer was refused. The captain of the *Galena* thought the gale would die down at sunset and he still had visions of saving his ship. When it didn't, he reconsidered his options and decided to take his yawl to shore with the five passengers and five crew. The remainder stayed aboard. Managing to reach the rocky beach safely, the captain led the wet and bedraggled survivors back to Alpena, several miles distant. The men left aboard were safely removed the following day, but the propeller was a total loss. The captain should have listened to his own premonition.[1]

Just south of Arch Rock on Mackinac Island there is a narrow trail running from the beach up the bluff to the Manitou Trail. In years past it was known as Wazhuska Trail in recognition of a powerful Indian medicine man.

When Henry R. Schoolcraft was Indian Agent on the island in the 1830s, he witnessed some of Wazhuska's potent medicine. Reputedly he was able to communicate with the spirits much as European spirit mediums claim to be able to contact "the other side."

On one occasion, Schoolcraft watched as Wazhuska was tied up with rope and wrapped tightly in a small canoe sail then placed in a rude pyramidal lodge. The structure was made of poles and skins and entirely closed up. The ends of the poles were dug deep into the ground preventing movement. After a moment, Wazhuska began to chant and the lodge swayed to his rhythm. A rustling sound came from the top of the lodge indicating the presence of the called-for spirit. Whoever the spirit was, it was invoked, then asked questions that were answered in a husky voice. The whole scene is eerily similar to the animations of parlor mediums in the United States and elsewhere, then and now. Schoolcraft was never convinced that Wazhuska wasn't using trickery, but neither could he prove he was.

Wazhuska claimed that he was born near the head of Lake Michigan in about 1753. Orphaned, he lived with an uncle under the care of his grandmother. He said that his spiritual powers came about when he was undergoing a long and severe fast as a young man.

He first used his power when on a war party in the Chicago area. His group was running out of food and fearful of ambush. When everything looked bleakest, he used his spiritual powers to find game and the position of their enemy.

He reputedly used his power again at Fort Mackinac in 1815. The commander of the fort was concerned when the boat from Detroit hadn't arrived with needed rations and winter supplies. He turned to Wazhuska to find out what happened to it. Using his spiritual power he told the commander that the boat was just below the mouth of the St. Clair River and when it would reach Mackinac. It arrived right on time.[2]

The November 22, 1879, loss of the 135-foot, 465-ton Canadian sidewheeler *Waubuno* is a classic example of dream intervention. Even the name, an Algonquian Indian word for "sorcerer" (or black magic, depending on the translation), lends itself to thinking about "things beyond." Ominously, it was also her second name since her launch in 1865, at Thorold, Ontario, on Lake Huron's Georgian Bay, as the *Wawatam*. The earlier name doubtless honored Chief Wawatam, an Ojibway leader who befriended Alexander Henry when he was a prisoner. Old sailors believed changing a name always affected a ship's luck.

The *Waubuno* was delayed in Collingwood on November 29 en route for Parry Sound, waiting out the worst of a strong northwest gale. Rather than stay aboard the cramped steamer, many passengers elected to sleep in a more comfortable local hotel. Two of the passengers were a Dr. W.H. Doupe and his young bride,

Eliza, both from Mitchell, Ontario. The trip on the *Waubuno* was to be part of their short honeymoon. They were heading for the small town of McKellar, near Parry Sound where Dr. Doupe would open his practice. That night Eliza had a terrifying nightmare. The following morning she described a "great weight pressing them (passengers) down." In her dream, she saw the crew and passengers being swallowed by the icy dark lake.

When the storm eventually lessened, and the captain blew his whistle at 4 a.m. to call the passengers back to the boat, she implored her husband for them not to board the steamer but to stay safe ashore. They could take another steamer. What difference did a day or two delay make? But her husband was adamant. As a man of science, he couldn't be swayed by a silly woman's dreams! Other passengers heard her protests and ominous explanation of the eerie dream. Some took heed and stayed behind. Others ignored the ranting of a "hysterical" woman and boarded the ship. The *Waubuno* steamed out of Collingwood and into Georgian Bay legend.

What actually happened will never be known, but the steamer perished in the cold and gloomy waters with all 24 souls aboard. The last man to see her in this world reportedly was the Christian Island lightkeeper as she passed two miles offshore. He noted that she appeared to be doing fine. Christian Island is about a third of the distance to Parry Sound. Once she left port, the storm increased in ferocity and the small steamer must have struggled mightily. Some hours later, lumberjacks near Moon River heard what they thought was the *Waubuno*'s lonely whistle, but paid it no special attention. When she didn't arrive at Parry Sound, a quick search was made. Her paddle box with the name painted on it was found, as was part of the Doupe's furniture and a single empty lifeboat. Every little island along the coast was combed in the desperate hope that at least one survivor had made it ashore. There were none. The searchers also found or accounted for every lifebelt carried by the steamer. Not one was ever used. Whatever happened was so quick that there wasn't time for an action as simple as putting on a lifebelt. The following spring, the hull was discovered upside down in a lonely bay near Moose Point on the bay's eastern shore. Marine men surmised that she capsized in heavy seas during the night of the gale. On things less tangible than dreams do hang our lives. If Dr. Doupe had only listened to his wife.[3]

It was later suggested that the *Waubuno* may have had significant structural problems. During a subsequent suit for liability, a ship's carpenter testified that in 1872, 1874 and 1877 the *Waubuno* came into the shipyard with bulwarks, stanchions and rail carried away as well as rotten timbers and braces. When he called the attention of the captain to it, the officer just told him to do the best he could and departed on schedule with the repair work incomplete. Other workers testified that the gallows frame of the engine was loose. A loose frame would allow the engine to shift in seaway, perhaps disabling the steamer. One of the wheelsmen on the last round trip before she was lost stated that her timbers were rotten, too, as he discovered by boring the decks. He claimed once to have overheard the engineer refuse to sail in her because he said the machinery would not stand the strain of a heavy gale.[4]

There is also a ghost associated with the old *Waubuno*. In the late 1980s, a pleasure boater stopped at Wreck Island for a swim and felt a strong presence of someone or something watching him. The island was named for its proximity to the disaster. He also briefly sighted the fleeting image of what he thought was a woman dressed in a dark colored, old-fashioned full-length dress. A search showed that he was alone on the island. So who or what did he see? Was it the wandering spirit of Mrs. Doupe or another of the *Waubuno*'s lost souls?

It's been said that misfortune comes in threes and so it proved for the owners of the *Waubuno*, the Georgian Bay Navigation Company. First it was the *Waubuno* in November 1879. Then the 162-foot *Manitoulin*, purchased to replace the *Waubuno*, burned with the loss of perhaps 40 lives on May 19, 1882. Finally the 136-foot *Asia*, chartered from the Northwestern Transportation Company to replace the *Manitoulin*, sank in Georgian Bay on September 14, 1882, with an estimated 123 lives lost. The board of directors was hard pressed to explain the unnatural trio of disasters.[5]

In 1906, 27 years to the day after the *Waubuno* perished, another vessel disappeared in Georgian Bay under a similar cloud of mystery. The small steamer *J.H. Jones* left her Owen Sound dock and sailed into a storm and complete oblivion. Just a single body from the 26 passengers or crew aboard was ever found. Only scattered wreckage along the shore testified to her end.[6]

The November 1869 gale that swept Lake Huron was a real hell-banger. Captain Dishrow and the old schooner *Volunteer* were caught out in the lake during the terrible storm. During the depth of the dark night, while the screaming wind rattled the windows and the very walls shook with the violent blasts, the captain's young granddaughter woke suddenly and excitedly telling her mother that she had seen her grandfather standing quietly by her bed. The young girl was the apple of the old captain's heart. He loved her more than life itself. The mother shrugged off the child's vision as only a nightmare. When the storm waters finally calmed and the damages totaled, the *Volunteer* and her captain grandfather were among the lost. Did he pay one last visit to a favorite grandchild? Was it just a nightmare or something more?[7]

A modern presumed lost mystery occurred in August 2005 when two people disappeared from their 27-foot Wellcraft cabin cruiser named *Sea's Life* en route from Belle River, Ontario, to Mackinac Island. The man and woman were both lawyers in their 30s and described as "vibrant and successful animal loving adventurers." One worked for the city of Detroit while the other was in private practice. Apparently neither had a dark secret capable of leaping forth from a closet to "do them in."

The run north from Belle River started on the morning of August 10 and took them through Lake St. Clair, up the St. Clair River to Port Huron and along the Michigan coast to Oscoda, where they spent the night at a marina. The next day it was on to Presque Isle just north of Alpena for lunch and fuel. Continuing northward, the woman called her family on a cell phone about 1:45 p.m. This was the last known contact with the couple.

After they failed to show up at the Grand Hotel where they had reservations, a search was initiated. The woman was supposed to call her family reporting their safe arrival. When she didn't, the family called the hotel and discovered that they hadn't checked in. At 9:10 a.m., the family contacted the Coast Guard.

During the subsequent search, the husband-and-wife crew of a 52-foot cruiser noticed the drifting *Sea's Life*. Both were surprised to see the smaller boat out in the prevailing rough water. They noticed that the boat was empty and a line was trailing astern with two blue

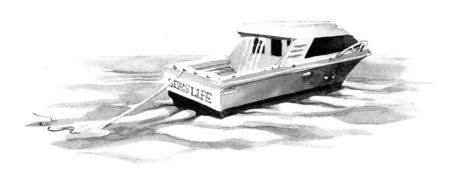

fenders at the end. Concerned with the situation, they contacted
the St. Ignace Coast Guard Station and discovered that the boat
was reported missing.

At 11:10 a.m. on August 12, the Coast Guard arrived, officially
finding *Sea's Life* idling two miles south of Marquette Island about
10 miles northeast of Mackinac Island. There was no evidence of
foul play. All electronics worked and life jackets were all aboard.
The stereo was still playing. Clothing and wallets were in the cabin.
The swim ladder was up and a rope trailed astern, although the two
blue boat fenders reported earlier were gone. An empty vodka
bottle was in the trash but boating friends of the woman reported
she never drank when she operated the boat.

The most intriguing clue is in the woman's running shoe found
lying on her boat deck with a knob from the boat's GPS bracket
strangely wedged in the sole. No rational explanation was ever
given as to how it happened, but it is certainly possible that the
knob had "backed out" from the mounting during the rough water
and vibration dropped it down on the deck unseen. The woman in
turn stepped on it, wedging the screw end into the thick sole.

The search for the missing couple covered 1,550 square miles
and took two days, certainly longer than a swimmer, supported by a
life jacket, could survive even in the comparatively warm 68-degree
water. U.S. and Canadian authorities used boats, planes and
helicopters. It was a fruitless effort. The woman's family picked up
the search when the official agencies stopped, looking by both
plane and boat. They, too, found nothing.

There is confusion over the boat's global positioning system
(GPS) data. One report claimed that it showed the boat deviating
from the planned course around 1 a.m. on August 12 and the speed
decreasing to 1 m.p.h. while it was on the east side of Bois Blanc

Island. At this point the boat was roughly 20 miles from Mackinac Island. A second report on the GPS claimed that it was only turned on at 1:36 a.m. on August 12, when the boat was east of Bois Blanc Island. From then on it just recorded a slow drift toward Marquette Island. A sonar search in the area where the GPS was reportedly activated failed to discover anything. Claims were also made that the earlier GPS data was intentionally erased. If so, why?

Two weeks later, the bloated body of the woman came ashore in Hammond Bay, on the Michigan mainland and about 30 miles from the boat. She was nude, wearing only a thin gold necklace, ring and very expensive Omega watch. As on the boat, there was no sign of foul play. At this writing, the body of the man is still missing.

Theories are cheap and there were a bunch hatched to explain the mystery. Did one of them fall in and the other attempt a rescue that went horribly bad? Did the pair stop to go swimming and leave the boat in neutral, but the gear slipped, causing it to run away from them? If so, why was it discovered in neutral later? Did the boat drift away from them? Was there some kind of medical emergency? Did they meet someone who "did them in?" If the couple stopped for a little "skinny dipping," why was the woman wearing her non-waterproof, very expensive Omega, which was reputedly her pride and joy? Since the man's body was never found, does this suggest foul play on his part? Was it a relationship gone sour, so sour only murder could solve the problem? Investigating police maintain that there is no evidence of foul play, but is this a ploy to smoke out the killer(s) by providing a false sense of security?

There is conflicting evidence on the relationship issue. Some claim that they were a perfect match and two people deeply in love. Others thought they were having problems. The great leap of logic, of course, is if there were problems, were they of the nature that could only be resolved by murder? In sum, the relationship issue is a non-issue. There also doesn't appear to be any actual motive. A violent assault would leave wounds of some nature on her body and there weren't any, at least as publicly released.

The Coast Guard said that waves were running 4-5 feet with the wind blowing 20 knots out of the southeast when the couple disappeared. This would have placed the seas and wind on their stern. The boat could easily have handled the conditions and both were experienced sailors. It isn't reasonable to conclude that they were thrown out of the boat by the waves especially considering that the woman was naked. Was one thrown in and the other went in to make a rescue only to be unable to regain the boat?

A published autopsy report of the woman revealed an elevated level of carbon monoxide in her blood. Investigators theorize that she could have become overcome with fumes from the boat motor while swimming. Carbon monoxide is called the silent killer. It is a colorless, odorless gas about the same density as air and is an exhaust product of internal combustion engines. The cause of death, however, was officially ruled as drowning. But if the Coast Guard weather claim of 20-knot winds is correct, it is an invalid conclusion. First, because no one would stop to go swimming in 4- to 5-foot waves and such strong winds and, second, the winds would rapidly blow away fumes from an idling engine. If the scenario involves the boat running downwind with the fumes boiling into the cockpit from astern and poisoning the woman, it would be assumed the man would also suffer the same fate. So how did the woman's body get into the water? There is far more to the mystery than the simplistic carbon monoxide explanation. The autopsy didn't reveal an elevated alcohol level beyond that consistent with decomposition.

Before going into private practice, the man was a criminal prosecutor. Could he and the woman been "rubbed out" by the mob for past sins? If so, there are far easier ways to do it than being "ambushed" in mid-Lake Huron. Could the pair have come across another boater and been murdered for the pure sport of it, without any logical reason? Stranger things have transpired.

Whatever happened is still unknown. Were there other forces involved? Strange and inexplicable things happen on the lakes. Does this mystery fall into that category? Like the infamous *Mary Celeste*, it is a case that will continue to fascinate.

The brig *Mary Celeste* left New York on November 7, 1872, bound for Europe with a cargo of industrial alcohol. Besides his seven-man crew, Captain Briggs brought his wife and young daughter. On December 4, 1872, another ship found her deserted and drifting 600 miles off Gibraltar. Everything on board was shipshape and in good order except that her yawl boat was missing as well as the ship's papers and chronometer. The last entry in the log on November 24, 1872, gave no indication of any problem. Many theories were advanced and investigations made, but none ever solved the mystery of the missing crew. Is the *Sea's Life* a modern-day *Mary Celeste*, an unsolvable mystery of the sea?[8]

CHAPTER 9

From Beyond the Stars

Just as there are strange and unexplained phenomena on land and water, so, too, are they in the air. The floating rock canoe of Mackinac Island could be looked at as an Indian UFO. The wife claimed that it was the spirit of her dead husband, but was it really something else?

UFOs are common in the Lake Huron environment. Simply put, some people claim to see them all the time. Remember, though, a UFO is an "Unidentified Flying Object," not necessary an interplanetary spacecraft filled with little green men from "Planet X."

In recent years, the U.S. Air Force declassified much of the material in Project Blue Book, the official investigation of UFOs. The material is voluminous and a rich source of sightings and possible explanations.[1]

On the night of July 29, 1952, a Michigan-based Air Force radar station tracked a UFO moving at 550 knots on a due north heading for 20 minutes. It was roughly west of Port Huron. Since three F-94B jet fighters were in the area doing practice intercepts of a Mitchell B-24 light bomber, one was directed to intercept and identify the unknown fast-moving target. Ground control directed the fighter pilot to a point four miles away and directly behind the UFO at an altitude of 21,000 feet. The pilot radioed back that he could see a "bright, flashing, colored light." He followed for 20 minutes at 550 knots, but couldn't catch up. The UFO was just too fast for the jet.

Initially the Air Force thought that the pilot could have been chasing the star Capella, which was in line with the fighter's line of flight. Later when they realized that both the aircraft and UFO were on the radar together, this was plainly impossible. A balloon was also disregarded, since even the jet stream couldn't carry one as fast as the radar tracked it. The case remains unresolved, truly an "unidentified flying object."[2]

It is easy to make fun of people claiming to "see strange things in the sky." Perhaps they had one drink too many or were just a bit daft to begin with. UFO reports based on the hard science of radar observations backed up by U.S. Air Force fighter pilots are more difficult to blow off.

One of the cases over Lake Huron is especially interesting. During the early morning hours of September 18, 1951, an Air Force ground radar station picked up a target at an estimated 6,000 feet altitude moving at great speed. The extreme velocity made determining altitude difficult. The UFO was initially picked up 40 miles east of Milwaukee. Eleven minutes later it was 50 miles west of Selfridge Air Base near Mount Clemens (northeast of Detroit), then 20 miles south of Milwaukee to 60 miles southeast of Selfridge to 60 miles south of Calumet, Michigan on the Upper Peninsula's Keweenaw Peninsula to 140 miles northeast of Oscoda, Michigan, on Lake Huron to 10 miles northeast of Port Huron to 30 miles southeast of Sault Ste. Marie to 60 miles northeast Port Huron to 60 miles south of Calumet to 65 miles northwest of Milwaukee to 100 miles northeast of Sault Ste. Marie to 10 miles north of Bay City. It was all over the sky and every move tracked by at least one Air Force radar station. The operators were also experienced men. They knew that what they were seeing was impossible, at least for any aircraft in their experience, but seeing is believing. Adjoining radar stations reported similar sightings.[3]

On May 16, 1958, a UFO was seen to crash into Smith's Bay, near Parry Sound, roughly 400 feet offshore. There was no sign of remains on the surface. The Royal Canadian Mounted Police was said to have investigated, but no report of what they found was ever released. A low flying UFO was observed flying over Georgian Bay on November 18, 1960. Reportedly it was smaller than a jet and entirely black. Other sightings placed it in the vicinity of Collingwood.[4]

A rash of UFO sightings were reported March 1999 in the Unionville area on Michigan's Thumb. Several folks reported strange lights hovering over their homes. Bright orange in color, they appeared to be shining from inside some kind of unknown flying craft. The lights would blink off and then on again while the

mysterious craft hovered motionless. One observer described the object as the size of a football field. Another said that it seemed to coalesce into six other light groups, move and reform into a triangle shape rotating on its axles. Other watchers said the formation was Z-shaped. Law enforcement phones rang "off the hook" with reports of the unknown aerial display. What happened that night was never explained.[5]

An observer in St. Clair Shores on the St. Clair River reported a spectacular sighting on November 16, 1999. At 7:10 p.m., she saw 10 to 15 bright balls of light with wavering tails all flying in a row. The woman was inside of her apartment on the 24th floor, so she had an unobstructed view of the action. The lights were moving east to west. Supposedly similar sightings by neighbors were also reported to local police.

On July 6, 2002, a husband and wife were out for a pleasant evening boat ride on lonely Lake Muskoka, just east of Georgian Bay. About 9:30 p.m., a bright light appeared on their port side, about 35 degrees above the horizon. It moved as the boat did. If the boat went faster, it went faster. If the boat turned, it turned. If the boat stopped, it stopped. It was weird to say the least. At first the couple was more amused than anything else, but unable to explain the creepy action of the light, returned as fast as they could to their lakeside cabin. All the way back the light kept pace with them. After they moored the boat and went inside the cabin, the light just drifted away finally dropping below the horizon. This type of incident leads to some fascinating speculation. What if the light was an extraterrestrial craft and it was piloted by a couple of aliens with a sense of humor? Perhaps one turned to the other and said something like, "Come on Sam (or whatever aliens call each other), let's have some fun with these two!" Maybe, just maybe …

Another strange sighting was at the mouth of the Thessalon River, Ontario, on northern Lake Huron. On July 19, 2002, three bizarre lights were reported in the North Channel. The area is very popular for yacht cruising, so witnesses were not sparse. The lights definitely weren't from an airplane or boat. Clear white in color, they seemed to be on or just below the surface until, whoosh, they shot skyward! One of them peeled off to the west and the others went east, both moving at high speed.[6]

Epilogue

It is strange the way some ghost stories beg to be told, but yet remain elusive. You know they are there. They have to be, but refuse to come out into the open. If you have ever walked past a long abandoned building or home, one that has stood the ravages of time but perhaps not received lavish maintenance, you understand what I am driving at. The empty windows staring outward to a dark night speak eloquently of the dead not yet buried. What evil lurks deep in the deserted depths of the old walls? Even buildings still occupied can reek of tales not told. The old admonition "if only the walls could speak" reminds us that mysteries still remain. It isn't just the structures of man that can hold such "presence." Land can, too.

Mackinac Island is a case in point. Ever since I started visiting the island a very long time ago I knew there had to be some great folklore connected with it, but it wasn't available. There was history all around. Documented, categorized, interpreted and duly sanitized in full compliance with acceptable, politically correct state of Michigan standards. But there wasn't any folklore or at least depressingly little of it. Remember, if history is what people did and perhaps why, folklore is what they felt or believed.

So I kept searching and digging for old tales not included in "official" histories. I asked questions and filed away answers. Gradually I built up a reasonable collection of material looking more at the "other" side of the island than is presented to the daily horde of marauding Fudgies from the authorized history.

While many of the old stories were dug out of very early publications, back when legend and lore held a higher position in society, some are more interesting because of their contemporary nature. This is true of other material in the book, too. Getting a firsthand account of a ghostly crew racing a spectral yacht or phantom hearse clattering along Main Street on a dark and rainy night adds a new angle to the topic. These kinds of tales, be they called folklore, legend or just ghost stories, are accounts that can be as contemporary as today. Certainly a "guess what I just saw" story is as accurate as pulling one out of a crinkled and cracking old newspaper or scrawled journal.

Are they true? The answer is yes and no. They certainly are all "true" ghost stories. Whether the observers imbibed in too much bottled spirits or not isn't for me to say. They saw what they saw and related it as best they could.

Remember, scientists have been investigating the paranormal for many years without finding a shred of evidence that it exists or doesn't. This doesn't mean they aren't still looking, but the answer remains elusive.

Fred Stonehouse

186

Endnotes

INTRODUCTION

[1] The Laurentian Shield, aka the Precambrian Shield, or Laurentian Plateau, is the earth's greatest area of exposed Archean rock and is covered with a thin layer of soil that forms the nucleus of the North American craton. The Shield has a deep, common, joined bedrock region in eastern and central Canada, covering more than half of Canada stretching north from the Great Lakes to the Arctic Ocean. It also includes most of Greenland and reaches into the United States as the Adirondack Mountains and the Superior Highlands.

CHAPTER 1

[1] *Detroit Free Press*, July 3, 1909.

[2] *Detroit Free Press*, July 3, 1859, March 9, 1850, October 22, 1859; *Buffalo Morning Express*, April 27, 1849; *Buffalo Republican*, July 11, 1853; *Cleveland Evening Herald*, August 15, 1856; *Toronto Globe*, October 22, 1859; Boatnerd.com, www.boatnerd.com; Stonehouse File, *Troy*; Paul J. Schmitt, "A Hard Luck Boat, Loss of the Propeller *Troy*," *Inland Seas*, (Winter 2000), pp. 294-300.

[3] Boatnerd, *Meteor* www.boatnerd.com/; Stonehouse File, *Meteor*.

[4] Boatnerd, *Globe* www.boatnerd.com/; *Detroit Free Press*, June 30, 1867.

[5] Mansfield, History of the Great Lakes, Volume II (Chicago: J.H. Beers and Company, 1899), pp. 17-18; *Detroit Post and Tribune*, May 17, 1883.

[6] Stonehouse Collection, *Fred A. Lee*.

[7] Boatnerd, *Fontana* www.boatnerd.com/; Stonehouse Collection, *Fontana*.

[8] Boatnerd, *Jamaica* www.boatnerd.com/; Stonehouse File, *Jamaica*.

[9] Boatnerd, *Montana,* www.boatnerd.com/; Stonehouse Collection, *Montana*.

[10] Michael M. Dixon, *When Detroit Rode the Waves* (Mervue Publications: 2001), pp. 141-159; Dana Thomas Bowen, *Lore of the Lakes* (Freshwater Press, Cleveland: 1940), pp. 180-188; The SS *Tashmoo* and Her Date With Doom, info.detnews.com/history/story/index.cfm?id=22&category=events.

[11] *Great Lakes Journal*, January, May 1939.

[12] Annual Report U.S. Life-Saving Service, 1904, p. 85; *John Duncan*, www.boatnerd.com.

CHAPTER 2

[1] Anonymous interview, circa 1985; Frederick Stonehouse, *Wreck Ashore, the U.S. Life-Saving Service on the Great Lakes* (Lake Superior Port Cities: Duluth, 1994), pp. 159-152.

[2] The *Marine City* burned on August 29, 1880, with the loss of approximately 20 lives.

[3] Ignis fatuous: "A wide variety of spectral lights, whose alleged purpose is to herald death or play tricks on travelers at night. It literally means 'foolish fire' and is so named because anyone who follows such a light is foolish."

[4] *Detroit Post*, September 15, 1884.

[5] Anonymous interview 1996.

[6] Fudgies: the term given to tourists who invade the island every summer day, mill around the downtown and fort area , buy vast amount of fudge and catch a ferry back to the mainland.

[7] Anonymous interview, 1999.

[8] Leo C. Lillie, *Historic Grand Haven and Ottawa County* (Grand Haven, Michigan: 1931), pp. 259-260; Boatnerd.com, www.boatnerd.com/swayze/shipwreck/s.htm

[9] *Blade-Crescent* (Sebewaing, MI), November 8, 1988; Dwight Boyer, *Strange Adventures of the Great Lakes* (New York: Dodd-Mead, 1974), pp. 61-73; John Kaufman, "*Hunter Savidge* Disaster recalled," *Inland Seas* (Fall 1965), pp. 233-235; Swayze, Shipwreck, p. 211; Mystery Schooner, Captain Ron Burkhart, www.pointeauxbarqueslighthouse.org/preserve/shipwrecks/MysterySchooner1.cfm

[10] *Iron Agitator* (Ishpeming, Michigan), April 17, 1886; Mansfield, History, pp. 826, 893.

[11] Boatnerd, www.boatnerd.com/; Russell Floren and Andrea Gutsche, "The Asia Mystery," *Inland Seas*, (Spring 1995), pp. 16-48; Stonehouse Collection, *Asia*; "The Steamer *Asia*, A Local Connection," www.pastforward.ca/perspectives/march_142003.htm; USQUE AD MARE, "A History of the Canadian Coast Guard and Marine Services" by Thomas E. Appleton, www.ccg-gcc.gc.ca/usque-ad-mare/chapter04-07_e.htm

[12] *Great Lakes Cruiser* magazine, October 1994, p. 45; Marine Collection, Rutherford B. Hayes Library, Fremont, Ohio; Runge Collection, Milwaukee Public Library, Milwaukee, Wisconsin; John M. Mills, Canadian Coastal and Inland Steam Vessels, 1809-1930 (Providence, Rhode Island: Steamboat Historical Society of America, 1979).; *Echo* (Wiarton, Ontario, November – December 1881; www.ontarioplaques.com/PlaqueText/Grey25a.html.

[13] Stonehouse Collection, *Kaliyuga* File.

[14] "Lost Cité" perdurabo10tripod.com/id1125.html; "Lost Cité," minufon.org/2002%20articles/UFORoundup_2002.htm; John O. Greenwood, Namesakes, 1900-1909 (Cleveland: Freshwater Press, 1987), p. 438.

[15] *New York Sun* , August. 20, 1883.

CHAPTER 3

[1] Stonehouse Collection, Les Cheneaux Islands.

[2] Anonymous interview, July 23, 1993; Anonymous interview, October 19, 2002.

[3] Right Rev. Frank O'Brien, *Names of Places of Interest of Mickinac Island*, Michigan, Bulletin On. 5 (Wyndoop Hallenback Crawford and Company: Lansing, Michigan, 1918), p. 44; Fred Landon, Lake Huron (Bobbs-Merrill: New York, 1944), pp. 74-89, 188-193.; The National Parks and National Historic Sites of Canada in Ontario, Fort St. Josepth, www.pc.gc.ca/voyage-travel/pv-vp/itm6-/page20_e.asp

[4] Samuel F. Cook, "Drummond Island, the Story of the British Occupation" (Author's edition: Lansing, Michigan, 1896), pp. 98-102; Jill Lowe Brumwell, "Drummond Island History, Folklore and Early People" (Black Bear Press, 2003), pp. 45-48; "Buried Antiques, The History of Penetanguishene" www.buriedantiques.com/historyofpenetanguishene.html

[5] Brumwell, *Drummond Island History*, pp. 45-48.

[6] Anonymous interview, March 1998; David D. Swayze, Shipwreck (Boyne City, Michigan: Harbor House Publishers, 1992, p. 165.

[7] Marion Kuclo, *Michigan Haunts and Hauntings* (Lansing, Michigan: Thunder Bay Press, 1992), pp. 119-123; Stonehouse File, Minnie Quay; Harbor Beach Forever, www.geocities.com/wlmmcn7/; Lost Cité, www.ghostzoo.com/forum/Partagium/viewthread.php?-68

[8] William C.S. Pellowe, *Tales From a Lighthouse Cafe* (Adrian, Michigan: Raisin River Publishing, 1960), pp. 77-78.

[9] Frederick Denny Larke, "The Story of Sacred Rock," Calcite Screenings (August 1929); Rogers City Historical Society.

[10] Lost Cité, www.alpenacvb.com/fall.htm; native burial grounds were often not treated with respect by Europeans. It is likely the burials simply disappeared when the native culture was disrupted.

[11] Lost Cité, www.ghostzoo.com/forum/Partagium/viewthread.php?tud=886; The Unofficial Monty Python Homepage, www.mwscomp.com/sound.html.

[12] *Saginaw Daily Courier* (Saginaw, Michigan) November 16, 1873.

[13] Port Huron Michigan, www.maritimecapitalgl.com/; Haunted Places in Michigan, theshadowlands.net/places/michigan.htm

[14] Lightship Huron, www.boatnerd.com/museums/huron/history.htm; anonymous interview, May 22, 2001.

[15] *The Chronicle*, Algonac-Clay Township Historical Society, Summer 1996, Volume 1, Issue 2; CBC News, "The road to Catholic sainthood: one miracle at a time," www.cbc.ca/news/background/catholicism/sainthood.html; Michigan's Harsens Island, www.rootsweb.com/~miharsen/; Harsensisland.com, www.harsensisland.com; Lost Cité, algonac-clay-history.org/VOLIISS2.htm; Lost Cité, www.algonac-clay-history.org/VOLIISS1.htim; River Scene, October 2005;

[16] Anonymous interviews, March 31- April 1, 2006; anonymous interviews, March 30 – April 1, 2006; e-mail, Beverly Wilkens, Idle Hour Yacht Club, June 7, 2006.

[17] Russell Floren and Andrea Gutsche, *Mysterious Islands.* (Toronto: Lynx Images, 1999) pp. 139-141.

[18] Dave Dempsey, *On the Brink, The Great Lakes in the 21st Century* (East Lansing: Michigan State University Press, 2002) p. 157-158.; *The Manitoulin Expositor*, www.manitoulin.ca; "This is Manitoulin, the Natural Destination – Mindemoya," www.manitoulin.ca/TIM/mindprov.html; "Mysteries of Canada, the Suspicious Death of Danny Dodge," www.mysteriesofcanada.com/ontario/dodge.htm; "The Aboriginal Peoples of Little Current," www.turners.ca/pages/main/manitoulin2.html; Mindemoya Computing and Design, www.mcd.on.ca/mcd/the-name.html

[19] Samuel F. Cook, *Drummond Island, The Story of The British Occupation 1815 - 1828* (Lansing, Michigan: 1896), pp. 103-110; Fred Landon, Lake Huron (Bobbs-Merrill: New York, 1944), pp. 198-99.

[20] John Maclean, *Canadian Savage Book, the Native Tribes of Canada* (William Briggs: Toronto, 1896), pp. 181-182.

[21] Russell Floren and Andrea Gutsche, *Ghosts of the Bay*. (Toronto: Lynx Images, 1995) pp. 134-136.

[22] Interview, Dr. Bell, January 24, 1995.

[23] Ontario Ghosts and Hauntings, Collingwood, Village of Departed Souls, www.torontoghosts.org/barrie/villageofdeparted.htm

[24] Ontario Ghosts and Hauntings, Port Severn, Bressette House, www.torontoghosts.org/barrie/bressette.htm

[25] Historical Information, History of Discovery Harbour, www.discoveryharbour.on.ca/english/historicalinfo.html; Ontario Ghosts and Hauntings, Penetanguishene, Discovery Harbor www.torontoghosts.org/barrie/disharb.htm; From a purely marketing perspective, it is much easier to try to convince tourists to visit "Discovery Harbour" than someplace called "Penetanguishene," something the average person can neither spell or pronounce.

[26] Haunted Places in Canada, Goderich www.theshadowlands.net/places/canada.htm; Canadian Corrections www.canadiancorrections.com: Ontario Gen Web, Huron County Heritage, Huron Goal www.geocities.com/heartland/meadows/8965/heritage.html#Huron%20Historic

[27] The Ouendat (Huron) Indian Lengend of Kitchikewanna, collections.ic.gc.ca/huronia/ghost/kitchi.htm.

CHAPTER 4

[1] Although Mackinaw is the preferred pronunciation today, historically Mackinac was also used, depending on the speaker's point of view and ethnic background. As would be expected, spelling varied, too, with Mackinack being a common variant.

[2] There is some controversy over where the name Michilimackinac came from. It is popular today to claim that it is from the Indian words "Michi," meaning "great," and "Mackinac," meaning "turtle," thus Michilimackinac became "great turtle," as it is claimed to resemble the hump of a mud turtle. A century ago, historians also translated the Ojibway *MichineMaukinouk* as the "place of giant fairies." The great

190

collector of Indian folklore and legends, Henry Schoolcraft, rationalizes the two meanings by saying that the spirits often took the form of a fairy. Go figure. Over time, the "Michili" faded from popular use and only "Mackinac" was left. John Read Bailey, M.D., *Mackinac Formerly Michilimackinac, A History and Guide Book with Maps* (Tradesman Company: Grand Rapids, Michigan, 1909), p. 34.

3 Prairie Ghosts, www.prairieghosts.com/small_pt.html; Dixie Franklin, *Haunts of the Upper Great Lakes* (Thunder Bay Press, Michigan, 1997), pp. 64-70; Stonehouse Collection, Mackinac Island.

4 Franklin, *Haunts*, pp. 7-16.

5 Lake Huron, p. 95.

6 Shadowlands, shadowlands.net/places/michigan.htm.

7 Lake Huron, pp. 95-96.

8 Lost Cité, www.juicenewsdaily.com/0205/news/haunted_michigan.html

9 Lost Cité, www.ghostzoo.com/forum/Partagium/viewthread.php?tid=116

10 Rootsweb, www.rootsweb.cm/~minmacki2/haunted_mackinac.html

11 Rootsweb, www.rootsweb.cm/~minmacki2/haunted_mackinac.html.

12 Lake Huron, pp. 94-95

13 Shadowlands, shadowlands.net/places/michigan.htm.

14 Rootsweb www.rootsweb.cm/~minmacki2/haunted_mackinac.html.

15 Internment.net, Fort Mackinac Post Cemetery, www.interment.net/data/us/mi/mackinac/ftmack/mackinac.htm

16 Anonymous interview, July 3, 2000.

17 Dwight H. Kelton, LL.D., Captain, U.S. Army, *Annals of Fort Mackinac* (John W. Davis and Son: Mackinac Island, 1890), pp. 57-60; Right Rev. Frank O'Brien, *Names of Places of Interest of Mackinac Island*, Michigan, Bulletin On. 5 (Wyndoop Hallenback Crawford and Company: Lansing, Michigan, 1918), pp, 71-72; Some sources also identify Robertson as Robinson. Given the similarity in names it is easy to see how the confusion occurred over time.

18 Anonymous interview, July 30, 1999.

19 Grace Franks Kane, *Myths and Legends of the Mackinacs and the Lake Region* (The Editor Publishing Company: Cincinnati, 1897), pp. 61-62; David A. Armour, Colonial Michilimackiac (Mackinac State Perks: Mackinac Island, 2000), pp. 10-11.

20 Kane, *Myths and Legends*, pp. 31-34; O'Brien, *Names of Places*, pp. 77-78.

21 Kane, *Myths and Legends*, pp. 67-68.

22 John Read Bailey, M.D., *Mackinac Formerly Michilimacknac, A History and Guide Book with Maps* (Tradesman Company: Grand Rapids, Michigan, 1909), pp. 35-36; Earliest Known History of Mackinac Island, www.nanations.com/ottawachippewa/earliesthistory.htm

23 Lighthouse Lane, Arch Rock, www.lighthouselane.net/archrock.html; O'Brien, *Names of Places*, p. 39: Indian Peoples.org, Indigenous Peoples Literature, www.indians.org/welker/archrock.htm; History of Mackinac Island – Sugar Loaf, Rock www.mackinac.com/content/general/history_sugarloaf.html; Lake Algonquin was formed by melting glaciers that existed in east-central North America at the time of the last ice age. Portions of Lake Algonquin are now Lake

Huron, Georgian Bay and inland portions of northern Michigan. While the lake varied in size, it was the largest during the post-glacial period, gradually shrinking to the current Lake Huron and Georgian Bay.

[24] Kelton, *Annals of Fort Mackinac*, pp. 62-66; O'Brien, Names of Place), p. 54.

CHAPTER 5

[1] Interview, Lynn Carr, August 16, 1995.

[2] Western Lights, Spectacle Reef, www.terrypepper.com/lights/huron/spectacle/spectacle.htm; Western Lights – Martin Reef www.terrypepper.com/lights/huron/martin_reef/martin-reef.htm; Stonehouse Collection, Spectacle Reef, Martin Reef.

[3] *Ann Arbor News*, December 16, 1989; Charles K. Hyde, *Northern Lights* (Lansing, Michigan: TwoPeninsula Press, 1986), p.66; interview, Dan McGee, May 21, 1994.

[4] Interview, Anna Hoge, March 12, 1996.

[5] William O. Thomson. *The Ghosts of New England Lighthouses*. (Salem, MA: Old Saltbox Publishing, 1993), pp.19,51.

[6] Hyde, Northern Lights, p. 93.

[7] *Detroit Free Press*, September 14, 1994; October 29, 1999; "Haunts of the Great Lakes," Great Lakes Cruiser, October 1995, pp. 42-43; Interview, Lorraine Parris, May 29, 1994; Interview, Anna Hoge, March 12, 1996.

[8] Interview, Ted Richardson, January 1994.

[9] Stonehouse Collection, Sturgeon Point Light.

[10] Stonehouse Collection, Forty Mile Point Lighthouse; interview, Mr. Comtois, February 17, 1994

[11] Interview, Pamela Kennedy, July 1, 1996; Stonehouse Collection, Pointe aux Barques Light.

[12] Anonymous interview, June 3, 1970.

[13] Stonehouse Collection, Tawas Station.

[14] Floren and Gutsche, *Ghosts of the Bay* pp. 269-271; Floren and Gutsche, *Mysterious Islands* pp. 126-137, Laura M. Gateman, *Lighthouses Around Bruce County* (Chesley, Ontario: Spinning Wheel Publications, 1991), pp. 38-39; Mansfield, *History of the Great Lakes*, p. 880; Stonehouse Files; Swayze, *Shipwrecks*, p. 199.

[15] Floren and Gutsche, Ghosts, pp. 56-59.

CHAPTER 6

[1] Letter, September 12, 1999; unidentified; interview, September 15, 1999, unidentified. ,

[2] *Grand Rapids Press*, June 26, 1976.

[3] *London Ontario Free Press*, July 12, 1975.

[4] *Detroit Free Press*, October 24, 1890.

[5] *Detroit News-Tribune*, August 8, 1897.

[6] *Great Lakes Journal*, October 1938.

[7] Floren and Gutsche, *Ghosts*, p. 195.

[8] *Owen Sound Sun Times*, July 23, 1948

[9] Author's File, Middle Island; Unpublished, mythical ms, "The Adventures of Marcel LaFontaine," Arkmanian University Archives.

CHAPTER 7

[1] Interview author and Dennis Hale, October, 1993, November 1995; Tim Juhl, Pat and Jim Stayer, *Sole Survivor, Dennis Hale's Own Story* (Lexington, Michigan: Lakeshore Charters and Marine Exploration, 1996), pp. 31-46: Stonehouse Collection; United States Coast Guard, Marine Board of Investigation Report, SS *Daniel J. Morrell*; Rev. Peter Van der Linden, *Great Lakes Ships We Remember*, (Cleveland, Ohio: Freshwater Press, 1979), pp. 298-299.

[2] Manuscript, "*Stamback* Loss," undated, unmarked; Although this story involves several Great Lakes, since the bulk of the action takes place in Lake Huron, I included it in this book.

CHAPTER 8

[1] Boatnerd, *Galena* www.boatnerd.com/; Stonehouse Collection, *Galena*.

[2] O'Brien, (*Names of Places*), pp. 83-84.

[3] *Canadian Coastal and Inland Steam Vessels* 1809 - 1930 , p. 124; John Columbo, *Mysterious Canada* (Toronto: Doubleday, 1988), pp. 145-146; C.N.J. Snider, "Schooner Days," *Toronto Telegram*, January 31, 1953, MXC, February 7, 1953, MXCI; W.R. Williams, "The Gale-Shattered *Waubuno*," *Inland Seas* (Spring 1965), pp. 52-55.

[4] Oswego Palladium, January 13, 1881.

[5] Landon, *Lake Huron* p. 322.

[6] Landon, *Lake Huron*, p. 311; Ship of the Month, *J.H. Jones* vaxxine.com/gblawson/jonesarticle.htm.

[7] William Ratigan, *Great Lakes Shipwrecks and Survivals* (Galahad Books, New York, 1960), pp. 98- 99.

[8] *Detroit Free Press*, August 26, 2005, January 14, 2006; Press Release, U.S. Coast Guard, Ninth District, August 13, 2005; *Detroit News*, August 25, September 16, 2005, February 13, 2006; Petoskey News-Record, March 4, 2006; Charles Rutherford Jr., www.charleyproject.org/cases/r/rutherford_charles.html; *Cheboygan News*, www.cheboygannews.com/articles/2006/02/28/news/mackinaw/news2.txt; Was Foul Play Behind Boating Accident, msnbc.msn.com/id/10793084/; Stempien-Rutherford, www.stempienrutherford.com/default.htm; 6 News, WLNS.Com; www.wlns.com/Global/story.asp?S=4070825&nav=0RbQ

CHAPTER 9

[1] Project Blue Book started in 1952 as a study of UFOs conducted by the United States Air Force. It was terminated in 1969. It was the last known UFO research project conducted by the Air Force.
The purpose was to determine if UFOs were a potential threat to national security.

To this end, thousands of reports were collected, analyzed and filed. Some 12,618 reports were studied. Researchers concluded that most were the result of natural phenomena or conventional aircraft. Some were certainly hoaxes. But 701 of the reports, about 6 percent, were considered unknown. Critics claim that it was all a cover up and the "government" continues to study UFOs and knows far more than it ever revealed.

[2] U.S. Air Force Project Blue Book, MAXW-PBB1-671-676.

[3] U.S. Air Force Project Blue Book, MAXW-PBB8-1576-1580.

[4] Unsourced; Canadian Government X-Files from Department of National Defense Microfilm Reel T3291.

[5] *Huron Daily Tribune*, March 17, 1999; Lost Cité, mimufon.org/Historical_folders/HistoricalArticles_90s.him.

[6] Para Researchers of Ontario www.pararesearchers.org/UFO/2002ufo/2002ufo.html.

Bibliography

BOOKS

Armour, David A. *Colonial Michilimackinac*. Mackinac State Parks: Mackinac Island, 2000.

Bailey, John Read M.D. *Mackinac Formerly Michilimackinac, A History and Guide Book with Maps*. Tradesman Company: Grand Rapids, Michigan, 1909.

Bowen, Dana Thomas. *Lore of the Lakes* (Freshwater Press, Cleveland: 1940.

Brumwell, Jill Lowe. *Drummond Island History, Folklore and Early People*, Black Bear Press, 2003.

Columbo, John. *Mysterious Canada*. Toronto: Doubleday, 1988.

Cook, Samuel F. *Drummond Island, the Story of the British Occupation* (Authors Edition: Lansing, Michigan, 1896.

Dempsey, Dave. *On the Brink, The Great Lakes in the 21st Century*. East Lansing: Michigan State University Press, 2002.

Dixon, Michael M. *When Detroit Rode the Waves*, Mervue Publications: 2001.

Boyer, Dwight. *Strange Adventures on the Great Lakes*. Dodd- Mead, New York, 1974.

Floren, Russell and Gutsche, Andrea. *Ghosts of the Bay*. Toronto: Lynx Images, 1995.

Floren, Russell and Gutsche, Andrea. *Mysterious Islands*. Toronto: Lynx Images, 1999.

Franklin, Dixie. *Haunts of the Upper Great Lakes*. Thunder Bay Press, Michigan, 1997.

Gateman, Laura M. *Lighthouses Around Bruce County*. Chesley, Ontario: Spinning Wheel Publications, 1991.

Gutsche, Andrea and Bisaillon, Cindy. *Mysterious Islands, Forgotten Tales of the Great Lakes*. Toronto: Lynx Images, 1999.

Greenwood, John O. *Namesakes, 1900-1909*. Cleveland: Freshwater Press, 1987.

Hyde, Charles K. *Northern Lights*. Lansing, Michigan: TwoPeninsula Press, 1986.

Jule, Jim and Stayer, Pat. *Sole Survivor, Dennis Hale's Own Story*. Lexington, Michigan: Lakeshore Charters and Marine Exploration, 1996.

Kane, Grace Franks. *Myths and Legends of the Mackinacs and the Lake Region*. The Editor Publishing Company: Cincinnati, 1897.

Kelton, Dwight H. LL.D., captain, U.S. Army. *Annals of Fort Mackinac*. John W. Davis and Son: Mackinac Island, 1890.

Kuclo, Marion. *Michigan Haunts and Hauntings*. Lansing, Michigan: Thunder Bay Press, 1992.

Landon, Fred. *Lake Huron*. Bobbs-Merrill: New York, 1944.

Lillie, Leo C. *Historic Grand Haven and Ottawa County*. Grand Haven, Michigan: 1931.

Maclean, John. *Canadian Savage Book, the Native Tribes of Canada*. William Briggs: Toronto, 1896.

Mansfield, John. *History of the Great Lakes, Volume II*. Chicago: J.H. Beers and Company, 1899.

Medium, A. *Revelations of a Spirit Medium*. New York, 1871.

Mills, John M. *Canadian Coastal and Inland Steam Vessels, 1809-1930*. Providence, Rhode Island: Steamboat Historical Society of America, 1979.

O'Brien, Right Rev. Frank. *Names of Places of Interest of Mickinac Island, Michigan, Bulletin On. 5*. Wyndoop Hallenback Crawford and Company: Lansing, Michigan, 1918.

Pellowe, William C.S. *Tales From a Lighthouse Café*. Adrian, Michigan: Raisin River Publishing, 1960.

Ratigan, William. *Great Lakes Shipwrecks and Survivals*. Galahad Books, New York, 1960.

Stonehouse, Frederick. *Wreck Ashore: the U.S. Life-Saving Service on the Great Lakes*. Lake Superior Port Cities Inc.: Duluth, 1994.

Swayze, David D. *Shipwreck*. Boyne City, Michigan: Harbor House Publishers, 1992.

Thomson, William O. *The Ghosts of New England Lighthouses*. Salem, MA: Old Saltbox Publishing, 1993.

Van der Linden, Rev. Peter. *Great Lakes Ships We Remember*. Cleveland, Ohio: Freshwater Press, 1979.

COLLECTIONS

Ivan Walton Collection, Bentley Historical Library, University of Michigan.

Letter, September 12, 1999; unidentified.

Marine Collection, Rutherford B. Hayes Library, Fremont, Ohio.

Press Release, U.S. Coast Guard, Ninth District, August 13, 2005.

Runge Collection, Milwaukee Public Library, Milwaukee, Wisconsin.

Asia, Stonehouse Collection

Fred A. Lee, Stonehouse Collection.

Fontana, Stonehouse Collection.

Forty Mile Point Lighthouse, Stonehouse Collection.

Galena, Stonehouse Collection.

Jamaica, Stonehouse Collection.

Kaliyuga, Stonehouse Collection.

Les Cheneaux Islands, Stonehouse Collection.

Martin Reef Lighthouse, Stonehouse Collection.

Mackinac Island, Stonehouse Collection.
Meteor, Stonehouse Collection.
Minnie Quay, Stonehouse Collection.
Montana, Stonehouse Collection.
Point aux Barques Lighthouse, Stonehouse Collection.
Sturgeon Point Lighthouse, Stonehouse Collection.
Spectacle Reef Lighthouse, Stonehouse Collection.
Tawas Station, Stonehouse Collection.
Troy, Stonehouse Collection.
United States Coast Guard, Marine Board of Investigation Report, SS *Daniel J. Morrell*, Stonehouse Collection.
Unsourced; Canadian Government X-Files from Department of National Defense Microfilm Reel T3291.
U.S. Air Force Project Blue Book, MAXW-PBB1-671-676.
U.S. Air Force Project Blue Book, MAXW-PBB8-1576-1580.

INTERNET
6 News, WLNS.Com, www.wlns.com/Global/story.asp?S=4070825&nav=0RbQ
Boatnerd, *Fontana*, www.boatnerd.com
Boatnerd, *Galena*, www.boatnerd.com
Boatnerd, *Globe*, www.boatnerd.com
Boatnerd, *Jamaica*, www.boatnerd.com
Boatnerd, *John Duncan*, www.boatnerd.com
Boatnerd, *Meteor*, www.boatnerd.com
Boatnerd, *Montana*, www.boatnerd.com
Boatnerd, *Troy*, www.boatnerd.com
Buried Antiques, "The History of Penetanguishene,"
  www.buriedantiques.com/historyofpenetanguishene.htm
Canadian Corrections, www.canadiancorrections.com
CBC News, "The road to Catholic sainthood: one miracle at a time,"
  www.cbc.ca/news/background/catholicism/sainthood.html
Charles Rutherford Jr., www.charleyproject.org/cases/r/rutherford_charles.html
Cheboygan News, www.cheboygannews.com/articles/2006/02/28/news/
  mackinaw/news2.txt
Earliest Known History of Mackinac Island, www.nanations.com/
  ottawachippewa/earlieshistory.htm
Ghosts of America, www.ghostsofamerica.com/states/mi.html
Harbor Beach Forever, www.geocities.com/wlmmcn7/
Harsensisland.com, www.harsensisland.com
Haunted Places in Canada, Goderich,
  www.theshadowlands.net/places/canada.htm
Historical Information, History of Discovery Harbour,
  www.discoveryharbour.on.ca/english/historicalinfo.html
History of Mackinac Island, Sugar Loaf Rock,
  www.mackinac.com/content/general/history_sugarloaf.html
Indian Peoples.org, Indigenous Peoples Literature,
  www.indians.org/welker/archrock.htm

Internment.net, Fort Mackinac Post Cemetery,
www.interment.net/data/us/mi/mackinac/ftmack/mackinac.htm
Lighthouse Lane, Arch Rock, www.lighthouselane.net/archrock.html
Lost Cité, algonac-clay-history.org/VOLIISS2.htm
Lost Cité, www.alpenacvb.com/fall.htm
Lost Cité, www.algonac-clay-history.org/VOLIISS1.htim
Lost Cité, www.ghostzoo.com/forum/Partagium/viewthread.php?tid=116
Lost Cité, www.ghostzoo.com/forum/Partagium/viewthread.php?-68
Lost Cité, www.ghostzoo.com/forum/Partagium/ viewthread.php?tud=886
Lost Cité, www.juicenewsdaily.com/0205/news/haunted_michigan.html
Lost Cité, mimufon.org/Historical_folders/HistoricalArticeles_90s.him
Lost Cité, minufon.org/2002%20articles/ UFORoundup_2002.htm
Lost Cité, perdurabo10tripod.com/id1125.html
Manitoulin Expositor www.manitoulin.ca
Michigan's Harsens Island, www.rootsweb.com/~miharsen
Mindemoya Computing and Design, www.mcd.on.ca/mcd/the-name.html
Mystery Schooner, Captain Ron Burkhart, www.pointeauxbarqueslighthouse.
org/preserve/shipwrecks/MysterySchooner1.cfm
Mysteries of Canada, the Suspicious Death of Danny Dodge,
www.mysteriesofcanada.com/ontario/dodge.htm
Ontario Gen Web, Huron County Heritage, Huron Goal, www.geocities.com/
heartland/meadows/8965/heritage.html#Huron%20Historic
Ontario Ghosts and Hauntings, Collingwood, Village of Departed Souls,
www.torontoghosts.org/barrie/villageofdeparted.htm
Ontario Ghosts and Hauntings, Penetanguishene, Discovery Harbor,
www.torontoghosts.org/barrie/disharb.htm
Ontario Ghosts and Hauntings, Port Severn, Bressette House,
www.torontoghosts.org/barrie/bressette.htm
Ontario Historic Sites, www.ontarioplaques.com/PlaqueText/Grey25a.html
The Ouendat (Huron) Indian Lengend of Kitchikewanna,
collections.ic.gc.ca/huronia/GHOST/KITCHI.HTM
Para Researchers of Ontario,
www.pararesearchers.org/UFO/2002ufo/2002ufo.html
Praire Ghosts, www.praireghosts.com/small_pt.html
Rootsweb, www.rootsweb.cm/~minmacki2/haunted_mackinac.html
Shadowlands, shadowlands.net/places/michigan.htm
Ship of the Month, *J.H. Jones*, vaxxine.com/gblawson/jonesarticle.eht
Stempien-Rutherford, www.stempienrutherford.com/default.htm
The Aboriginal Peoples of Little Current, www.turners.ca/pages/main/
manitoulin2.html
This is Manitoulin, the Natural Destination, Mindemoya,
www.manitoulin.ca/TIM/mindprov.html
The SS *Tashmoo* and Her Date With Doom,
info.detnews.com/history/story/index.cfm?id=22&category=events
The Steamer ASIA, A Local Connection,
www.pastforward.ca/perspectives/march_142003.htm
The National Parks and National Historic Sites of Canada in Ontario, Fort St.

Josepth www.pc.gc.ca/voyage-travel/pv-vp/itm6-/page20_e.asp
The Unofficial Monty Python Homepage www.mwscomp.com/sound.html
Usque Ad Mare, A History of the Canadian Coast Guard and Marine Services by
Thomas E. Appleton, www.ccg-gcc.gc.ca/usque-ad-mare/chapter04-07_e.htm
Was Foul Play Behind Boating Accident, msnbc.msn.com/id/10793084/
Western Lights, Martin Reef,
    www.terrypepper.com/lights/huron/martin_reef/martin-reef.htm
Westerm Lights, Spectacle Reef,
    www.terrypepper.com/lights/huron/spectacle/spectacle.htm

INTERVIEWS
Anonymous interview, June 3, 1970.
Anonymous interview, July 23, 1993.
Anonymous interview, 1996.
Anonymous interview, March 1998.
Anonymous interview, 1999.
Anonymous interview, July 30, 1999.
Anonymous interview, September 15, 1999.
Anonymous interview, July 3, 2000.
Anonymous interview, May 22, 2001.
Anonymous interview, October 19, 2002
Anonymous interviews, March 31- April 1, 2006.
Dan McGee interview, May 21, 1994.
Dr. Bell interview, January 24, 1995.
Anna Hoge interview, March 12, 1996.
Ted Richardson interview, January 1994.
Lorraine Parris interview, May 29, 1994.
Author and Dennis Hale interview, October, 1993, November 1995.
Beverly Wilkens, Idle Hour Yacht Club e-mail, June 7, 2006.

NEWSPAPERS
Ann Arbor News, December 16, 1989.
Blade-Crescent (Sebewaing, Michigan), November 8, 1988.
Buffalo Morning Express, April 27, 1849.
Buffalo Republican, July 11, 1853.
Detroit Free Press, July 3, 1859, March 9, 1850, October 22, 1859.
Detroit Free Press , June 30, 1867.
Detroit Free Press , October 24, 1890.
Detroit Free Press , July 3, 1909
Detroit Free Press , September 14, 1994; October 29, 1999.
Detroit Free Press , August 26, 2005, January 14, 2006.
Detroit News, August 25, September 16, 2005, February 13, 2006.
Detroit News-Tribune, August 8, 1897.
Detroit Post and Tribune, May 17, 1883.
Detroit Post, September 15, 1884.
Cleveland Evening Herald, August 15, 1856.
Echo (Wiarton, Ontario) November-December 1881.

Grand Rapids Press, June 26, 1976.
Great Lakes Journal, October 1938.
Great Lakes Journal, January, May 1939.
Huron Daily Tribune, March 17, 1999.
Iron Agitator (Ishpeming, Michigan), April 17, 1886.
London Ontario Free Press, July 12, 1975.
New York Sun, August. 20, 1883.
Oswego Palladium, January 13, 1881.
Owen Sound Sun Times, July 23, 1948.
Petoskey News-Record, March 4, 2006.
River Scene, October 2005.
Saginaw Daily Courier (Saginaw, Michigan) November 16, 1873.
Toronto Globe, October 22, 1859
Toronto Telegram, January 31, 1953, February 7, 1953.

PERIODICALS

"Annual Report U.S. Life-Saving Service, 1904."
Floren, Russell and Gutsche, Andrea. "The Asia Mystery," *Inland Seas*, (Spring 1995).
Great Lakes Cruiser , October 1994.
"Haunts of the Great Lakes," *Great Lakes Cruiser*, October 1995.
Kaufman, John. "*Hunter Savidge* Disaster Recalled," *Inland Seas*, Fall, 1965.
Larke, Frederick Denny. "The Story of Sacred Rock," *Calcite Screenings*, August 1929, Rogers City Historical Society.
Schmitt, Paul J. "A Hard Luck Boat, Loss of the Propeller *Troy*," *Inland Seas*, Winter 2000.
The Chronicle, Algonac-Clay Township Historical Society, Summer 1996, Volume 1, Issue 2.
Williams, W.R. "The Gale-Shattered *Waubuno*," *Inland Seas*. Spring 1965.

Index

Tawas, Michigan 31
Ten 38
The "Snows" 46
The Les Cheneaux Club 46
Thessalon River, Ontario 183
"This Time For Keeps" 106
Thorold, Ontario 173
Three Brothers 29
Thunder Bay Island 11, 41, 136, 166
Thunder Bay Island Lighthouse 136
Tinkiss, Duncan 35
Tobermory, Ontario 33
Toledo, Ohio 1, 30
Tonkin, Fred 40
Toronto 98
Traverse City, Michigan 2, 35
Treaty of Ghent 60
Tripp, Amos 146
Trotter, David 29
Troy 2-4
Truman, Harry 106

U

U.S. Life-Saving Service 17, 19, 29
U.S. Life-Saving Service Station 16
Undersea Research Associates 29
Unionville, Michigan 181
Universal Studios 107

V

Valkyries 99
Venice of America 72
Victorian Age 38
Vishnu Purana 41
Volunteer 176

W

Wahsoona 98
Wallaceburg, Ontario 7
Walpole Island 12
Wanakita 98
War of 1812 56, 60, 100, 121
Wasaga Beach 151
Waubuno 173-175
Wawanosh (chief) 127
Wawashkamo Golf Course 100, 111
Wawatam (chief) 121
Wazhuska 172-173
Wazhuska Trail 172
Welland Canal 32
Wenona 172

West Bay City, Michigan 159
White Cloud Island 36-37
White Star Line 11
White Star Steamship Line 73
Wiarton, Ontario 36-37
Williams, Esther 106
Williams, G. Mennen 111
Windsor, Ontario 159
Witchcraft 25-26
World War II 74
Wreck Ashore 19
Wreck Island 175

Y

Yellowstone National Park 101
York (Toronto) 95
Yuma 8

About the Author

Frederick Stonehouse holds a Master of Arts degree from Northern Michigan University and has authored 30 books on maritime history. Among them are his first *Haunted Lakes, Haunted Lakes II, Shipwreck of the Mesquite* and *Wreck Ashore, the U.S. Life-Saving Service on the Great Lakes*, published by Lake Superior Port Cities, and the *Wreck of the Edmund Fitzgerald*.

Frederick Stonehouse

He is the recipient of the 2006 Association for Great Lakes Maritime History Award for Historic Interpretation. The prestigious award is presented annually in recognition of an individual making a major contribution over many years to the interpretation of Great Lakes maritime history. He has also been a consultant for the U.S. National Parks Service and Parks Canada.

His articles have been published in *Lake Superior Magazine, Skin Diver* and *Wreck and Rescue Journal*. He is president of the Board of Directors of the U.S. Life-Saving Service Heritage Association and the Marquette Maritime Museum. He has taught Great Lakes maritime history at both Northern Michigan and Central Michigan universities and appeared as an on-air expert for the History Channel and National Geographic Society as well as in numerous regional media outlets. He lives in Marquette, Michigan, with his wife, Lois, and son, Brandon. See www.frederickstonehouse.com for additional details.

Other Books in the Series

Ghostly Tales and Legends from the Mystical Inland Sea

by Hugh E. Bishop

ISBN 978-0-942235-55-5

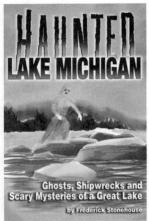

Ghosts, Shipwrecks and Scary Mysteries of a Great Lake

by Frederick Stonehouse

ISBN 978-0-942235-72-2

Related Titles

ISBN 978-0-942235-30-2

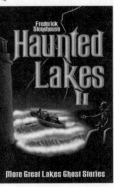

ISBN 978-0-942235-39-5

ISBN 978-0-942235-71-5

Watch for Haunted Lake Erie & Haunted Lake Ontario in the future at

www.lakesuperior.com

Also from Lake Superior Port Cities Inc.

Lake Superior Magazine (Bimonthly)

Lake Superior Travel Guide (Annual)

Hugh E. Bishop:

The Night the Fitz Went Down
Softcover: ISBN 978-0-942235-37-1

**By Water and Rail: A History of
Lake County, Minnesota**
Hardcover: ISBN 978-0-942235-48-7
Softcover: ISBN 978-0-942235-42-5

Haunted Lake Superior
Softcover: ISBN 978-0-942235-55-5

Haunted Minnesota
Softcover: ISBN 978-0-942235-71-5

**Lake Superior, The Ultimate
Guide to the Region**
Softcover: ISBN 978-0-942235-66-1

Bonnie Dahl:

Superior Way, Third Edition
Softcover: ISBN 978-0-942235-49-4

Joy Morgan Dey, Nikki Johnson:

Agate: What Good is a Moose?
Softcover: ISBN 978-0-942235-73-9

Daniel R. Fountain:

**Michigan Gold,
Mining in the Upper Peninsula**
Softcover: ISBN 978-0-942235-15-9

Marvin G. Lamppa:

Minnesota's Iron Country
Softcover: ISBN 978-0-942235-56-2

Daniel Lenihan:

**Shipwrecks of Isle Royale
National Park**
Softcover: ISBN 978-0-942235-18-0

Betty Lessard:

Betty's Pies Favorite Recipes
Softcover: ISBN 978-0-942235-50-0

James R. Marshall:

**Shipwrecks of Lake Superior,
Second Edition**
Softcover: ISBN 978-0-942235-67-8

**Lake Superior Journal:
Views from the Bridge**
Softcover: ISBN 978-0-942235-40-1

Howard Sivertson:

**Schooners, Skiffs & Steamships:
Stories along Lake Superior
Water Trails**
Hardcover: ISBN 978-0-942235-51-7

Tales of the Old North Shore
Hardcover: ISBN 978-0-942235-29-6

The Illustrated Voyageur
Hardcover: ISBN 978-0-942235-43-2

**Once Upon an Isle:
The Story of Fishing Families
on Isle Royale**
Hardcover: ISBN 978-0-962436-93-2

Frederick Stonehouse:

**Wreck Ashore: United States
Life-Saving Service, Legendary
Heroes of the Great Lakes**
Softcover: ISBN 978-0-942235-58-6

Shipwreck of the Mesquite
Softcover: ISBN 978-0-942235-10-4

Haunted Lakes (the original)
Softcover: ISBN 978-0-942235-30-2

Haunted Lakes II
Softcover: ISBN 978-0-942235-39-5

Haunted Lake Michigan
Softcover: ISBN 978-0-942235-72-2

Haunted Lake Huron
Softcover: ISBN 978-0-942235-79-1

Julius F. Wolff Jr.:

**Julius F. Wolff Jr.'s
Lake Superior Shipwrecks**
Hardcover: ISBN 978-0-942235-02-9
Softcover: ISBN 978-0-942235-01-2

For a catalog of the entire Lake Superior Port Cities collection
of books and merchandise, write or call:

Lake Superior Port Cities Inc.
P.O. Box 16417 • Duluth, MN 55816-0417
Outlet Store: 310 E. Superior St. #125 • Duluth, MN 55802
1-888-BIG LAKE (888-244-5253) • 218-722-5002
www.lakesuperior.com • E-mail: guide@lakesuperior.com